GED® TEST
Social Studies Prep 2015

KAPLAN
PUBLISHING
New York

ACKNOWLEDGEMENTS

Special thanks to the team that made this book possible:
Arthur Ahn, Mikhail Alexeeff, Gina Allison, Kim Bowers, Erik Bowman, Julie Choi, Margaret Crane, Alisha Crowley, Lola Dart, Boris Dvorkin, Paula Fleming, Tom Flesher, Joanna Graham, Allison Harm, Gar Hong, Kevin Jacobson, Wyatt Kent, Jennifer Land, Heather Maigur, Terrence McGovern, Eli Meyer, Kathy Osmus, Anthony Parr, Rachel Pearsall, Neha Rao, Rachel Reina, Teresa Rupp, Scott Safir, Glen Stohr, Alexandra Strelka, Lee Weiss, and many others who have shaped this book over the years.

Published by Kaplan Publishing, a division of Kaplan, Inc.
395 Hudson Street
New York, NY 10014

Printed in the United States of America

10 9 8 7 6 5 4 3 2 1

ISBN: 978-1-62523-237-3

Kaplan Publishing books are available at special quantity discounts to use for sales promotions, employee premiums, or educational purposes. For more information or to purchase books, please call the Simon & Schuster special sales department at 866-506-1949.

CONTENTS

KAPLAN'S GED® TEST BOOK AND ONLINE CENTER

Congratulations on your decision to pursue high school equivalency, and thank you for choosing Kaplan for your GED® test preparation.

You've made the right choice in acquiring this book—you're now armed with a GED® Social Studies test preparation program that is the result of years of researching the GED® tests and teaching thousands of students the skills they need to succeed. You have what you need to pass the GED® Social Studies test and score higher; the next step is to make the commitment to your study plan.

The next section will tell you everything you need to know to take advantage of your book and your Online Center.

YOUR BOOK

This book contains a complete study program, including the following:

- Detailed instruction covering the essential concepts for Social Studies
- Time-tested and effective methods and strategies for every question type
- A Pretest designed to help you diagnose your strengths and weaknesses
- Hundreds of practice questions, followed by answer explanations
- A timed, full-length Social Studies Practice Test

YOUR ONLINE CENTER

Your Kaplan Online Center gives you access to additional instruction and practice materials to reinforce key concepts and sharpen your GED® test skills. The following list summarizes the resources available to you:

- An additional full-length Social Studies Practice Test, so that you can practice the computer-based question formats used on the actual test
- Analysis of your performance on your Practice Test, including detailed answer explanations for the computer-based practice test
- Video lessons featuring Kaplan's top instructors

GETTING STARTED

Studying for the GED® test can be daunting, and with so many resources available to you, it may not be clear where to begin. Don't worry; we'll break it down one step at a time, just as we will with the GED® test questions that you will soon be on your way to mastering.

GETTING STARTED

1. Take the diagnostic Pretest.
2. Create a study plan.
3. Register your Online Center.
4. Learn and practice using both this book and your Online Center.
5. Work through the Practice Tests to gauge your progress.

STEP 1: TAKE THE DIAGNOSTIC PRETEST

It's essential to take the diagnostic Pretest before you begin to study. Doing so will give you the initial feedback and diagnostic information that you will need to achieve your maximum score. Place enough importance on completing the Pretest—turn off your cell phone, give the tests your full attention, and learn from your performance.

Once you have finished your Pretest, check your answers starting on page 17. Mark the questions that you got correct and **carefully read the answer explanations** of those that you got wrong.

When you have finished the Pretest, make a list of the questions that you got correct and use that list to fill out the Kaplan GED® Test Study Planner on page 20. Use the results to target your weak areas.

Another option is for you to go online and enter your answers so that the Kaplan Online Center can generate your results. Note which sections and which question types you need to target.

Review the detailed answer explanations in the book to better understand your performance. Look for patterns in the questions you answered correctly and incorrectly. Were you stronger in some areas than others? This analysis will help you target your study time to specific concepts.

STEP 2: CREATE A STUDY PLAN

Use what you've learned from your initial Pretest to identify areas for closer study and practice. Take time to familiarize yourself with the key components of your book and Online Center. Think about how many hours you can consistently devote to GED® test study.

Schedule time for study, practice, and review. It works best for many people to block out short, frequent periods of study time throughout the week. Check in with yourself frequently to make sure you're not falling behind your plan or forgetting about any of your resources.

Step 3: Register Your Online Center

Register your Online Center using these simple steps:

1. Go to **kaptest.com/booksonline.**
2. Follow the on-screen instructions for GED®. Please have your book available.

Access to the Online Center is limited to the original owner of this book and is nontransferable. Kaplan is not responsible for providing access to the Online Center to customers who purchase or borrow used copies of this book. Access to the Online Center expires one year after you register.

Step 4: Learn and Practice

Your book and Online Center come with many opportunities to develop and practice the skills you'll need on Test Day. Depending on how much time you have to study, you can do this work methodically, covering every unit and lesson, or you can focus your study on those content areas that are most challenging to you. You will inevitably need more work in some areas than in others, but the more thoroughly you prepare, the better your score will be.

Initially, your practice should focus on mastering the needed skills and not on timing. Add timing to your practice as you become familiar with skills and methods.

Step 5: Work Through the Practice Tests

As you move through your GED® studies, take advantage of both the full-length Social Studies Practice Test available in this book and also the one in your Online Center.

Review your Practice Test results thoroughly to make sure you are addressing the areas that are most important to your score. Allot time to review the detailed explanations so that you can learn from your mistakes and review the relevant chapters in the book for additional study.

If you find that you would like access to more of Kaplan's instructional content or practice material, look into our other subject books, our comprehensive GED® preparation books, or our On Demand course option available at **kaptest.com/GED.**

Thanks for choosing Kaplan. We wish you the best of luck on your journey to completing your high school equivalency and taking a vital step toward college and career readiness.

GED® TEST OVERVIEW

The GED® test is a widely used examination that demonstrates high school equivalency as well as college and career readiness. It includes the reading, writing, thinking, and problem-solving skills needed for postsecondary educational programs and for the world of work. This means that your high school equivalency diploma is not an end in itself—it is the springboard to more education, to better-paying jobs, and to more rewarding career paths.

Take Four Subtests in Four Content Areas

Reasoning through Language Arts—2.5 hours (one 10-minute break)

- Roughly 50–55 questions
- Includes 1 extended written response to reading passages—up to 45 minutes

Mathematical Reasoning—1 hour, 55 minutes

- Roughly 40–45 questions
- First section—5 questions, no calculator allowed
- Second section—calculator allowed (Texas Instruments TI-30XS MultiView™ calculator)

Social Studies—1.5 hours

- Roughly 30–35 questions
- Includes 1 extended written response to passages and/or graphics—up to 25 minutes

Science—1.5 hours

- Roughly 30–35 questions
- Includes 2 short-answer written responses to passages and/or graphics—up to 10 minutes each

You can read detailed information about the test in the *About the Test* section.

Respond to Seven Computer-Based Question Formats

To test a range of skills, the GED® test uses a variety of computer-based question formats. You will see examples of each type of question in *GED® Computer-Based Testing* and in the *About the Test* section. When you take the test, you will use these question formats:

- **Multiple-choice**—click to choose from four choices (A through D).
- **Fill-in-the-blank**—type a word, a phrase, or numbers in a box.
- **Drag-and-drop**—move words, numbers, or objects across the computer screen.
- **Drop-down**—select from menus embedded in text on the computer screen.
- **Hot spot**—click on graphics on the computer.
- **Short-answer**—write a paragraph or two of explanation in response to passages or graphics or a combination of the two.
- **Extended response**—compose a well-developed and supported response to passages or graphics or a combination of the two.

Read and Write Throughout the Test

You will read and interpret passages and word problems on all four tests. In addition, three out of four subtests (*Reasoning through Language Arts, Social Studies,* and *Science*) require that you read a passage or two and compose a response about what you have read.

The type of writing that you will use is called *evidence-based writing*, which means that you need to cite specific evidence from the readings in your response. This is a key characteristic of the type of writing that is required in workplaces and in educational programs. This book contains special lessons and practice activities to help you write effectively on all three of the subtests.

Perform Math Skills Throughout the Test

In addition to the questions on the *Mathematical Reasoning Test*, math items also appear on the *Science Test* and the *Social Studies Test*.

On all three of these tests, you may use either a hand-held or an on-screen version of the Texas Instruments TI-30XS MultiView™ calculator to use with math items. If you wish to use a hand-held version of the calculator, you may need to take one with you on test day. **You are strongly encouraged to purchase a hand-held version of this calculator to use with this study guide.** You can buy this calculator at stores that carry office and school supplies and through online vendors. See the section entitled *How to Use the Calculator* for instructions about calculator functions.

Use the GED Testing Service® MyGED™ Internet Portal

MyGED™ is a personalized online program that will be your entry point to all test activities, including scheduling testing and retesting (if necessary), viewing score reports, ordering transcripts and your diploma, and investigating your next steps in making the transition to college or to a career.

Take the Test: Understand Your Score

Each GED® Test is scored on a scale from 100 to 200. There are three possible scores that you can receive on the GED® Test:

- **Not Passing**—lower than 150 on any of the four tests. You can reschedule up to two times a year to retake any or all of the tests.
- **GED® Passing Score**—at or higher than the minimum score (150 per test) needed to demonstrate high school equivalency–level skills and knowledge. Points on one test do not carry over to the others; that is, if you score 200 on one and 100 on another, that is not equivalent to scoring 150 on both. You need to score 150 on each of the four tests.
- **GED® Score with Honors**—at or higher than the minimum needed (170 per test) to demonstrate career and college readiness

Your score is determined by the number of points you earn on each test, but questions vary in point value. Therefore, there is no fixed number of questions you need to get correct on each test in order to pass or pass with honors.

GED® COMPUTER-BASED TESTING

The GED® Test is delivered on a computer. That means that you will need to familiarize yourself with basic computer skills and computer-based question formats in order to succeed on the test.

NOTE: *The GED® Test on computer is only offered at official Pearson Vue Testing Centers. Any Internet-based test that claims to be the GED® Test is* not *the actual test. At the MyGED™ portal, you can access study resources, take a practice test, or schedule your test. You cannot take the real GED® test online.*

To become familiar with the computer-based functions, you should review the GED® Test Tutorial available through the GED® Testing Services website. Before you take the actual test, you can practice computer-based testing functions with the Practice Test available in Kaplan's Online Center and with the GED® Testing Service's GED Ready™ Test.

COMPUTER-BASED TESTING FUNCTIONS AND TOOLS

The GED® Test uses many computer **functions**, some of which you may already know. It also offers specific **tools** that you will utilize in different test areas.

Use the **mouse** to

Tab through the pages of a reading passage

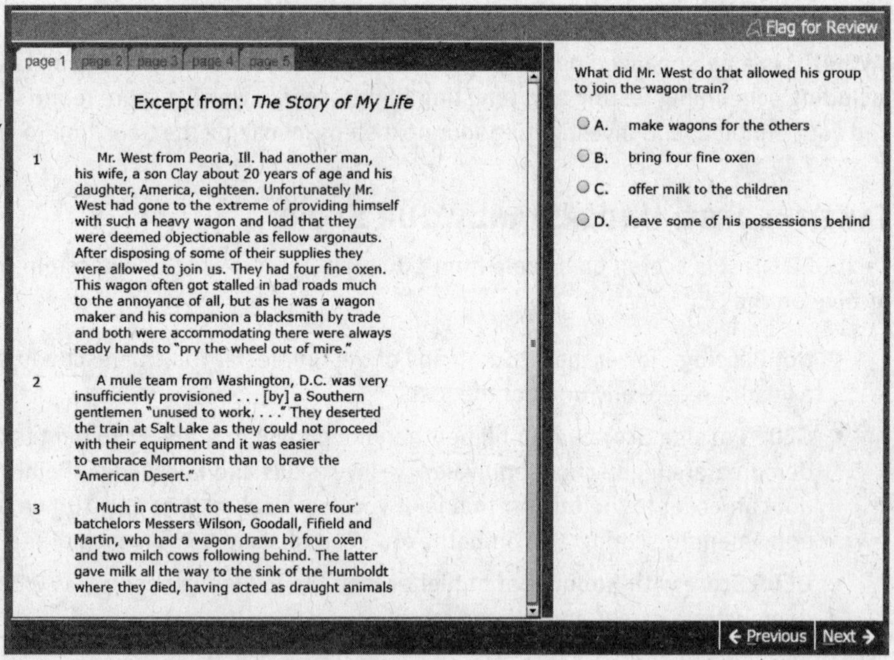

Scroll up and down a page when a scroll bar appears

Click on Previous and Next navigation buttons to move forward or backward

Use the **mouse** to (continued)

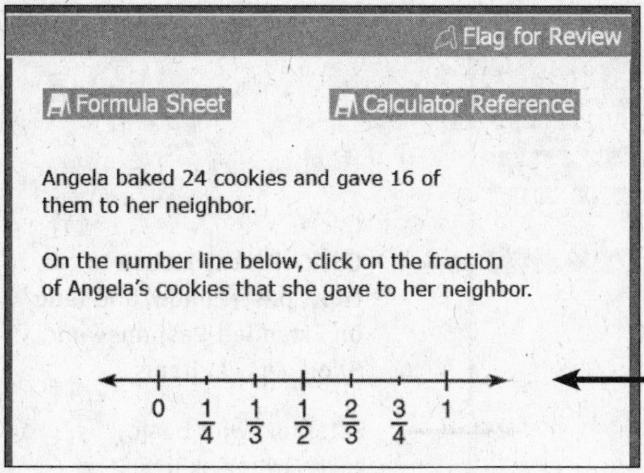

Click on an answer choice, a "Select" menu, or a point on a graphic

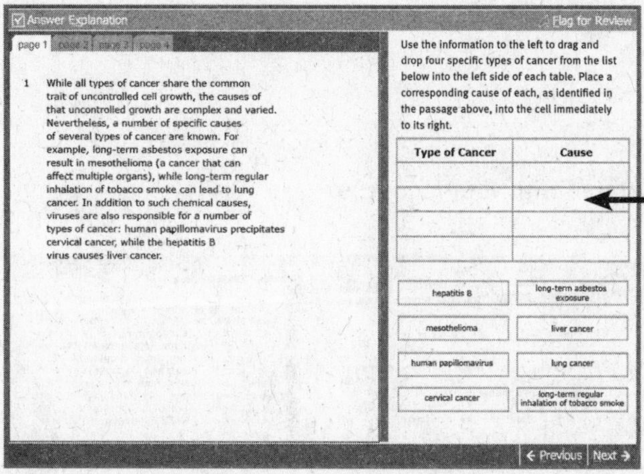

Drag and drop text, numbers, or images into a shape on the computer screen

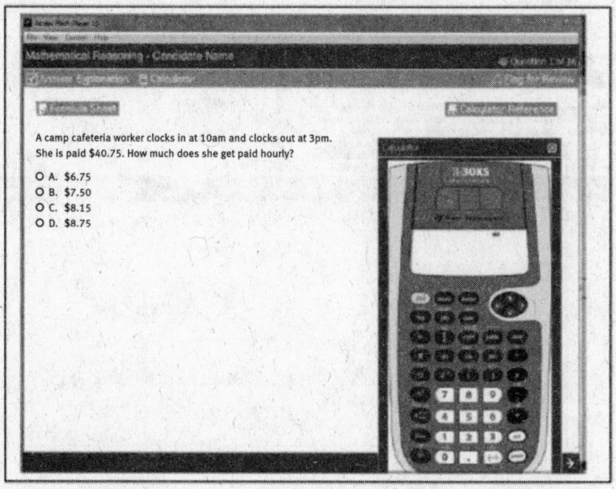

Click to open, move, and close information windows and math resources—such as the calculator, formula sheet, or symbol toolbar

Use **word processing skills** to

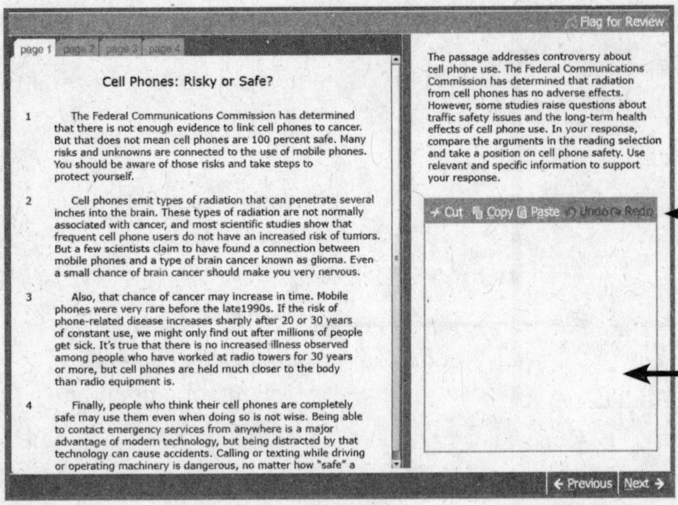

Click with the mouse to **cut, copy, paste, undo,** and **redo** on Extended-Response and Short-Answer items

Enter text with basic keyboarding skills in text boxes (shown here) and fill-in-the-blank questions

Use **the online highlighter,** operated with your mouse, to

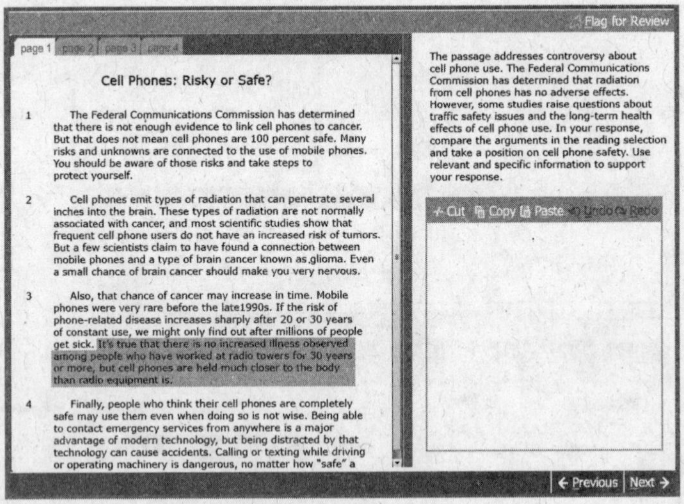

Highlight specific information that you will use as evidence in writing your Extended Responses and Short Answers.

Use the offline, **erasable wipe-off board**, which will be provided at the testing center, to

Plan your Extended Response (*Reasoning through Language Arts* and *Social Studies Tests*) and Short Answers (*Science Test*) before you begin writing

Use as scrap paper to do math problems on the *Mathematical Reasoning Test* and the *Social Studies* and *Science Tests*

Use three **onscreen test-tracking tools** at the top of the computer screen to

- **See how much time you have left:** ***Time Remaining*** shows how much time is left to complete each test.
- **Monitor your progress** through each test by viewing the ***Question Line.*** You can check how far you have progressed and how many more questions you need to answer. Budget your time carefully to allow for these writing tasks:
  - 45 minutes for the Extended Response at the end of the first section of the *Reasoning through Language Arts Test*
  - 25 minutes for the Extended Response at the end of the *Social Studies Test*
  - 10 minutes for <u>each</u> of the Short Answer questions that are interspersed with other questions in the *Science Test*
- **Click** on the ***Flag for Review*** if you are unsure of an answer. (You should never skip a question.) If you click on it, the flag will display in yellow and will be marked on the Review Screen.

At the end of each test, if you have time left, you can use the **Review Screen** to go back and review questions that you marked.

HOW TO USE THE CALCULATOR

You will use math skills throughout the *Science* and *Social Studies Tests* as well as on the *Mathematical Reasoning Test*. The following pages provide instruction about the calculator and other tools you will have access to on test day.

Calculation Tools

Calculator For most of the *Mathematical Reasoning Test* and portions of the *Science* and *Social Studies Tests*, you will be able to use either a hand-held or an on-screen version of the **Texas Instruments TI-30XS MultiView™ scientific calculator**. You can access the on-screen calculator by clicking on this icon. You can also take your own hand-held TI-30XS MultiView™ calculator to use on test day.

Calculator

If you forget how to use a specific calculator function, you will be able to access a ***Calculator Reference Sheet*** from the computer screen by clicking on this icon. That reference sheet is reprinted in the back of this book.

Calculator Reference

Accessing the Symbol Selector Toolbar

On some fill-in-the-blank problems, you may need to use a symbol from the symbol selector toolbar. This is not available for all problems, but this icon shows up when you need the toolbar:

Æ Symbol

When you **click** on this icon, a new window will open up with these symbols:

Æ Symbol

∏	f	≥	≤	≠	^{2}	^{3}	|	×	÷	±	∞	√
+	−	(	)	>	<	=						

Click on a symbol to insert it in the correct place in an expression, equation, or inequality. When you are finished with the toolbar, **click** on the "X" at the top of the window to close the window.

If you do not know all of these symbols now, copy them on a piece of paper or in a math notebook. Use a GED® *Mathematical Reasoning Test* study resource to improve your familiarity with mathematical symbols.

Using the Wipe-Off Board

At the testing center, you will also be given a wipe-off board to serve as scratch paper. Even with all of the computer-based tools, you may still feel the need for some scratch paper to do the following:

- Write down the relevant numbers that you need to answer a specific question.
- Solve the problem by hand and use the calculator to check your work.
- Make a drawing or a diagram to help you picture a situation that is described in a problem.

At the testing center, you will be provided with a wipe-off board and dry erase marker, similar to the material shown at the right. Make use of the board throughout the test and ask for a new one if you feel that you need it.

Using the Texas Instruments TI-30XS MultiView™ Calculator

When you encounter questions in this book that involve math, you may use a calculator. We strongly encourage you to practice with the same calculator you will use on test day, namely the **TI-30XS MultiView™** calculator. Remember: You do not have to use the calculator to solve problems; only use it if it is relevant to the problem or if you believe it will be helpful.

Below is a picture of the hand-held version and some issues to keep in mind.

- The hand-held version has an On/Off button at the lower-left hand side.
- To use the on-screen version of the calculator, **click** the calculator icon (see page xiii) to open the calculator in a new window. Use your mouse to **drag** the calculator to the side of the computer screen so that it does not cover the problem. When you are finished with a calculation, **click** on the "X" at the top of the window to close the calculator.
- When you are finished with a calculation, use the ***enter*** button. (There is no "equal sign" button on this calculator.)
- Use the ***white numeric keypad*** to enter numbers, the decimal point, and the negative sign (–) for a negative number such as –13 .
- The ***operation keys,*** on the right, allow you to add, subtract, multiply, and divide. (Use the minus sign here for subtraction; use the negative sign (–) on the keypad to indicate a negative number.)

TI-30XS MultiView™ Calculator

Photo used with permission from TI. http://education.ti.com.

- Use the bright green ***2nd button*** at the left of the calculator to activate the *2nd functions* (in bright green) above the keys. Some of the main ones are square root, exponent, percent, and mixed number functions.
- The ***four arrows*** at the top right of the calculator allow you to move the ***onscreen cursor*** up, down, left, or right as needed. The ***delete*** key to the left of the arrows allows you to correct mistakes as you work.
- Every time you begin a calculation, press the ***clear*** button above the ***operation keys*** to clear the calculator's memory.

You are encouraged to purchase a hand-held version of the Texas Instruments TI-30XS MultiView™ calculator for practice as you work through this book. You can buy one at office or school supply stores or online.

Basic Calculator Functions

Look at the reproduction of the calculator below and follow the examples that demonstrate how to use the calculator's **operation keys**.

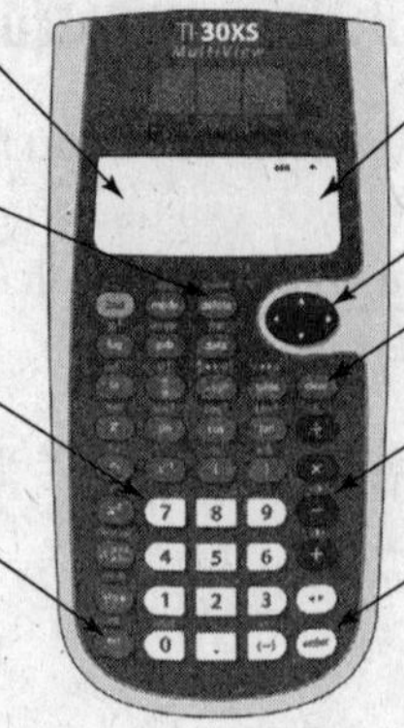

Example 1: Add 63 + 97 + 58 + 32 + 81.

1. Always clear a calculator before starting a new computation. On the TI-30XS MultiView™, use the *clear* key. — [clear]
2. Enter each number followed by the plus sign. As you type, the numbers and plus signs will appear on the calculator's screen. If you make a mistake, press *delete* to go back and reenter a number. — 63 [+] 97 [+] 58 [+] 32 [+] 81
3. Press *enter* to find the total. — [enter]

The total, **331**, will appear on the right-hand side of the display: **331**

Example 2: Find the difference between 15,789 and 9,332.

1. Always clear a calculator before starting a new computation. — [clear]
2. Enter the greater number first, followed by the minus operator. **NOTE:** Use the minus key that is on the right side of the calculator with the other operation symbols. Don't use the (–) key at the bottom of the calculator; that key is used to enter a negative number. — 15789 [−]
3. Enter the number being subtracted. — 9332
4. Press the *enter* key to find the answer. — [enter]

The answer **6457** will appear on the right-hand side of the display. **6457**

Example 3: Find the product of 309 and 68.

1. Always clear a calculator before starting a new computation. — [clear]
2. Enter the first number, followed by the multiplication operator. (The multiplication sign will appear in the display as an asterisk rather than an ×, but the *multiplication key* looks like an ×.) — 309 [×]
3. Enter the next number. — 68
4. Press the *enter* key to find the product. — [enter]

The answer **21012** will appear on the right-hand side of the display. **21012**

Example 4: Divide 12,456 by 12.

1. Always clear a calculator before starting a new computation. — [clear]
2. Enter the number to be divided first, followed by the division operator. — 12456 [÷]
3. Enter the number you are dividing by. — 12
4. Press the *enter* key to find the quotient. — [enter]

The answer **1038** will appear on the right-hand side of the display. **1038**

Using the *2nd* Key for a Second Function

To access some of the functions on the TI-30XS MultiView™, you need to press the *2nd* key in the upper left corner of the keypad. This bright green key will activate the second function also shown in green above the corresponding key. To access the second function of a key, press the *2nd* key first—do not press it at the same time as the function key. High-lighted below are two commonly used second functions—square root and percent. Use the process shown here for all *2nd* function keys.

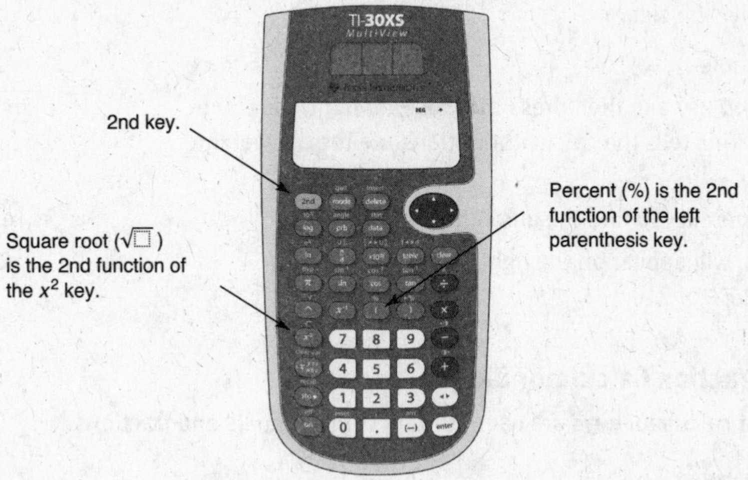

Example 5: Find the square root of 169.

Step	Keys to Press	On the Display
1. Always clear a calculator before starting a new computation.	clear	
2. Recognize that square root is a *2nd* function over the x^2 key. Press the *2nd* key. (Note that the term *2nd* now appears in the upper left corner of the display.)	2nd	2nd
3. Next, press the x^2 key to activate the square root function in green over the key. You will see a blinking cursor under the square root.	$\sqrt{}$ / x^2	$\sqrt{\square}$
4. Now that you have the square root function, enter the number. The number will appear under the square root symbol in the display.	169	$\sqrt{169}$▶
5. Press the *enter* key to find the square root. The answer, **13**, will appear on the right-hand side of the display.	enter	$\sqrt{169}$ 13

Remember: For all *2nd functions*, (1) press the *2nd* key first to activate the *2nd* function, (2) press the key, and (3) enter the numbers.

Example 6: Find the part if you are given the percent and the whole. Find 10 percent of 500.

Step	Keys to Press
1. Always clear a calculator before starting a new computation.	clear
2. Enter the number you want to find the percent of.	500
3. Press the multiplication sign.	×
4. Enter the percent number.	10
5. Press the *2nd* key and then press the open, or left, parenthesis key to activate the percent function.	2nd % / (
6. Press the *enter* key to find the answer.	enter

The answer, **50**, will appear on the right-hand side of the display. Ten percent of 500 is 50. **50**

Example 7: Find the percent if you are given the whole and the part. What percent of 240 is 60?

1. Always clear a calculator before starting a new computation. clear
2. Enter the part. 60
3. Press the division sign. ÷
4. Enter the whole. 240
5. Press the *2nd* key and then press the close, or right, parenthesis symbol. This tells the calculator to translate the answer into a percent. 2nd ►%)
6. Press the *enter* key to find the answer. enter

The answer, **25%**, will appear on the right-hand side of the display. Sixty is 25% of 240. **25%**

Decimal and Fraction Calculator Skills

Several important calculator keys are used to work with decimals and fractions.

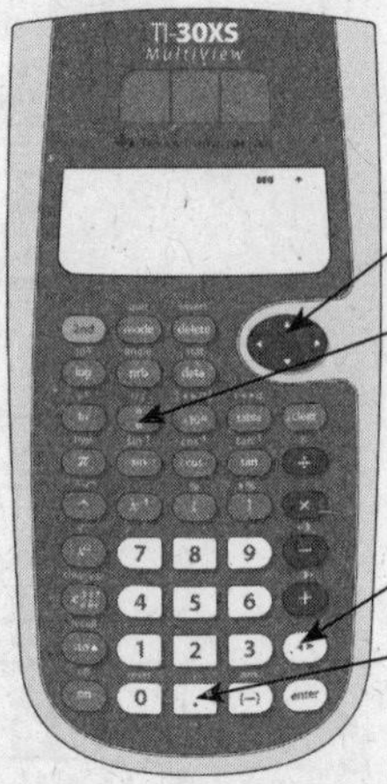

Cursor keys move the cursor on the screen up, down, left, and right.

The **fraction key** is used to enter fractions; the **mixed number 2nd function** is in green above it.

The **toggle key** changes between equivalent fraction and decimal forms of a number.

The **decimal point** key enters a decimal point.

Calculator **decimal operations** are performed in the same way that you use operations with whole numbers. You need to use the **decimal point key** ⊙ under the 2 in the white **numeric keypad**. Practice with these examples:

To solve this problem...	Press these keys...	The right-hand side of the display reads...
$3.89 + 2.5$	3.89 + 2.5 enter	6.39
$5.2 - 0.78$	5.2 - .78 enter	4.42
0.9×15	.9 × 15 enter	13.5
$1.7 \div 2$	1.7 ÷ 2 enter	0.85

You will use several calculator functions to work with **fractions** and **mixed fraction operations.** First practice entering fractions and converting to decimals.

Example 8: Reduce $\frac{56}{448}$ to lowest terms and then convert to a decimal.

	On the Display
1. Clear the calculator.	
2. Press the $\frac{n}{d}$ button to enter a fraction. Enter 56 at the blinking cursor, in the numerator.	$\frac{56}{\square}$
3. Use the down cursor key (▼) to enter 448 in the denominator.	$\frac{56}{448}$
4. Press (enter) to reduce the fraction to lowest terms, which appears on the right of your screen: $\frac{1}{8}$	$\frac{56}{448}$ $\frac{1}{8}$
5. To express the fraction as a decimal, press the toggle button: (◄►). The decimal 0.125 appears on the right display.	$\frac{1}{8}$ ◄► 0.125

A fraction answer may appear in the form of an improper fraction. In order to change an improper fraction to an equivalent mixed number, use the green 2nd function over this key:

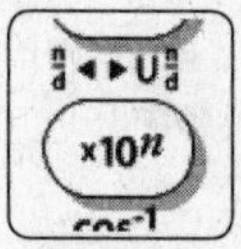

Now practice operations with **mixed fractions** using the *2nd function* key.

Example 9: A plastic pipe is to be cut into pieces measuring $1\frac{7}{8}$ feet. The original pipe was $20\frac{5}{8}$ feet long. How many pieces can be cut from the pipe?

	Keys to Press	On the Display
1. Clear the calculator	(clear)	
2. Recognize that a mixed fraction is a green *2nd* function: $\cup\frac{n}{d}$ over the $\frac{n}{d}$ key. Press the (2nd) key and the $\frac{n}{d}$ key. Note both a whole number and a blinking fraction cursor on the display.	(2nd) $\frac{n}{d}$	$\blacksquare\frac{\square}{\square}$
3. Enter the number being divided first–the whole pipe: $20\frac{5}{8}$. Enter 20, then follow the direction of the on-screen arrow and press the right arrow button to move to the fraction cursors. Enter 5 and then use the down arrow to enter the 8. Exit the fraction by pressing the right arrow again.	20 (►) 5 (▼) 8 (►)	$20\frac{5}{8}$
4. Press the division key. Then follow the same process with the second number: $1\frac{7}{8}$, starting with the 2nd function: $\cup\frac{n}{d}$	(÷) (2nd) $\frac{n}{d}$ 1 (►) 7 (▼) 8 (►)	$20\frac{5}{8}\div1\frac{7}{8}$
5. Press the (enter) button for the solution. The answer 11 for **11 pieces** appears on the right side of the screen.	(enter)	$20\frac{5}{8}\div1\frac{7}{8}$ 11

As you read above, you can use the percent functions of your calculator to solve percent problems. You can also solve these problems by converting a percent to either a fraction or a decimal. Study the examples below.

Example 10: What is 25% of 120? Try both decimals and fractions.

	On the Display
Change 25% to the decimal (.25), multiply times 120, and press (enter). **30** is on the right of the display.	.25*120 30
Change 25% to the fraction $\frac{25}{100}$ using the $\frac{n}{d}$ key, multiply times 120, and press (enter). **30** is on the right of the display.	$\frac{25}{100}$*120 30

Using either decimals or fractions, you can find that **30** is 25% of 120.

When you use the *percent 2nd* function, you don't have to convert the percent to a fraction or decimal. Practice this function below to multiply to find the **part** when you are given the rate (percent).

Example 11: What is 65% of $360?

	Keys to Press	On the Display
1. Type the base, 360, and press the multiplication sign.	360 (×)	360*
2. Type the rate (65). Press the 2nd function key and engage the percent 2nd function—over the (key. Then press (enter).	65 (2nd) (% () (enter)	360*65% 234

The amount **$234** is 65% of $360.

You can use the percent function to divide to find the **base** when given the rate.

Example 12: Ned paid $150 for a stereo. The amount Ned paid was 20% of the original cost. What was the original cost of the stereo?

	Keys to Press	On the Display
1. Enter the base, 150, and press the division sign.	150 (÷)	150÷
2. Enter 20 and press the 2nd function key and the (key. Then press *enter.*	20 (2nd) (% () (enter)	150÷20% 750

The original cost of the stereo appears on the right of the display: **$750**.

Expressions and Calculator Skills

The TI-30XS MultiView™ calculator, like most scientific calculators, uses algebraic logic, which means that it follows the correct order of operations.

You need to practice using a scientific calculator with algebraic logic. You can find out whether your calculator uses algebraic logic by running this simple test.

Press: 4 (×) 3 (x^2) (enter) (Your calculator may have an equal sign instead of an *enter* button.)

If the display reads **36**, your calculator uses algebraic logic.

If the display reads **144**, your calculator does not use algebraic logic.You should find another calculator to practice for the GED® Test.

You can use a calculator to evaluate an expression that contains several operations.

Example 13: Find the value of the expression $2x^2 + 3x - 5$ when $x = -4$.

When you come to the variable *x*, enter –4 by pressing (–) 4. The (–) key is called the **change sign key.**

Press: 2 ((–) 4) x² + 3 × (–) 4 – 5 enter

The right side of the display reads 15.

The value of the expression is **15.**

Expressions sometimes contain grouping symbols to show a different order of operations. You can enter grouping symbols on a scientific calculator. On the TI-30XS MultiView™, the grouping symbols (and) are found above the 8 and 9, respectively. When you enter the left, or open, parenthesis, (, the calculator waits until you enter the right, or closing, parenthesis,), before it calculates what is inside the symbols.

Example 14: Find the value of the expression $2(x+4) + \frac{5x}{3}$ when $x = 6$.

Press: 2 × (6 + 4) + 5 × 6 ÷ 3 enter.

The right side of the display reads **30.**

The value of the expression is **30.**

You can also use your calculator for only part of an expression.

Example 15: Find the value of the expression $\frac{3x+6}{2} + \sqrt{225}$ when $x = 4$.

Substitute 4 for *x* in the first part of the expression and calculate the results by hand or using your calculator: $\frac{3(4)+6}{2} = \frac{12+6}{2} = \frac{18}{2} = 9$.

Now use your calculator to find the square root of 225.

Press: 2nd x² 225 enter. The right side of the display reads 15.

Add the results of the two steps: $9 + 15 = \mathbf{24}$.

For more information about performing math skills on the GED® Test, consult a study resource for the *Mathematical Reasoning Test*, such as *Kaplan's GED® Test Mathematical Reasoning Prep.*

Pretest

The purpose of this pretest is to help you decide what you need to study to pass the actual GED® Social Studies Test. You will use the pretest along with the explanations and the study planner that follows to determine what course of study works best for you.

This pretest is specially designed to make your study as efficient as possible. If you want to see what the actual GED® Social Studies Test looks like, look at the *Practice Test* beginning on page 115.

1. **Take** the pretest:

    - **Social Studies, pages 2–15**
        - Part I: Social Studies Practices—10 Questions
        - Part II: Social Studies Content—25 Questions
        - Part III: Extended Response

    Most of the questions are in multiple-choice format. There is one extended response activity in this pretest.

    - For the **multiple-choice questions,** you may fill in the circles next to the correct answers in this book, or you can write your answers on a separate piece of paper.
    - You can the **extended response** on a computer or, if one is not available, on a sheet of paper.

      NOTE: Writing your responses on a computer is preferable because you will be composing your responses on a computer when you take the GED® test. However, if you do not have a computer available when you take these pretests, write your responses on paper so that you can evaluate your writing samples.

2. **Check** your answers with the *Pretest Answers and Explanations* that begin on page 17.
3. **Fill in** the *Pretest Study Planner* on page 20. These charts will allow you to target your problem areas so that you can study in the most efficient manner.
4. **Use the study planner** on page 20 to map out your work. Once you have completed your study, take the *Practice Test* on pages 115-129.

Part I: Practices—10 Questions

Directions: You may fill in the circles next to the correct answers or write your answers on a separate piece of paper. You MAY use your calculator if desired.

Question 1 refers to the following passage.

With the passage of the Fifteenth Amendment in 1870, all African Americans were given the right to vote throughout the United States. However, many Southern states quickly enacted legislative barriers to disenfranchise these new voters. Provisions such as poll taxes, literacy tests, and the grandfather clause prevented many African Americans from exercising their rights. For nearly one hundred years, these restrictions persisted in many Southern states. The civil rights movement, which gained national momentum in the 1950s, sought to address this unequal treatment in voting rights laws. Finally, in 1965, the Voting Rights Act provided for federal oversight of states that had previously raised unfair barriers to African American voting and outlawed discriminatory measures such as poll taxes and literacy tests. Voter participation among African Americans dramatically increased in the following years.

1. Which of the following describes the author's main idea?

   - A. The Voting Rights Act of 1965 ended discrimination in all areas of American society.
   - B. The main effect of the Voting Rights Act of 1965 was to empower individual states to end discriminatory measures against African American voting.
   - C. The Voting Rights Act of 1965 gave the federal government oversight of state elections to end barriers against African American voting.
   - D. The Fifteenth Amendment did not end racism in Southern states.

Question 2 refers to the following passage.

To address the nation's financial insolvency after the Revolutionary War, George Washington turned to his secretary of the treasury, Alexander Hamilton. Hamilton proposed creating a national bank, which would help to pay back the nation's debt and stabilize the nation's currency. Immediately, Hamilton faced stiff opposition from those who believed in a **strict construction** of the Constitution; they believed that Congress and the president could only exercise powers specifically written in the Constitution. Because the Constitution did not give the power to create a national bank, Hamilton's actions would be unconstitutional. In response, Hamilton offered a justification for the constitutionality of his bank based on a **loose construction** of the Constitution, meaning that Congress could use the Necessary and Proper Clause of the Constitution to stretch its power beyond what was specified in the words of the document. In Washington's first great test of presidential leadership, he sided with Hamilton and the idea of a national bank.

2. What is meant by the term "construction" in the passage?

   - A. building
   - B. creation
   - C. interpretation
   - D. structure

Questions 3 and 4 refer to the following passage.

In an attempt to make consumers more aware of the nutritional value of the foods they purchase, the Food and Drug Administration (FDA) is attempting to impose strict new regulations on all food retailers. These regulations would require that the caloric information of each food product be clearly posted on the premises, typically through signs that would be expensive to create and maintain. While these regulations would place a financial burden on all food retailers—an expense that would necessarily be passed on to consumers—the regulations would be particularly devastating to smaller restaurants, grocery stores, and convenience stores that offer fresh food items. To relieve this burden on smaller businesses, Congress has proposed the Common Sense Nutritional Disclosure Act, which would exempt smaller food establishments that primarily sell prepackaged foods from having to post on-site information. Also, under this legislation, restaurants that take most of their orders remotely can post caloric information online.

3. What is the author's point of view regarding the FDA's new food regulations?

   - A. The FDA's new regulations would place a financial hardship on small food retailers.
   - B. The FDA's new regulations would help consumers choose foods of a higher nutritional value.
   - C. The FDA's new regulations would have a more severe financial impact on chain restaurants than on smaller food retailers.
   - D. The FDA's new regulations would give food retailers more diverse options for displaying caloric information.

4. Which one of the following words points to the author's viewpoint regarding the FDA's strict new regulations?

   - A. "aware"
   - B. "strict"
   - C. "devastating"
   - D. "remotely"

Questions 5 and 6 refer to the following paragraph.

It is known that a significant quantity of oil exists within the Arctic National Wildlife Refuge (ANWR) of Alaska. Shockingly, there are many who would have us ignore this incredible resource housed right within our national borders. One commonly cited reason against drilling for oil in the ANWR is that the drilling process would endanger the existence of the porcupine caribou, whose calving grounds encompass much of the region. But science has shown us that as many as 99 percent of all the species that once existed on Earth are now extinct, and the vast majority of these extinctions were not caused by humans. Clearly, then, extinctions are a sad but natural aspect of life on Earth, and we have no reason not to drill in the ANWR.

5. Which of the following statements is a correct evaluation of the argument?

   - A. The argument is valid, because it relies on scientific evidence that has been shown to be true.
   - B. The argument is valid, because extracting oil would bolster the national economy.
   - C. The argument is invalid, because it confuses correlation with causation.
   - D. The argument is invalid, because it attempts to refute one reason against doing something while ignoring other possible reasons.

6. Which of the following considerations, if true, best illustrates why the author's evidence is inadequate?

   - A. Some people depend on the porcupine caribou for food.
   - B. People who call themselves "scientists" may make claims that are long held to be true yet are eventually shown to be false.
   - C. There is not enough oil in the ANWR to have a measurable impact on global oil prices.
   - D. Extracting oil from the ANWR would reduce the foreign trade deficit.

Questions 7 and 8 are based on the following information and map.

After World War II, Germany was split into two nations: democratic West Germany and communist East Germany. West Germany was under the control of the victorious Allies, who formed an alliance called the North Atlantic Treaty Organization (NATO). In 1955, NATO decided to allow West Germany to join NATO and to rearm. In response, the U.S.S.R. (that is, the Soviet Union) and a number of communist Eastern European countries formed what they called a "Treaty of Friendship, Co-operation, and Mutual Assistance," commonly referred to as the Warsaw Pact. In the Warsaw Pact, the communist countries agreed to band together if one of them was attacked, and the smaller communist countries agreed to put their military forces under the command of the Soviet Union.

Source: Central Intelligence Agency

7. Some historians believe that, in forming the Warsaw Pact, the Soviet Union wanted to create a buffer between itself and NATO countries. How does the map support that view?
   - A. The map indicates that many of the World War II Allies joined the Warsaw Pact, but not until the 1960s.
   - B. The map shows that most of the Warsaw Pact countries lay between the Soviet Union and Western countries, including France, West Germany, and Great Britain.
   - C. The map shows that the Warsaw Pact involved the building of a wall between the Soviet Union and Western Europe.
   - D. The map indicates that the Soviet Union was made up of smaller republics on its western border.

8. The map could be used to dispute which one of the following claims?
   - A. In forming the Warsaw Pact, the Soviet Union greatly increased its access to oceanic coastline.
   - B. In forming the Warsaw Pact, the Soviet Union wished to increase its trade with Africa.
   - C. The Warsaw Pact benefitted Bulgaria and Romania no less than the Soviet Union.
   - D. The Warsaw Pact initially included Albania.

Question 9 refers to the following table and map.

Average Yearly Rainfall in New England	
State	**Avg. Rainfall/Year**
Connecticut	47 inches
Maine	41 inches
Massachusetts	45 inches
New Hampshire	42 inches
Rhode Island	44 inches
Vermont	39 inches

Source: netstate.com

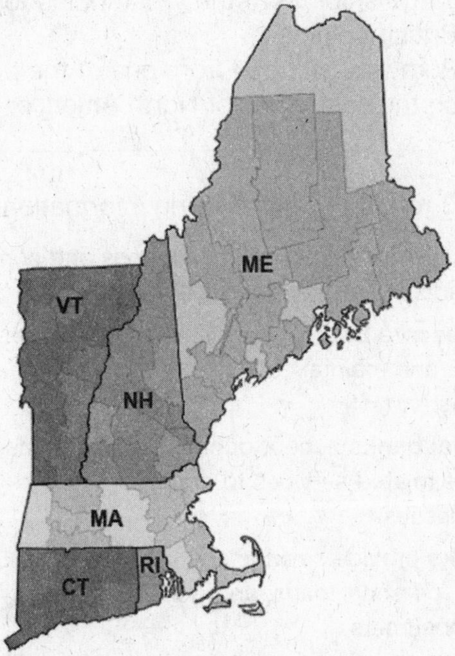

9. What is the average (arithmetic mean) yearly rainfall, in inches, of the three northernmost states in New England?

- A. $40\frac{2}{3}$
- B. 41
- C. 42
- D. $43\frac{1}{3}$

Question 10 refers to the following graph.

The graph below shows the percent of people who voted in presidential elections from 1996 to 2012.

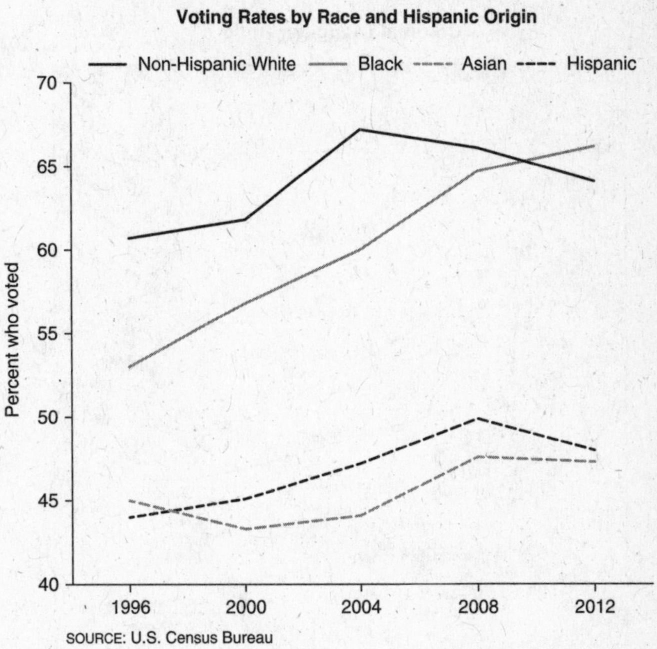

10. Over the period illustrated by the line graph, the rate at which eligible black voters participated in presidential elections

- A. fluctuated up and down, but ended higher than it began
- B. steadily increased, surpassing that of white voters in the 2012 elections
- C. increased sharply in the middle of the time period shown on the graph before dropping back closer to its original level
- D. was consistently lower than the rates of most other races and ethnic groups

Answers and explanations start on page 17.

PART II: SOCIAL STUDIES CONTENT—25 QUESTIONS

Directions: You may fill in the circles next to the correct answers or write your answers on a separate piece of paper.

Questions 1 and 2 refer to the following map.

Colonial Triangular Trade

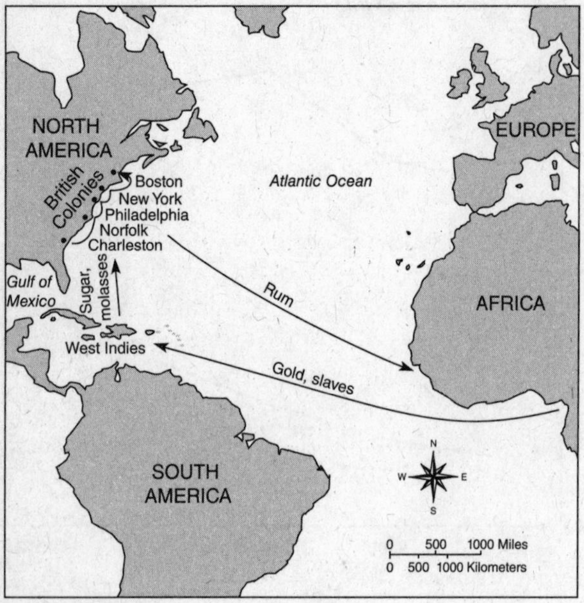

1. Based on this map, what were the three sides of the triangle in the triangular trade?
   - A. Europe to the West Indies; the West Indies to Africa; Africa to the British colonies
   - B. the West Indies to the British colonies; the British colonies to Africa; Africa to the West Indies
   - C. the West Indies to England; England to the British colonies; the British colonies to Africa
   - D. South America to Africa; Africa to the West Indies; the West Indies to the British colonies

2. Which statement is a conclusion based on the map rather than a supporting detail from the map?
   - A. Cargo ships never had to sail empty on any leg of a profitable triangular journey.
   - B. The journey of Africans from Africa to the Americas was called the Middle Passage.
   - C. Slaves sometimes were transported on cargo ships from the West Indies to the British colonies.
   - D. Rum was shipped from one of the ports on the east coast of North America.

Question 3 refers to the following information.

Several types of U.S. banking institutions and some of their main services are described below.

Federal Reserve Banks control the nation's monetary policy and maintain stability of the banking and financial systems.

Commercial banks accept deposits, make loans, and provide related services to corporations and other businesses.

Retail banks provide savings and checking accounts, mortgages, personal loans, and debit and credit cards to consumers.

Community development banks serve residents and spur economic development in low- to moderate-income areas.

Credit unions provide their members with checking and savings accounts, mortgages, and other services at a lower interest rate than other financial institutions.

3. At which type of financial institution would the ABC Printing Company be most likely to take out a loan to finance the purchase of a new printing press?
   - A. Federal Reserve Bank
   - B. commercial bank
   - C. retail bank
   - D. community development bank

Questions 4 and 5 refer to the following passage.

Somerville has had a long history of corruption. From the 1960s to the 1980s, its mayor, councilors, and tax assessors were involved in a complex network of bribery and favors. The "strong-mayor" system of government is responsible for this corruption; in the history of Massachusetts, all but a single instance of municipal corruption occurred under a strong-mayor government. Because that tainted system is still in place to this day in Somerville, the current mayor must be viewed with strong suspicion.

4. Which of the following words or phrases is based on the author's opinion, not fact?

- A. long history
- B. tainted system
- C. bribery
- D. mayors, councilors, and tax assessors

5. Is the author's conclusion properly supported by evidence?

- A. Yes, because the corruption in Somerville spreads beyond the office of the mayor.
- B. Yes, because 20 years of corruption can accurately be called a "long history."
- C. No, because there is no mention of criminal investigation or charges.
- D. No, because no indication is given that the current mayor will behave as past mayors did.

6. Most Americans believe it is their duty as citizens to take part in our system of government.

Which of the following actions represents participation in government?

- A. pursuing higher education
- B. displaying the American flag
- C. volunteering at a hospital
- D. serving on a jury

7. In many Latin American countries, control passes back and forth between military and civilian rule. Generally, when a civilian government rules, it tries to improve conditions for the nation's citizens, but these attempts lead to turmoil and civil unrest. In response, the military takes power and imposes strict controls on the populace. Such shifts have taken place in Argentina, Peru, and Chile in recent decades.

Which of the following is highly valued by those who favor military rule?

- A. social welfare
- B. freedom
- C. democracy
- D. law and order

Questions 8 and 9 refer to the following chart.

Presidential Powers in Several Nations

Constitutional Power	U.S.A.	South Africa	France	Mexico
Controls armed forces	✔	✔	✔	✔
Approves legislation	✔	✔	✔	✔
Appoints executive branch officials	✔	✔	✔	✔
Appoints judges	✔	✔	✔	✔
Appoints prime minister			✔	
Dissolves legislature			✔	

8. Which of the following is a difference between the powers of the U.S. and French presidents?
   - A. The U.S. president controls the armed forces, and the French president does not.
   - B. The U.S. president approves legislation, and the French president does not.
   - C. The French president has the power to dissolve the legislature, while the U.S. president does not.
   - D. The French president has the power to appoint judges, while the U.S. president does not.

9. Which of the following statements is a conclusion based on the chart rather than a detail?
   - A. The president of South Africa cannot dissolve the legislature.
   - B. Of all the presidents shown, the French president has the greatest variety of powers.
   - C. The president of Mexico has the power to appoint judges.
   - D. The U.S. president has the power to approve legislation.

Question 10 refers to the following paragraph.

After the Civil War, southern states passed Jim Crow laws, which kept whites and blacks apart in public places like restaurants, buses, and restrooms. In an 1896 case, *Plessy v. Ferguson*, the U.S. Supreme Court upheld a Louisiana law requiring separate railroad cars for white and black passengers. The Court ruled that it was constitutional to have "separate but equal" facilities for whites and blacks and other minorities. The Court reasoned that "legislation is powerless to eradicate racial instincts or to abolish distinctions." One justice dissented, saying that the decision was "inconsistent with the personal liberty of citizens, white and black."

10. Which of the following statements is an opinion rather than a fact?
    - A. In the late 1800s, many southern states passed Jim Crow laws to keep whites and blacks separate in public places.
    - B. In Louisiana, a law required separate railroad cars for white and black passengers.
    - C. *Plessy v. Ferguson* was an 1896 Supreme Court case that challenged the Louisiana law related to segregated railroad cars.
    - D. The U.S. Supreme Court ruling in *Plessy v. Ferguson* was wrong because it infringed on freedoms guaranteed in the Constitution.

Questions 11 and 12 refer to the following paragraph and chart.

When the U.S. government cannot cover its expenses, it borrows money by selling bonds. It pays back the principal and interest on the bonds over a period of many years. The national debt is the total amount the U.S. government owes at any particular point in time. In 2010, this was about $13.2 trillion.

One way of measuring the national debt is by computing the per capita national debt. The per capita national debt is the total national debt divided by the population of the United States. The graph below shows the per capita national debt every five years from 1990 to 2010.

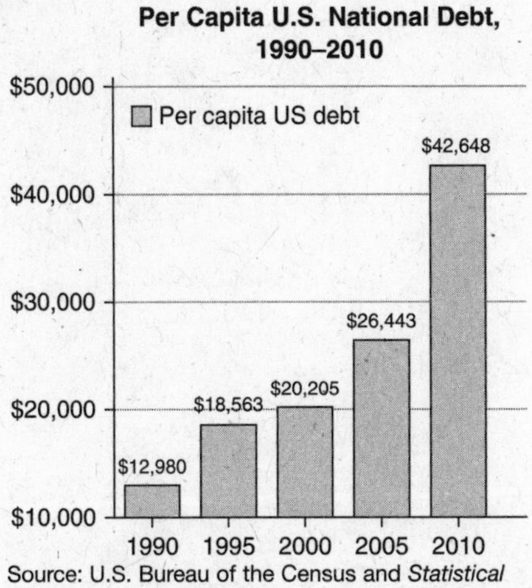

Source: U.S. Bureau of the Census and *Statistical Abstract of the United States*.

11. Which of the following conclusions is supported by the data in the paragraph and the graph?
   - A. The nation's debt increased at a faster rate than did the U.S. population during the period shown on the graph.
   - B. Every person in the United States owed an average of $20,000 to the government in the year 2000.
   - C. In 1990, the U.S. government owed every American about $13,000.
   - D. The U.S. government sold about $5.7 trillion worth of bonds in 2000.

12. Which action would enable the U.S. government to reduce its debt?
   - A. postpone payment of that debt
   - B. pay interest to foreign investors
   - C. pay interest to U.S. investors
   - D. raise taxes and cut spending

Question 13 refers to the following paragraph.

The ninth-century BCE collapse of the Mayan empire is often attributed to a massive drought. But new geological and archaeological evidence from the Yucatan peninsula in Mexico shows that the Maya engaged in massive deforestation, clearing land for crops and burning the wood to bake bricks for their cities and temples. Modern weather models show that the destruction of native vegetation could have contributed to as much as 60 percent of the dry weather that is believed to have ended this civilization.

13. According to the theory presented in the paragraph, what was the effect of Mayan deforestation of the Yucatan peninsula?
   - A. The Mayans needed more land to grow crops.
   - B. Scientists discovered new evidence in the geological record.
   - C. A drought was significantly worsened due to lack of native vegetation.
   - D. Baking bricks required an enormous amount of wood.

Question 14 refers to the following map.

Great Britain during the Industrial Revolution, 1830

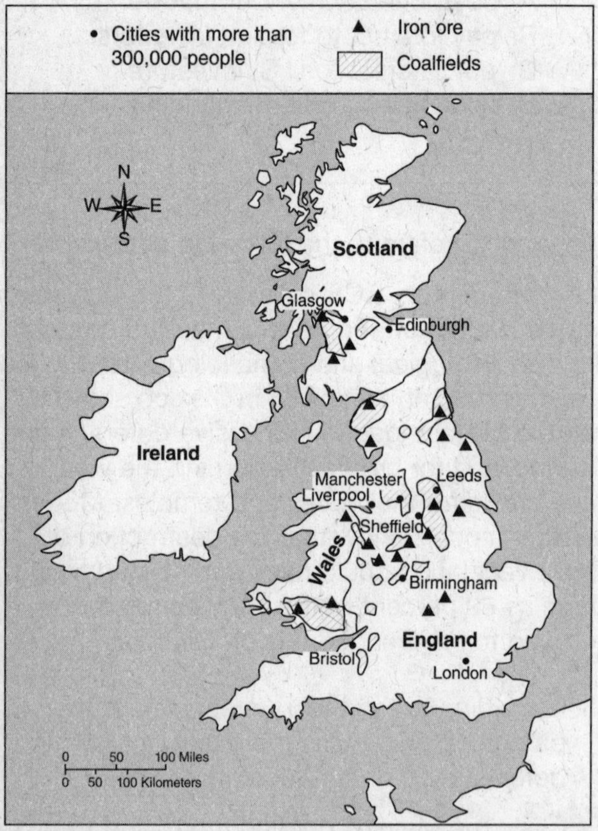

14. Which of the following is a conclusion based on the map rather than a supporting detail from the map?

- A. The Industrial Revolution took place in Great Britain around the year 1830.
- B. More than 300,000 people lived in Sheffield around 1830.
- C. Many cities had large populations because nearby coal and iron ore deposits meant jobs.
- D. There was a large area with coal deposits in southern Wales around 1830.

15. When a nation follows a policy of appeasement, it makes concessions to an aggressor in order to preserve the peace.

Which of the following is an example of appeasement?

- A. Italy's support of Spanish Nationalists in the Spanish Civil War in the late 1930s
- B. Great Britain's acceptance of Germany's takeover of Austria and Czechoslovakia in the late 1930s
- C. Germany's 1939 invasion of Poland, which started World War II
- D. Japan's alliance with Germany and Italy in 1940, which created the Rome-Berlin-Tokyo Axis

Questions 16 through 18 refer to the following poster.

Source: Library of Congress. Artist Dan Sayre Groesbeck.

16. The person who designed this poster used irony to make a point. Behind this irony was an assumption with which the designer expected viewers to agree.

    Which of the following statements summarizes this assumption?

    - A. People will give to the war effort because they are doing well economically.
    - B. Financing the war requires selling bonds and raising taxes.
    - C. During wartime, people have little money to spend on their sons.
    - D. People value the lives of their children more than they value money.

17. During which war was this poster part of a government advertising campaign?

    - A. the Civil War
    - B. World War I
    - C. World War II
    - D. the Vietnam War

18. If the government were running a similar advertising campaign today, which medium would probably reach the most people?

    - A. posters
    - B. leaflets and brochures
    - C. print ads in financial newspapers
    - D. television ads on primetime

Question 19 refers to the following table.

The Five Most Populous American Colonies, 1750

Colony	Population (estimate)
Massachusetts	188,000
Pennsylvania	119,700
Connecticut	111,300
Maryland	141,000
Virginia	231,000

Source: U.S. Bureau of the Census

19. Which of the following statements is supported by the data in the chart?

    - A. The population of all of the American colonies was less than 700,000.
    - B. Virginia had more than twice as many people as Maryland.
    - C. Most of the population of Massachusetts was of English origin.
    - D. The population of the colony of New York was smaller than that of Connecticut.

Questions 20 through 22 refer to the following paragraph and flowchart.

The U.S. Civil Service system is designed to ensure that people are appointed to government positions because of their skills and abilities rather than because of their political affiliation. Over 90 percent of federal jobs are covered by civil service rules. The typical steps in applying for a civil service job are shown below.

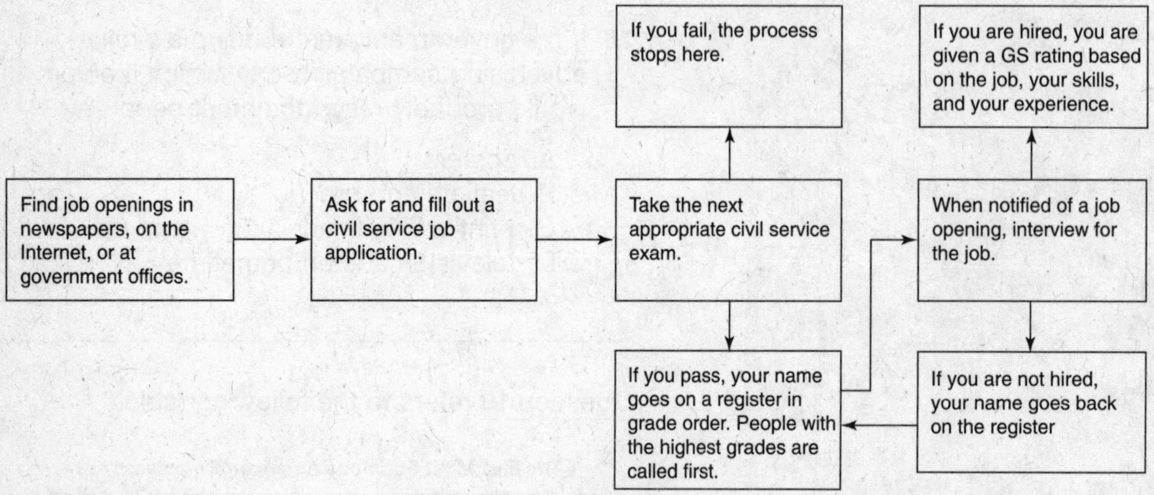

20. Which of the following is the best title for the flowchart?
    - A. A History of the Civil Service
    - B. The Qualifications of Civil Service Workers
    - C. Applying for Civil Service Jobs
    - D. Interviewing for a Civil Service Job

21. What does a civil servant's GS rating probably affect most?
    - A. salary
    - B. length of service
    - C. job security
    - D. education level

22. On which of the following values does the structure of the Civil Service system primarily rest?
    - A. patriotism
    - B. equal opportunity
    - C. freedom of speech
    - D. respect for seniority

Questions 23 and 24 refer to the following graphs.

Interest Rates for Conventional Mortgages

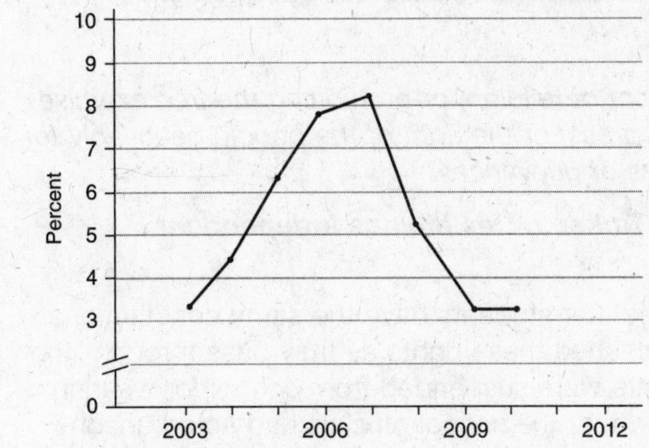

Source: U.S. Bureau of the Census

U.S. Mortgage Debt Outstanding

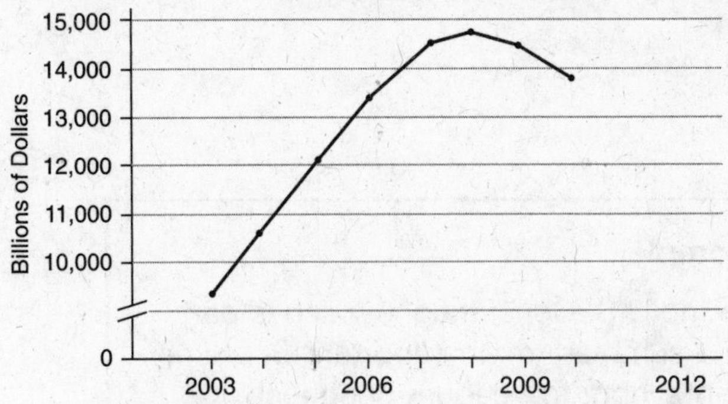

Source: U.S. Bureau of the Census

23. In 2005, what were the approximate interest rate and approximate total mortgage debt outstanding for a conventional mortgage?
    - A. 8 percent and $13,000 billion
    - B. 4 percent and $11,000 billion
    - C. 6 percent and $12,000 billion
    - D. 6 percent and $9,000 billion

24. Based on the graphs, how do mortgage interest rates and total mortgage debt outstanding compare?
    - A. Interest rates rise in direct proportion to decreases in total mortgage debt outstanding.
    - B. The higher the interest rate, the lower the total mortgage debt outstanding.
    - C. The lower the interest rate, the higher the total mortgage debt outstanding.
    - D. As interest rates rise and then fall, the total mortgage debt will move similarly but not at the same rate.

25. A culture hearth refers to the center of a culture—the source of its ideas, values, customs, fashions, and practices. An example of an ancient culture hearth was the area along the Nile River in Egypt. The agricultural, economic, social, artistic, and religious ideas and practices that grew up there spread through trade to other areas of the ancient world.

    Which of the following is an example of a modern culture hearth with worldwide influence?
    - A. Pyongyang, capital of North Korea, which has a 95 percent literacy rate
    - B. Ottawa, capital of Canada, with a population of about one million
    - C. New Zealand, which exports wool and textiles
    - D. Hollywood, California, which produces movies and television shows, enjoyed around the world

Answers and explanations start on page 17.

Part III: Extended Response

Directions: Read both of the selections and the writing prompt and answer the questions that follow.

Questions 1 through 5 are based on the process of writing a response to a reading selection.
NOTE: Do not start writing your response until you are asked to do so at question 4.

First Amendment to the U.S. Constitution

Congress shall make no law respecting an establishment of religion, or prohibiting the free exercise thereof; or abridging the freedom of speech, or of the press; or the right of the people peaceably to assemble, and to petition the Government for a redress of grievances.

Public School Students Have Free Speech Rights: *Tinker v. Des Moines Independent Community School District* (1969)

This landmark U.S. Supreme Court decision recognizes that students have the same constitutional rights as every other American citizen. Students do not shed these rights as they pass through "the schoolhouse gate." The case arose when three students were suspended from school for wearing armbands to protest the Vietnam War. The Court found that the school officials had acted unconstitutionally in suppressing the students' free speech rights. The Court, however, recognized that school officials need some flexibility and control of students in order to fulfill the educational role of the school. Thus, school officials may prohibit student conduct which "materially disrupts or involves substantial disorder in the classroom."

Bill of Rights Curriculum Guide, American Civil Liberties Union of Minnesota

Writing Prompt

The first selection is the First Amendment to the U.S. Constitution, which is part of the Bill of Rights. The second selection is a summary of an important Supreme Court case relating this amendment to students' right to freedom of speech.

Write a response to these selections that analyzes how the case applies the concept of "free speech" in the First Amendment to students. Also explain the implications of the Court's statement that school officials need flexibility and therefore can prohibit some student conduct.

Use relevant and specific information from the reading selection and your general knowledge to support your response.

Unpack the Writing Prompt and Plan Your Response

1. What two things does the prompt ask you to write about?

   A. ____________________

   B. ____________________

2. What is the main point you will make about 1.A above?

   ____

3. What are three main points you will make about 1.B above?

   ____

   ____

   ____

Draft, Revise, and Edit Your Response

4. On a computer or on a piece of paper, write a response to the prompt.
5. On the computer or on the paper, make revisions to improve your response and edit to correct errors in grammar, usage, spelling, capitalization, and punctuation.

The *Extended Response Evaluation Guide* starts on page 19.

STOP

Congratulations! You have completed the GED® Social Studies Pretest.

Reminder: your next step is to check your answers with the Pretest Answers and Explanations and fill in the study planner that follows those explanations.

PRETEST ANSWERS AND EXPLANATIONS

Part I: Social Studies Practices, page 2

1. **C. The Voting Rights Act of 1965 gave the Federal Government oversight of state elections to end barriers against African American voting.** The passage described the historical events that led to the Voting Rights Act, and how this legislation ended the voting discrimination that certain states enacted after the passage of the Fifteenth Amendment.

2. **C. interpretation** According to the passage, the terms "strict construction" and "loose construction" refer to different ways in which people interpret the range of powers that the Constitution grants to the federal government.

3. **A. The FDA's new regulations would place a financial hardship on small food retailers.** According to the passage, smaller food retailers would feel more of the burden than larger establishments, and the Common Sense Nutritional Disclosure Act seeks to relieve this burden.

4. **C. "devastating"** This word highlights the author's point of view that the FDA's new regulations would be especially harmful to smaller food retailers.

5. **D. The argument is invalid, because it attempts to refute one reason against doing something while ignoring all the others.** The paragraph states that possible danger to the porcupine caribou is "one commonly cited" reason against drilling in the Arctic National Wildlife Refuge. This implies that there are other reasons as well. Thus, the author's conclusion that "we have no reason not to drill in the ANWR" is unsupported, since the author has attempted to refute only one of the possibly many reasons against drilling in the refuge.

6. **A. Some people depend on the porcupine caribou for food.** The primary evidence in this argument is that almost all of the species that have ever lived on Earth have gone extinct, and the vast majority of these extinctions happened naturally. The author uses this evidence to argue that the human threat to the porcupine caribou isn't a big deal. However, the author fails to consider the possibility that human-caused extinctions are worse than naturally-occurring ones. Choice (A) shows that the loss of the caribou by human hands would cause a severe problem: the loss of a major food source for some people.

7. **B. The map shows that most of the Warsaw Pact countries lay between the Soviet Union and Western countries, including France, West Germany, and Great Britain.** The passage states that the World War II Allies, which included France and Great Britain, formed NATO. It also states that West Germany was allowed to join NATO. And the map makes clear that the smaller Warsaw Pact countries lay geographically between those nations and the Soviet Union.

8. **A. In forming the Warsaw Pact, the Soviet Union greatly increased its access to oceanic coastlines.** Although most of the Warsaw Pact countries touched a body of water, most of their borders were land borders, and two of the Warsaw Pact countries were completely landlocked.

9. **A. $40\frac{2}{3}$** The three northernmost states are Maine (ME), New Hampshire (NH) and Vermont (VT). To find the average, sum the rainfall of each state and divide by 3: $\frac{41+42+39}{3} = 40\frac{2}{3}$.

10. **B. steadily increased, surpassing that of white voters in the 2012 elections** The solid gray line corresponds to the rate at which black voters participated in presidential elections. It increases consistently from year to year, and shows the highest rate of all groups in the 2012 election.

Part II: Social Studies Content, page 6

1. **B. the West Indies to the British colonies; the British colonies to Africa; Africa to the West Indies** According to the map, the West Indies exported sugar and molasses to the British colonies in North America. The British colonies exported rum to Africa. Finally, Africa exported slaves and gold to the West Indies. The trade routes formed a triangle.

2. **A. Cargo ships never had to sail empty on any leg of a profitable triangular journey.** This is a general conclusion that is supported by the details of the map, which show goods traveling along each leg of the triangular trade route. Therefore, a very profitable journey must have meant a ship carried cargo on each leg of the route. The remaining options state details that may or may not be confirmed by the map.

3. **B. Commercial bank** According to the descriptions, commercial banks provide services to businesses and other corporations. None of the other descriptions describe financial institutions making loans to companies. They focus either on national financial systems or on individual borrowers.

4. **B. tainted system** "Tainted" is a loaded word that indicates the author's belief that a "strong-mayor" system is inherently corrupt.

5. **D. No, because no indication is given that the current mayor will behave as past mayors did.** A strong-mayor system may enable, but does not guarantee, corruption. Past corruption is not by itself enough reason to have a strong suspicion toward the current government.

6. **D. serving on a jury** Serving on a jury, like voting, is a civic duty of each citizen. It is a way to participate in the judicial branch of government. Note that although choice (B), displaying the American flag, is a patriotic act, it does not involve participating in government

in any way and so is not a way of participating in the political system.

7. **D. law and order** The hallmark of military rule is strict control over the citizenry; in other words, law and order.

8. **C. The French president has the power to dissolve the legislature, while the U.S. president does not.** The checkmark in the last row under "France" indicates that the French president can dissolve the legislature. The U.S. president does not have this power.

9. **B. Of all the presidents shown, the French president has the greatest variety of powers.** This statement is a conclusion, a generalization based on the details in the chart. Choices (A), (C), and (D) are specific details from the chart.

10. **D. The U.S. Supreme Court ruling in *Plessy v. Ferguson* was wrong because it infringed on freedoms guaranteed in the Constitution.** This statement is a rephrasing of the dissenting justice's opinion, or belief, about the case. The other statements are all facts from the paragraph.

11. **A. The nation's debt increased at a faster rate than did the U.S. population during the period shown on the graph.** You can tell this is true because the per capita debt figure increased steadily from 1990 to 2010. This would happen only if the debt increased faster than the population of the United States.

12. **D. raise taxes and cut spending** You can conclude from the text that to cut the national debt, the U.S. government would have to increase income (raise taxes) and lower costs (cut spending).

13. **C. A drought was significantly worsened due to lack of native vegetation.** According to the passage, the deforestation caused a significant portion of the drought that led to the Mayan collapse. Choices (A) and (D) are both causes, not effects, of the deforestation.

14. **C. Many cities had large populations because nearby coal and iron ore deposits meant jobs.** Coal and iron ore were among the most important raw materials of the Industrial Revolution. By examining the relationship of the location of the cities to that of the coalfields and iron ore deposits, you can conclude that Great Britain's most populous cities (with the exception of London) were large partly because of their proximity to the important raw materials of the Industrial Revolution. The remaining statements are details from the map.

15. **B. Great Britain's acceptance of Germany's takeover of Austria and Czechoslovakia in the late 1930s** Of all the options, this is the only one that has the element of concession without opposition that is the hallmark of appeasement.

16. **D. People value the lives of their children more than they value money.** This is the underlying assumption of the poster: that Americans have been willing to send their sons into battle where they risk their lives, but haven't been donating money to the war cause with equal willingness. The poster thus plays upon their sense of guilt.

17. **B. World War I** The poster is dated 1917, so the war is World War I.

18. **D. television ads on prime time** Today, the government could probably reach the most people with television ads rather than print ads, because so many people watch television.

19. **D. The population of the colony of New York was smaller than that of Connecticut.** Since the chart shows the five colonies with the largest populations in 1750, it follows that any colony not listed has a population smaller than that of Connecticut, which ranked fifth. The other options are not supported by the data in the table.

20. **C. Applying for Civil Service Jobs** This title best describes what the flowchart shows—the steps in applying for a civil service job.

21. **A. salary** The GS rating of a job, based on the job description and the candidate's skills and experience, is directly related to the salary level of the position. The other options would not be affected by the GS rating.

22. **B. equal opportunity** Since Civil Service jobs are open to all who apply and are awarded on merit, they are designed to provide equal opportunity for employment, regardless of gender, race, ethnicity, party affiliation, or other factors.

23. **C. 6 percent and $12,000 billion** Locate 2005 on each graph. (Note that each tic mark on the horizontal axis indicates a year, even if it is not labeled.) The first graph shows the mortgage interest rate was about 6 percent in 2005. The second graph shows the total outstanding mortgage debt was about $12,000 billion in 2005.

24. **D. As interest rates rise and then fall, the total mortgage debt will move similarly but not at the same rate.** Look at the general trend shown by each graph. Note that as interest rates rise and fall, the mortgage debts rise similarly but fall at a different rate.

25. **D. Hollywood, California, which produces movies and television shows, enjoyed around the world** The movies and television shows that originate in Hollywood are distributed worldwide, helping to spread American popular culture to other nations.

Part III: Extended Response, page 14

Your responses to question 1 may vary but should be similar to the following:

1. **A.** Explain how the Supreme Court case applied the idea of free speech to students.

   B. Discuss what it means that school officials can prohibit some student conduct.

Your responses to questions 2 and 3 may vary. Sample responses are below.

2. The Supreme Court said that students have free speech, but only if that freedom doesn't lead to disorder in the classroom.
3. (1) The Supreme Court said that school officials can control speech that leads to disorder in the classroom. (2) It's very important that students be able to study without disruption. (3) But the ruling also means that it's up to the discretion of school officials to decide how much free speech constitutes a disruption.
4. **Drafting Checklist** Check off each task that you performed. Give yourself a score of 0–5 based on how many checks you made.

   _______ I wrote an introduction to my response based on my central idea (thesis statement).

   _______ I developed several paragraphs responding to the prompt.

   _______ In my response, I cited specific evidence from the text to support my central idea.

   _______ In my response, I provided additional relevant information based on my own knowledge and perspectives.

   _______ I wrote a conclusion that summarized my position or restated my central idea in a different way.

5. **Revising and Editing Checklist** Check off each task that you performed. Give yourself a score of 0–6 based on how many checks you made.

   _______ My piece was well organized, or I improved its organization so that one idea relates to another.

   _______ I made sure that my sentences were complete, clear, and correct.

   _______ Each of my paragraphs has a central idea and supporting evidence from the text.

   _______ My piece has a clear beginning, middle, and ending.

   _______ I corrected subject-verb agreement, pronoun agreement, and verb tense errors.

   _______ I have corrected punctuation, capitalization, and spelling.

KAPLAN GED® SOCIAL STUDIES TEST STUDY PLANNER

Take the Pretest, starting on page 1. Check your answers in the Pretest Answers and Explanations. Use the results to fill in the charts below so that you can target the areas that need the most work.

Part I: Social Studies Practices, 10 Questions

Circle the *Question Numbers* that you answered correctly in the second column. Write the *Number Correct* in the third column. Compare your "number correct" to the "mastery" number in the fourth column. If you do not have time to review all of the *Social Studies Practices* sections, target your study to the *Content Areas* in which you did not score at the mastery level.

Content Area	Question Numbers	Number Correct	Mastery/Total
Determine Central Idea and Draw Conclusions, Interpret Words and Ideas, and Analyze Relationships Between Materials Pages 26–29 and 34–37	1, 2		**2 out of 2**
Analyze Author's Purpose and Point of View and Evaluate Author's Reasoning and Evidence Pages 30–33	3, 4, 5, 6		**3 out of 4**
Interpret Data and Statistics Pages 38–39	7, 8, 9, 10		**3 out of 4**

Part II: Social Studies Content, 25 Questions

Circle the *Question Numbers* that you answered correctly in the second column. Write the *Number Correct* in the third column. Compare your "number correct" to the "mastery" number in the fourth column. If you do not have time to review all of the *Social Studies Content* sections, target your study to the *Content Areas* that need the most work.

Content Area	Question Numbers	Number Correct	Mastery/Total
U.S. History Pages 46–59	1, 2, 10, 16, 17, 18, 19		**5 out of 7**
Civics and Government Pages 60–73	4, 5, 6, 7, 8, 9, 20, 21, 22, 23		**7 out of 10**
Economics Pages 74–85	3, 11, 12, 24		**3 out of 4**
Geography and the World Pages 86–101	13, 14, 15, 25		**3 out of 4**

About the GED® Social Studies Test

The GED® *Social Studies Test* evaluates your ability to understand, interpret, and apply information. You will have 90 minutes to answer 35 questions that are based on reading passages and interpreting graphics such as charts, graphs, diagrams, editorial cartoons, photographs, and maps.

You will need a minimum score of 150 to pass the *Social Studies Test*, which is one of the four tests you will need to pass in order to earn a high school equivalency diploma.

Content Areas

Civics and Government (50%) topics include modern and historic governments, constitutional government, levels and branches of the U.S. government, the electoral system, and the role of the citizen.

U.S. History (20%) topics stretch from colonialism and the American Revolution through the Civil War and Reconstruction into the modern era of industrialization, immigration, two world wars, the Cold War, and the movements for equal rights.

Economics (15%) topics include basic economics concepts and systems, the government and the economy, and labor and consumer economics issues.

Geography and the World (15%) topics cover major stages in world history as well as the relationship among resources, the environment, and societies.

Social Studies Practices

In addition to testing your understanding of social studies passages and graphics, questions are based on your understanding of major skills, called **Social Studies Practices,** and these skills introduce this unit on pages 26–45. After you study these practices, you will reinforce them as you work through the unit. They include the following:

- Determine **Central Ideas, Inferences, Hypotheses,** and **Conclusions.**
- Analyze **Words, Events,** and **Ideas** in Social Studies Contexts.
- Analyze Author's **Purpose** and **Point of View.**
- Evaluate Author's **Reasoning** and **Evidence.**
- Analyze and Integrate **Relationships Within and Between Social Studies Materials.**
- Interpret Data and Statistics in **Graphs** and **Charts.**
- Find the Center in a Statistical Data Set, Including **Average, Median,** and **Mode.**

Computer-Based Social Studies Test Question Formats

You will work with six question formats on the Social Studies Test. Many of the questions will be in the familiar multiple-choice format, but you will need to be acquainted with the other formats as well.

Multiple-choice questions have four options (A through D). You will **click** on the best answer.

> Which statement correctly describes a significant way that aristocracy differs from democracy as a political system?
>
> ◯ A. In an aristocracy, power is always directly exercised by the people.
> ◯ B. In an aristocracy, power is concentrated in the hands of a small group.
> ◯ C. In an aristocracy, all adults are equal before the law.
> ◯ D. In a democracy, all laws are seen as divinely ordained.

Fill-in-the-blank questions will require you to **type** a word, phrase, or number in a box that appears on the screen.

GED® TEST TIP

Fill-in-the-blank questions can have only one correct answer. Find a specific number, word, or phrase in the passage or graphic to type in the box or complete a computation if required by the question.

> Type the appropriate state name in the box.
>
> The number of representatives in Congress from the state of [ ] is twice the number of representatives in Congress from the state of Pennsylvania.

Drop-down questions give you the opportunity to **click** on the correct response to complete a statement.

> An industrial economy exists within a web of complex relationships. Goods must first be [Select...] before they can be sold, but no goods can be sold without [Select...] to buy them. The largest group of buyers are ordinary citizens, who cannot buy without [Select...], the most common source of which is [Select...], frequently earned through employment in the production of goods.

Hot-spot items consist of a graphic image or images. You will need to **click** on one or more "points" or graphics on the screen.

Which two charts relate to the concept of inflation? Click on the two charts that you want to select.

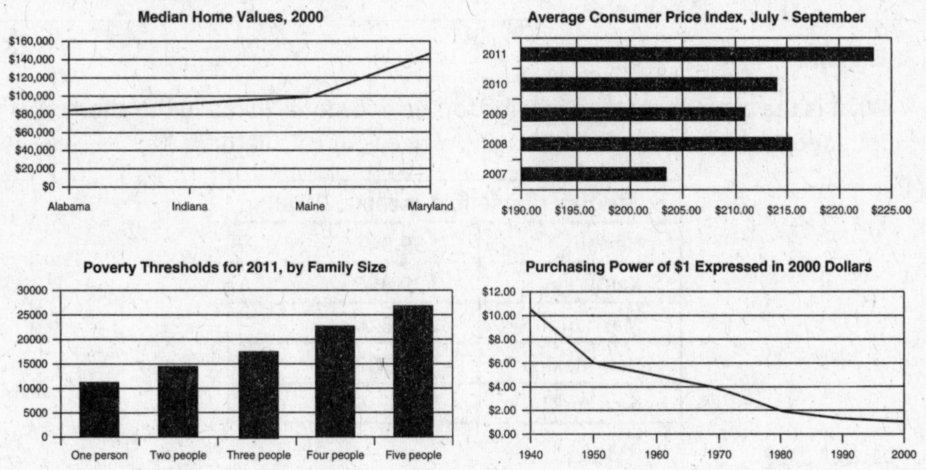

Drag-and-drop items require you to **click** on a small image, words, or numerical expression and to **drag** and **drop it** in a specified location on the computer screen.

Click on five bars and drag them onto the graph to show the number of Americans that speak each of the five languages indicated.

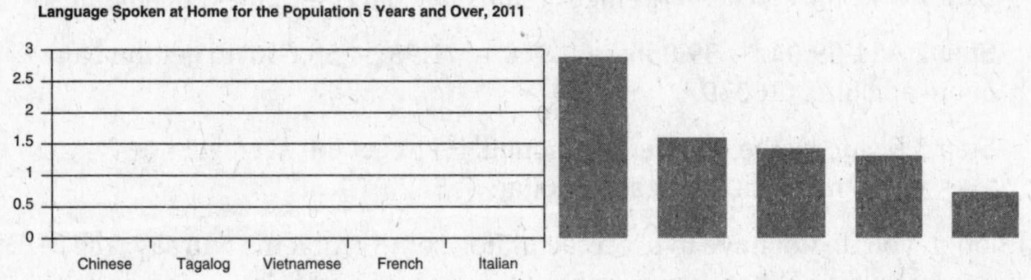

An **Extended-Response** item requires you to **type** in a *text box* in response to a **prompt** based on one or more short passages, a graphic, or a combination.

You will have 25 minutes at the end of the *Social Studies Test* to read the materials and to plan, write, and revise your response.

In your response, develop an argument for the main cause behind the Great Depression, and the major step taken to recover. Incorporate relevant and specific examples from the paragraph and your own knowledge of the issue and the circumstances surrounding the time of the Great Depression.

Type your response in the box. This task may require 25 minutes to complete.

GED® TEST TIP

The Extended Response will be the last question on the Social Studies Test. *Carefully watch both the **Time Remaining** and **Question** bars at the top of the computer screen. Make sure you are allowing yourself 25 minutes for this task.*

Math Problems on the *Social Studies Test*

Many social studies investigations use mathematics. For that reason, there will be math questions on the *GED® Social Studies Test*. You will focus on math skills in this unit with the Social Studies Practices lesson on pages 38–39 and with problems that have this symbol: Calculator.

Example

What is the average median income for the five states listed in the chart, rounded to the nearest dollar? You MAY use your calculator.

Median Household Income, 2011	
Hawaii	\$59,047
Kentucky	\$39,856
Maryland	\$68,876
New Mexico	\$41,982
New York	\$50,636

A. \$41,952

B. \$50,338

C. \$52,079

D. \$52,200

Solution

Step 1 Write the equation: Average = sum of amounts ÷ number of amounts.

Step 2 Add 59,047 + 39,856 + 68,876 + 41,982 + 50,636 to get the sum of the amounts (260397).

Step 3 Divide by the number of amounts (5) to get the average: 60397 ÷ 5 = 52079.; round to the nearest dollar: C. \$52,079.

Although you do not have to use a calculator, some problems will say: *You MAY use your calculator*. When you see that language, the calculator icon appears at the top of the screen. If you cannot remember how to use the calculator, you can open the online ***Calculator Reference Sheet.*** Both links are shown below.

Calculator | Calculator Reference

You can **click** the links to ***open, move,*** and ***close*** both the online ***Texas Instruments TI-30XS MultiView™*** calculator and the ***Calculator Reference Sheet***. You will want to move them on the computer screen so that they don't block the problem. Also remember that you will have an ***off-line wipe-off board*** that you can use as scratch paper.

GED® TEST TIP

You are encouraged to purchase a hand-held version of the Texas Instruments TI-30XS MultiView™ calculator for practice as you work through this book. You can buy one at office or school supply stores or from online vendors.

Extended-Response Questions on the Social Studies Test

Social scientists and students communicate about their work in writing. To reflect that, the *GED® Social Studies Test* has an Extended-Response item. You will focus on writing Extended Responses in this unit with the Social Studies Practices lesson on pages 40–41.

The Extended-Response items are based on one passage, two passages, a graphic, or a combination. You will compose your answer in a textbox similar to the one below.

page 1 | page 2

Quotation

"Our progress in degeneracy appears to me to be pretty rapid. As a nation, we began by declaring that 'all men are created equal.' We now practically read it 'all men are created equal, except negroes.'"

— Abraham Lincoln, in a personal letter, 1855

Excerpt

One hundred years of delay have passed since President Lincoln freed the slaves, yet their heirs, their grandsons, are not fully free. They are not yet freed from the bonds of injustice. They are not yet freed from social and economic oppression. And this Nation, for all its hopes and all its boasts, will not be fully free until all its citizens are free. ... We preach freedom around the world, and we mean it, and we cherish our freedom here at home, but are we to say to the world, and much more importantly, to each other that this is the land of the free except for the Negroes; that we have no second-class citizens except Negroes; that we have no class or caste system, no ghettoes, no master race except with respect to Negroes?

— John F. Kennedy, in his Civil Rights Address, 1963

In your response, develop an argument about how the concerns in the quotation from Abraham Lincoln's letter endured to the time President Kennedy delivered the Civil Rights Address. Incorporate relevant and specific evidence from the quotation, the excerpt, and your own knowledge of the historical context of the address, the letter, and the Civil Rights movement of the 1960s to support your analysis.

Cut | Copy | Paste | Undo | Redo

Read the prompt carefully and use the **online highlighter** to target specific facts and information that you will use in your response. An effective response must answer the questions and use relevant and specific evidence from the source material as well as your knowledge about the issue.

Your response is expected to be an example of "**evidence-based writing.**" Since the Extended Response is worth more than other kinds of questions, take time to understand the question, write a thesis statement to articulate your position, plan your response, and cite at least three relevant facts from the information to back up your position. Conclude with a strong summary of your position.

As with other writing tasks on the GED® Test, you have word processing tools that you can **click** on at the top of the toolbox that will allow you to do the following:

- **Cut** (remove extraneous ideas or correct mistakes)
- **Copy** and **Paste** (move words and ideas to improve your writing)
- **Undo** or **Redo** (use if you change your mind or want to change it back)

GED® TEST TIP

As you write your Extended Response, make sure that you keep in mind the three types of criteria on which your work will be judged:

- *Creation of Argument and Use of Evidence*
- *Development of Ideas and Organizational Structure*
- *Clarity and Command of Standard English Conventions*

LESSON

1

SOCIAL STUDIES PRACTICES

Determine Central Idea and Draw Conclusions

Key Ideas

- *Social Studies Test* presentations consist of text, graphics, or a combination of the two.
- Comprehending social studies material requires understanding the central idea or point and its supporting details.
- *Social Studies Test* questions also require you to make inferences in order to draw conclusions.

GED® TEST TIP

To answer GED® test questions based on a passage or graphic, ask yourself, "What is the main point? What evidence or details are used to support it? What conclusion can I draw?"

The **central idea** of a passage or graphic is its topic or main point. This is supported by **details** or **examples**.

At the outset of the Revolutionary War, the American colonies had a small navy of only 31 ships. To contest the far superior number of vessels in the British fleet, the colonies employed privateers, independent ships authorized to harass and capture enemy merchant and cargo ships. Armed with more than 14,000 guns, American privateers captured well over 2,000 enemy ships. These figures demonstrate how difficult it would have been, without the aid of privateers, for the colonies to win their independence against a larger, better equipped British Navy.

▶ What is the topic of this passage?

(1) the importance of colonial privateers to winning the Revolutionary War
(2) the fact that American privateers captured well over 2,000 enemy ships

Choice **(1)** is correct. The main point of the passage is that privateers were crucial to the colonies' success in their war for independence. The number of ships captured by privateers, referred to in choice (2), is used to support that point.

One skill needed to understand social studies information is the ability to **draw conclusions** from what you read or see. This skill requires you to go beyond what is directly stated and make an inference about what is meant or implied.

▶ Which of the following conclusions can be drawn based on this graph?

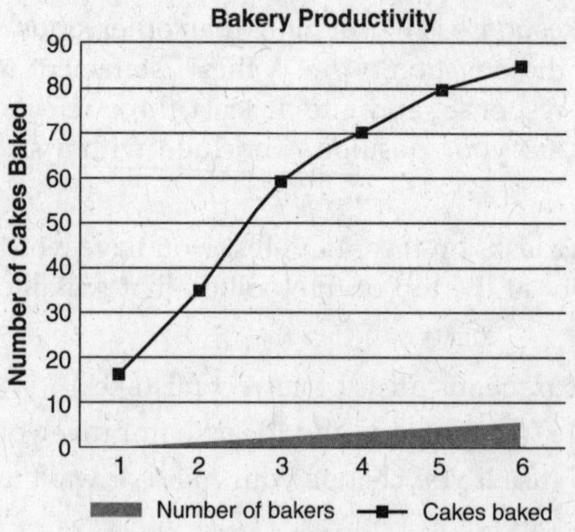

(1) The productivity of a bakery is based on a number of factors.
(2) The productivity of the bakery rises when more bakers are added.

You were correct if you selected choice **(2)**. As you look at the graph, the line—the number of cakes baked—rises steeply when more bakers are added. This associates the productivity of the bakery with the number of bakers. Choice (1) may well be true, but it is not a conclusion based on this graph.

PRACTICE 1

Questions 1 through 3 are based on the following passage.

Theater was one of the most popular forms of art in ancient Greece, and one form of drama—tragedy—was central to Greek culture. Tragedies told familiar stories from Greek myths and epics, but actors portrayed the main roles, and a chorus narrated the background of the story and commented upon the action. These serious dramas centered on a main character who displayed exceptional attributes but also had a tragic flaw that caused his downfall. This flaw was often hubris, which is excessive pride or overconfidence.

1. Which of the following is the topic of the paragraph?

A. the superiority of Greek theater
B. the standard forms of Greek drama
C. the characteristics of Greek tragedy
D. the most popular Greek tragedies

2. Which of these details supports the central idea?

A. Theater was one of the most popular Greek art forms.
B. Tragedies were more important than comedies in ancient Greece.
C. Greeks thought flaws other than hubris were not tragic.
D. The main character in Greek drama has a tragic flaw that causes his downfall.

3. Which of these conclusions is supported by the paragraph?

A. Ancient Greeks did not expect to see an original story each time they attended the theater.
B. Playwrights in ancient Greece also wrote myths and epics.
C. Tragedies in ancient Greece were judged on the basis of how serious their stories were.
D. Only highly cultured people attended tragedies in ancient Greece.

Questions 4 and 5 are based on this graphic.

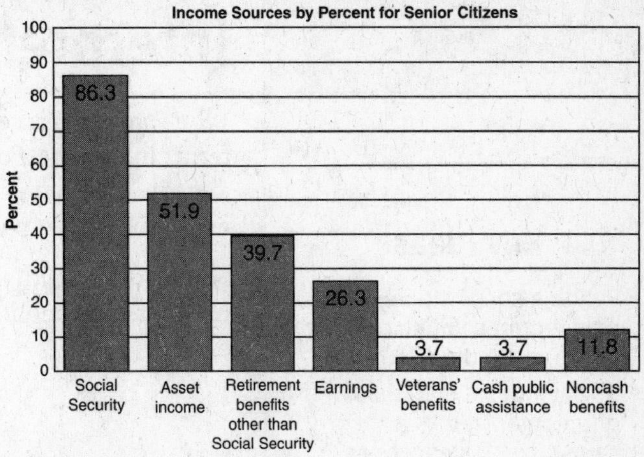

Source: Social Security Administration

4. The graph answers which of the following questions?

A. What is the dollar value of the income for senior citizens?
B. How much do senior citizens have in savings accounts?
C. How many senior citizens are dependent upon veterans' benefits for their retirement income?
D. Where do the incomes of senior citizens come from?

5. Which of the following conclusions can be drawn from this graph?

A. More senior citizens need to continue to work in order to make ends meet now than in the past.
B. Social Security benefits are the most widespread means of support for most senior citizens.
C. Senior citizens who receive income from veterans' benefits also receive benefits from public assistance.
D. Senior citizens who do not receive Social Security benefits get income from one or more other sources.

Answers and explanations start on page 102.

LESSON

2

SOCIAL STUDIES PRACTICES

Interpret Words and Ideas

Key Ideas

- Reading social studies materials requires understanding key terms in their context.
- Social studies material is often organized as a sequence of events or as steps in a process.
- Analyzing social studies materials often involves relating causes to effects.

GED® TEST TIP

To learn key social studies terms, pay close attention to the meaning of the words in ***bold type*** *in the history, government, economics, and geography sections of this unit.*

When you interpret social studies materials, you need to understand key **terms** in context. For instance, on page 62, the word *articles* is presented. You already know an everyday use of the word, such as "articles of clothing," but in the context on page 62, an *article* refers to a section of the U.S. Constitution.

Some social studies material is organized in **chronological** or time order. Look at the timeline below and answer a question about the sequence of events.

Inventions in the 1870s

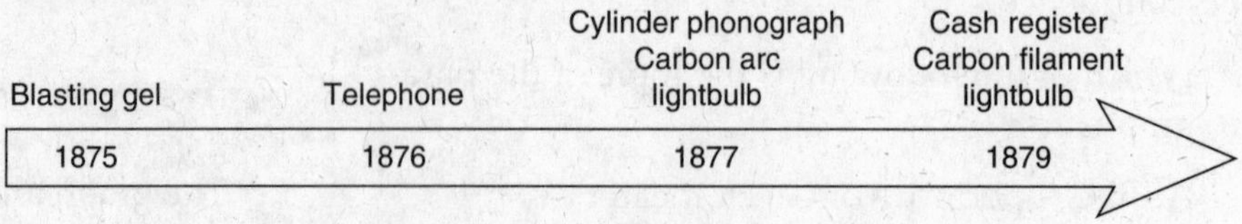

► Which of the following events preceded the invention of the carbon arc lightbulb?
  (1) invention of the telephone
  (2) invention of the carbon filament lightbulb

Timelines are read left to right from oldest to most recent, so choice **(1)** is correct. Choice (2) refers to the carbon filament lightbulb, invented in 1879, a year after the carbon arc lightbulb.

Another way that social studies material is organized is by **cause and effect**, which is another way of asking "What resulted from this action?" or "What made this event happen?" Read the following paragraph to practice this skill.

The prices of goods and services are determined by the relationship between supply and demand. When supply exceeds demand, sellers must lower prices to stimulate sales; on the other hand, when demand exceeds supply, consumers bid up prices as they compete to purchase items or services that they desire.

► Based on the theory of supply and demand, under which of the following scenarios would prices be most likely to rise?
  (1) The demand for a product exceeds that product's supply.
  (2) Producers and sellers advertise a product in order to stimulate demand for that product.

Choice **(1)** is correct. According to the law of supply and demand, prices rise when demand outpaces supply. Choice (2) describes a situation in which producers and sellers advertise to stimulate demand for their product, but without knowing whether the supply is limited, we cannot conclude that this would cause the price to increase.

PRACTICE 2

Questions 1 through 3 are based on this passage.

From 1820 to 1870, more than 7.5 million immigrants arrived on U.S. shores. That was more people than the entire U.S. population in 1810. Almost all of these immigrants came from Northern Europe, and a majority were Catholic. Historians have often focused on what "pushed" these emigrants out of Europe. During the 1840s, for example, Germany experienced a series of crop failures that, combined with social upheaval triggered by rapid industrialization in urban areas, produced riots, civil unrest, and open rebellion. During the same years, Ireland saw the infamous "potato famine" strike poor and working-class Irish families, killing an estimated 700,000 people.

While those crises spurred Europeans to emigrate, a variety of factors created a simultaneous "pull" to immigrate to the United States. Letters home from friends and family members who had immigrated earlier often described the United States as a "land of plenty" and related stories of successful employment and plentiful land. Steamship companies offering passage across the Atlantic advertised with posters that showed majestic scenes of American abundance.

1. According to the passage, which of the following was a cause of Northern European immigration to the United States in the 1840s and 1850s?

   A. Americans' desire to double the population of the United States
   B. efforts by Northern European governments to reduce the number of people living in poverty
   C. political and social instability in some Northern European countries
   D. efforts to spread Catholicism to the United States

2. Based on the passage, which one of the following was most likely to have been featured on a steamship company poster?

   A. a folk-art painting depicting the life of the rural poor in the United States
   B. a portrait of an American politician from the 1840s
   C. a poster advertising an American product
   D. a painting of pioneers settling and farming productive prairie land

3. Which of the following results of Northern European immigration to the United States in the mid-1800s can be inferred from the passage?

   A. a spread of poverty in the United States
   B. a decline in political upheaval in Northern Europe
   C. a growth in the population of the United States
   D. a number of Americans converting to the Catholic faith

Questions 4 and 5 are based on this timeline.

The Great Dust Bowl

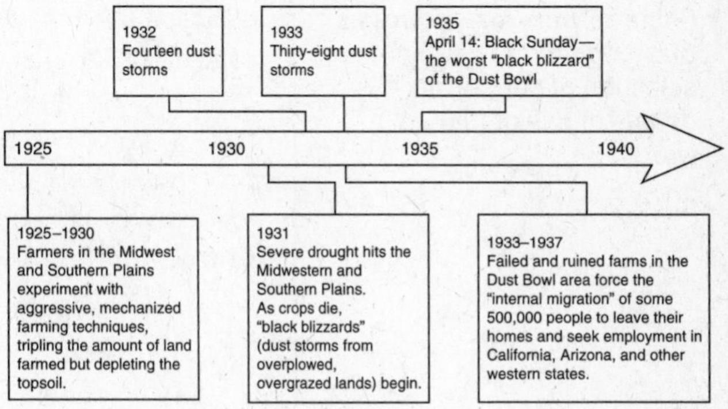

4. Given the information in the timeline, which of the following would be a flawed inference?

   A. Mechanized farming contributed to dust storms.
   B. Internal migration led to overgrazing.
   C. Severe drought contributed to "black blizzards."
   D. Some farmers left the Dust Bowl before the worst dust storm hit the region.

5. Which of the following could have been a cause of the Great Dust Bowl?

   A. "black blizzards"
   B. internal migration
   C. depleted topsoil
   D. failed farms

Answers and explanations start on page 102.

LESSON

3

SOCIAL STUDIES PRACTICES

Analyze Author's Purpose and Point of View

Key Ideas

- Social studies material may be written to inform or to persuade.
- Thoughtful readers need to take an author's purpose and point of view into account.
- Some authors may express a bias or point of view by the selection of supporting details or use of loaded words.

GED® TEST TIP

You may be provided with a newspaper editorial, an online blog commentary, or a speech. Ask yourself, "What is the author's viewpoint? How are facts and evidence organized to be convincing? How are words chosen to have an impact?"

Any author of social studies material has a viewpoint and a purpose. Social studies material can have many purposes, such as to inform or educate (for example, a textbook or magazine article). Other materials, such as newspaper editorials and online blogs, are used to convince people of a point of view.

An author's **point of view** is his or her way of looking at the world. Some social scientists follow a method of examining the facts and coming to a conclusion. In other cases, an author may start with a point of view and assemble facts or evidence to support it.

When you read social studies materials, determine whether an author has a **bias**, a tendency to see one point of view. A bias is not a bad thing in and of itself (after all, we all have biases), but you should take the author's bias into account. An extreme form of bias is **propaganda**, in which an author tries to convince people to act and think as the author wants. Authors of propaganda selectively include certain facts and ignore others, or they use loaded words to trigger emotional responses. Use the following example to practice finding the author's point of view.

> Until the 1980s, most anthropologists mistakenly estimated the native population in North America at the time of Columbus's expedition in 1492 to be somewhere between 2 million and 7 million people. They based these estimates on the number of Native Americans alive at the time of their first contact with European explorers and settlers. However, the estimates ignored the impact of infectious diseases, such as smallpox, which traveled much faster than humans did and would have decimated the native population before Europeans made contact with native people.

► What is the author's point of view about the population of North America in 1492?

(1) that it was not exactly 2 million people or 7 million people but was somewhere in between those two numbers
(2) that it was probably much larger than 7 million people

Choice **(2)** is correct. The author points out a reason to think that anthropologists prior to the 1980s undercounted the native population. Answer (1) gives the estimate of most anthropologists prior to the 1980s.

► Which of the following words is a clue to the author's viewpoint?

(1) ignored
(2) estimated

The correct choice is **(1)**. The author believes that the anthropologists' estimates were flawed because they ignored relevant information about the impact of diseases on the native population. Choice (2) misses the author's point; he doesn't fault them for estimating, but rather for ignoring evidence when they made their estimates.

PRACTICE 3

Questions 1 through 3 are based on the paragraph and poster below.

During World War I, the U.S. National War Garden Commission began a campaign to encourage private citizens to grow their own food as a means of supporting the war effort. This practice became very popular. With increased private food production, the government could reserve much of the cheaper, mass-produced food for the troops. The money saved in feeding soldiers freed up resources for other military needs. In addition, planting war gardens, also known as victory gardens, gave American citizens a sense of empowerment.

Source: Library of Congress Poster by James Montgomery Flagg

1. Which of the following best describes the poster's use of the word *victory*?

A. ambiguous
B. informative
C. propagandistic
D. impersonal

2. What is meant by the poster's caption "Every Garden a Munition Plant"?

A. War gardens require a great deal of time to cultivate.
B. Citizens who plant war gardens encourage a sense of community in their hometowns.
C. Citizens who plant war gardens help supply the war effort with essential resources.
D. War gardens provide an excellent opportunity to learn about gardening, canning, and food drying.

3. The author's primary purpose in writing the paragraph accompanying the poster is most likely to

A. describe war gardens and explain their popularity in the United States
B. encourage patriotism and continued support for a strong United States military
C. distinguish the efforts of American citizens during World War I from those of citizens in other countries
D. rebut the accusations of those who claimed that civilians did not do enough to support the U.S. war effort in World War I

Question 4 is based on the following dialogue.

Congresswoman Burns: The new organic food safety regulations are likely to increase the average cost of some food staples. The costs are justified, however, by the peace of mind that comes from knowing your food is safe and healthy.

Concerned Citizen: Rising prices are a cancer eating away at our families. High costs will drive people away from healthy foods and wind up harming our children's diets. Instead of buying wholesome, natural products, parents will feed their kids fast food.

4. Which of the following constitute "loaded" words the Concerned Citizen uses to support her point?

A. high costs
B. fast food
C. a cancer
D. our children's diets

Answers and explanations start on page 102.

LESSON

4

SOCIAL STUDIES PRACTICES

Evaluate Author's Reasoning and Evidence

Key Ideas

- An author's point of view may be supported by facts, opinions, and reasoned judgment.
- While reading, analyze whether information is a fact, an opinion, or a conclusion based on reasoning or evidence.
- A careful reader evaluates whether an author supports his or her claims with evidence.

Social studies authors in print and online publications use a variety of strategies to support their viewpoints. They may use the following:

- **Facts**—information that can be proven to be true
- **Opinions**—beliefs about a concept or situation
- **Judgments**—conclusions that are supported by reasons and evidence

On the GED® *Social Studies Test*, you need to read carefully to distinguish among these three concepts.

► Indicate whether each of the following statements is a fact (F), an opinion (O), or a judgment (J).

(1) ___ Because it raises the amount employers will pay in payroll taxes, the new tax bill may contribute to higher unemployment.

(2) ___ Last year, manufacturing output in our state rose by 4.6 percent over the previous year.

(3) ___ We should limit the role played by the federal government in formulating energy policy for our region of the country.

Statement (1) is a **judgment;** the author's conclusion (that the bill may increase unemployment) is based on evidence (that the bill raises payroll taxes). Statement (2) is a **fact;** the truth or falsity of the statement can be checked against empirical data. Statement (3) is an **opinion;** the author makes a recommendation (limit the role of the federal government) but offers no evidence or reasoning to support it.

GED® TEST TIP

When you read an author's viewpoint, ask yourself, "What is the claim being made? Is evidence provided to support this claim? Is the evidence relevant to the claim and sufficient and credible enough to support it?"

To be credible, a author needs to support his or her claims with evidence. Part of your job on the Social Studies Test is to answer questions about whether or not an author's claims are supported.

Delaware was the first state to ratify the U.S. Constitution. Because of its history of favorable corporate tax policies, Delaware is today home to 63 percent of Fortune 500 corporations. There is no doubt then that Delaware's freedom-of-information act, requiring the state government to respond within 15 days of a request, should serve as a model for similar acts in other U.S. states.

► Does the author support the claim of the passage?

(1) Yes, because he believes and asserts that there is no doubt about the truth of the claim.

(2) No, because he asserts the truth of the claim without offering evidence relevant to the claim.

Choice **(2)** is correct. The author's claim is that Delaware's freedom-of-information act should serve as a model for similar acts in other states, but the other statements in the passage are irrelevant to that claim. Choice (1) is incorrect because stating a claim firmly ("no doubt") does not provide *support* for the claim.

PRACTICE 4

1. Consultant: A reliable energy supply is vital to developing a stable economy in Cambodia, a country still recovering from decades of civil war and genocide in the late 1970s in which millions of Cambodians were killed. Damming the Mekong River could solve Cambodia's energy supply problems. However, since the Mekong flows through China, Myanmar, Laos, and Thailand before it reaches Cambodia, regional cooperation will be necessary.

   Which of the following is an opinion, and not a fact, presented by the consultant?

   A. Damming the Mekong could solve Cambodia's energy problems.
   B. The Mekong River flows through several countries before reaching Cambodia.
   C. Cambodia experienced civil war.
   D. Millions of Cambodians were killed in the late 1970s.

Question 2 is based on this cartoon referencing the labor movement of the early 20th century.

Protected by George Matthew Adams.

SPITING HIMSELF.

—Morris for the George Matthew Adams Service.

Source: Literary Digest 9/6/19. Originally from the George Matthew Adams Service (Morris).

2. Which of the following represents the viewpoint of the cartoonist?

   A. Strikes can achieve better working conditions.
   B. Strikes have a detrimental impact on workers.
   C. Farmworkers are more likely to engage in strikes than are factory workers.
   D. Strikes should hamper production.

3. Historian: Ancient Greece was the greatest of the early civilizations. While the Babylonians may have had arithmetic and ancient Egypt built the pyramids, ancient Greece gave us our first taste of democracy.

   Which of the following is a fact that the historian uses to support her opinion?

   A. Ancient Greece was the greatest early civilization.
   B. Babylonians made use of arithmetic.
   C. The pyramids were built in ancient Egypt.
   D. Ancient Greece pioneered democracy.

Question 4 is based on the following chart.

The Articles of Confederation were the predecessor to the United States Constitution.

	The Articles of Confederation	The Constitution
Federal Court System	No system of federal courts	Court system exists to deal with issues between citizens, states
Regulating Trade	No provision to regulate interstate trade	Congress has the right to regulate trade between states
Executive Power	No executive with power; president merely presided over Congress	Executive branch is headed by president who chooses Cabinet and has checks on power of judiciary and legislature
Raising an Army	Congress could not draft troops; depended on states to contribute forces	Congress can raise an army to deal with military situations
Sovereignty	Sovereignty resides in states	The Constitution is the supreme law of the land
Taxes	Congress could ask states to pay taxes	Congress has the right to levy taxes on individuals

4. Which of the following is a conclusion supported by the table above, rather than a detail stated in the table?

   A. The Constitution allows Congress to enforce collection of taxes, whereas the Articles of Confederation did not.
   B. The Constitution grants more power to the federal government than did the Articles of Confederation.
   C. There were no national armed forces before the Constitution was drafted.
   D. Trade was not nationally regulated by the Articles of Confederation.

Answers and explanations start on page 102.

LESSON

5

SOCIAL STUDIES PRACTICES

Analyze Relationships Between Materials

Key Ideas

- Social studies materials may use graphics to illustrate key concepts.
- Circle, bar, and line graphs visually portray social studies information.
- Maps are drawings that show places and regions with keys, compasses, and scales.

GED® TEST TIP

When you interpret a social studies graphic, carefully read the title and all labels and keys to make sure that you correctly understand the main idea and the type of information being displayed.

Content Presented in Graphic Format

Social studies content is often presented in graphic form. Two of the most useful displays are graphs and maps.

Circle graphs are used to show how a whole is divided into parts; they show fractions or percents.

Line graphs and **bar graphs** organize material by using labels on the bottom axis and values on the side.

Sanchez Family Budget

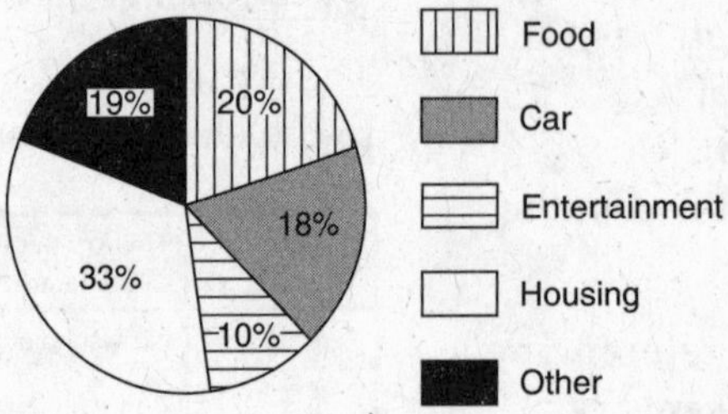

Divorce Rates for Five Countries in the Western Hemisphere*

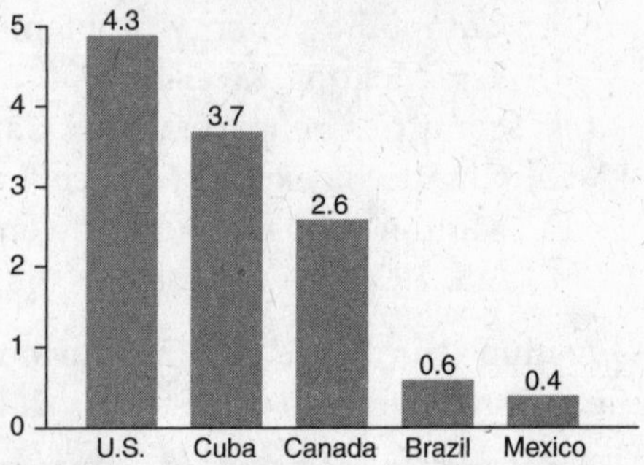

* Per 1,000 population

Maps may use a **legend** (also called the **key**) to explain symbols, a **compass rose** to indicate directions, and **scales** to determine distances.

Europe's Climate

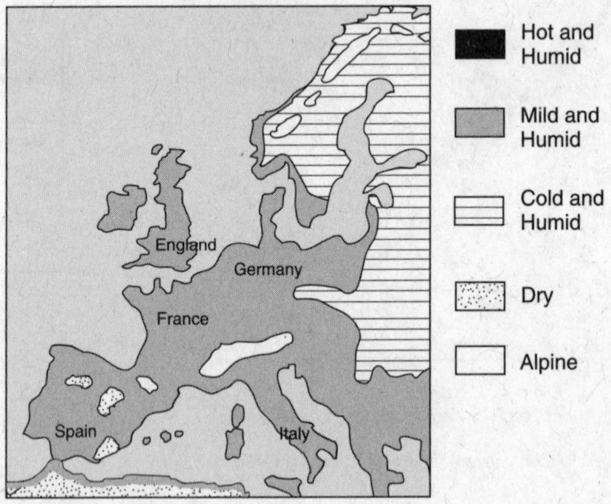

► According to the map, what is England's climate?

(1) mild and humid

(2) cold and humid

The correct answer here is choice **(1)**. To interpret information on a map, note any labels printed directly on the map—in this case, England appears just to the left and slightly above the center. Then check the legend to see whether the color, shading, or symbols shown give additional information. On this map, England is shown in gray, indicating that its climate is "mild and humid."

PRACTICE 5.1

1. According to the circle graph on p. 418, the greatest portion of the Sanchez family's budget is spent on which two items?
   A. housing and food
   B. housing and entertainment
   C. food and car
   D. entertainment and other

2. Which of the following statements is supported by the bar graph on p. 418?
   A. Cuba has the highest divorce rate in the hemisphere.
   B. Mexico has the lowest divorce rate in the hemisphere.
   C. Mexico's divorce rate is decreasing.
   D. Brazil has a higher divorce rate than Mexico.

Questions 3 and 4 refer to the following graph.

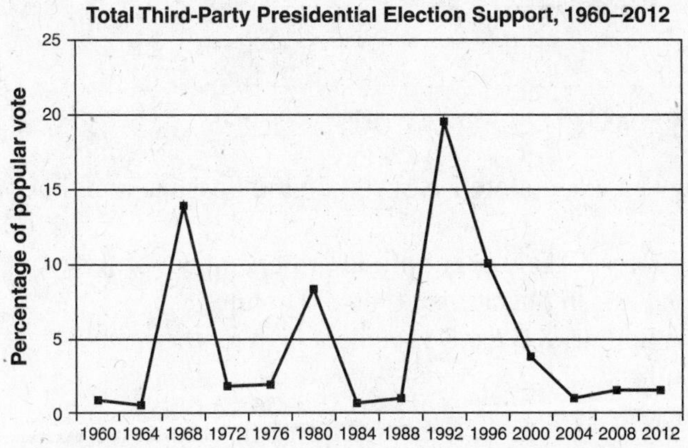

3. Based on the graph, you may validly infer that support for third-party candidates Select... during the 1980s and 1990s.
   - steadily increased
   - steadily decreased
   - neither increased nor decreased
   - fluctuated

4. The graph can be used to disprove which one of the following claims?
   A. Third-party candidates have not enjoyed significant support in the 21st century.
   B. The third-party candidate who garnered the most support since 1960 was Ross Perot in 1992.
   C. Third party candidates have never captured more than 10 percent of the popular vote in any presidential election.
   D. In most elections, all third-party candidates combined get less than 5 percent of the popular vote.

Questions 5 and 6 are based on the following map.

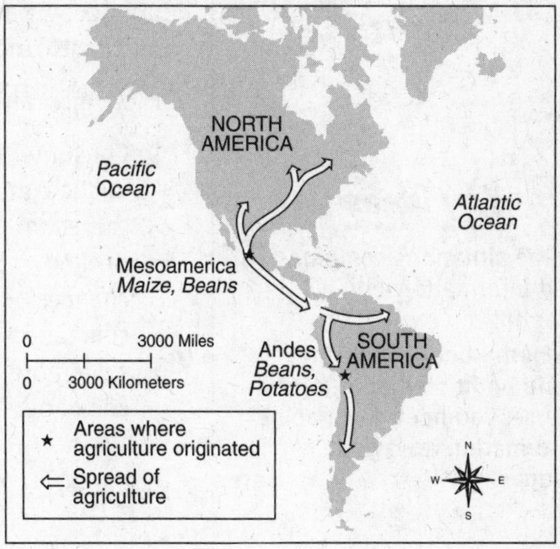

5. What does this map show?
   A. political boundaries in the ancient Americas
   B. physical features of the Americas
   C. how agriculture spread in the Americas
   D. all ancient civilizations of the Americas

6. Which of the following statements is supported by the information on the map?
   A. Both the Andes civilization and Mesoamerica domesticated maize.
   B. Both the Andes civilization and Mesoamerica domesticated beans.
   C. Agriculture developed in the Andes civilization before it did in Mesoamerica.
   D. Agriculture spread more rapidly northward than southward.

Answers and explanations start on page 103.

Integrating Text and Graphic Content

In reading social studies materials and the materials you encounter in daily life, you often have to combine text information with a graphic. For example, an online article about a conflict in Africa may have a map. A newspaper graph with information about new immigrants in your community may accompany a story about their contributions to local health care and manufacturing industries.

Practice combining information with the passage and graphic below.

> Consumer confidence is an economic indicator that reflects how optimistic consumers are about their personal finances, given the state of the economy. When consumer confidence shows a monthly trend of decline month after month, consumers are pessimistic about their chances of finding and keeping good jobs. When their confidence is low, consumers spend less—especially on nonessential items—and tend to save more of their money. On the other hand, when confidence is high, consumers will make more discretionary, or optional, purchases.

Consumer Confidence by Month in Country X

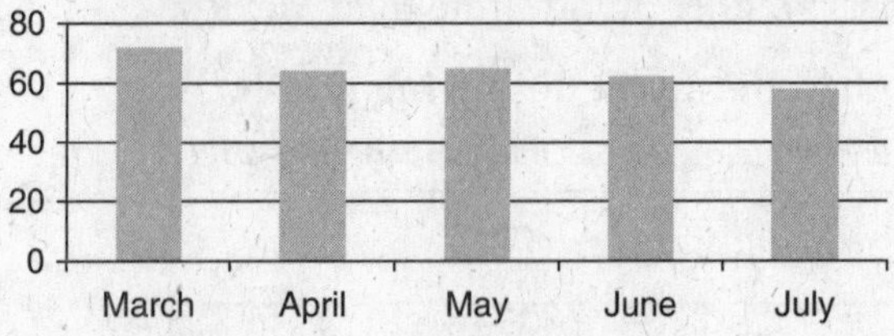

► Which of the following is a valid inference based on the passage and the graph above?

(1) Consumers in Country X likely spent a higher percentage of their income on luxury items in March than they did in July.

(2) Unemployment in Country X is likely to remain high for the remainder of the year shown.

Choice **(1)** is correct. The graph shows that the trend in consumer confidence has generally been in decline from March through July. The text tells you that when consumer confidence is lower, consumers are less likely to spend, especially on nonessential goods. These two statements combined support choice (1). Choice (2) cannot be inferred from the information in the passage or that in the graph. Neither of those sources provides a basis to make a prediction about future unemployment.

Key Ideas

- Some situations combine text information with a graphic.
- To better understand the main point or supporting evidence, you need to combine information from both sources.

GED® TEST TIP

When you see text accompanied by a graphic, read the questions carefully. Some questions may ask about the text or the graphic individually. Others may ask you to combine information from both sources.

PRACTICE 5.2

Questions 1 through 3 relate to the following passage and map.

The sea otter (*Enhydra lutris*) is a marine mammal native to the coasts of the northern and eastern North Pacific Ocean. At one time, sea otters populated the entire coast of what is now the state of California and farther south along Mexico's Baja California coastline. Prior to 1741, the sea otter population worldwide is estimated to have been 150,000–300,000.

Between 1741 and 1911, however, sea otters were hunted extensively for their fur, and the world population fell to just 1,000–2,000 individuals. By 1911, the wild sea otter population in California was limited exclusively to a small area around Monterey Bay.

Fortunately, an international ban on hunting, conservation efforts, and programs to reintroduce the sea otter into previously populated areas have contributed to numbers rebounding, and the species now occupies about two-thirds of its former range. Despite these successes, sea otter populations in California have declined, and the sea otter remains classified as an endangered species.

Current Range of the Sea Otter in California

* Maps and ranges not to scale

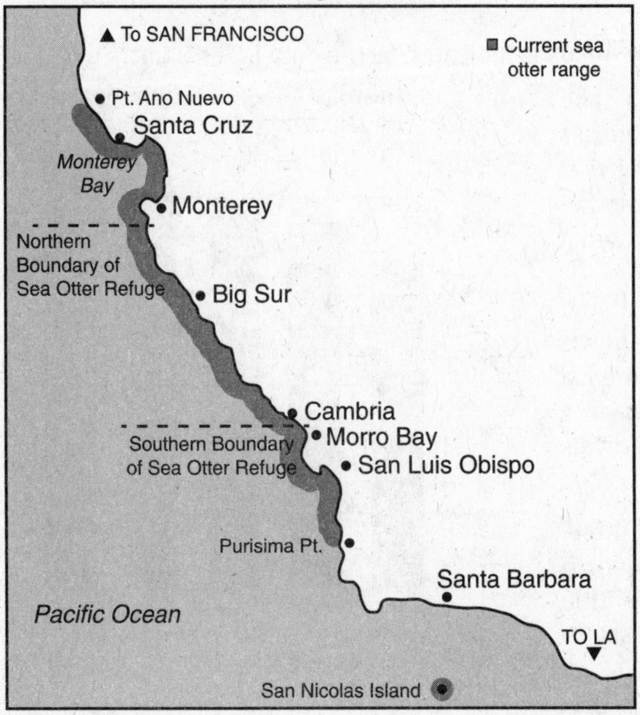

1. According to the passage, which one of the following statements about the sea otter is true?

   A. Sea otter conservation efforts have been more successful in areas outside of California than they have been within California.
   B. Sea otter populations were threatened by water pollution as well as by extensive hunting.
   C. The sea otter population is now about two-thirds of its pre-1741 number.
   D. Sea otters have been able to live in habitats from which they were once eliminated.

2. Which of the following conclusions can be drawn from the information in the passage and the map?

   A. Sea otters will soon have the same range they had prior to 1741.
   B. Sea otter habitat has been restored only within the boundaries of the Sea Otter Refuge.
   C. Sea otters are still hunted in the area north of Point Ano Nuevo.
   D. The current range of the sea otter in California is larger than it was in 1911.

3. The author of the passage would be most likely to agree with which of the following statements about the information in the map?

   A. The range of sea otters shown on the map indicates that sea otter conservation programs are no longer needed.
   B. The range of sea otters shown on the map is identical to the range of sea otters prior to 1741.
   C. Without conservation efforts and reintroduction programs, the range of sea otters in California would be smaller than what is shown on the map.
   D. Ten years from now, the range of sea otters in California will be larger than what is currently shown on the map.

Answers and explanations start on page 103.

LESSON

6

SOCIAL STUDIES PRACTICES

Interpret Data and Statistics

Key Ideas

- Tables and graphs are commonly used to present data in social studies materials.
- A measure of central tendency is used to summarize data with one number.
- Bar graphs are used to compare data, and line graphs are used to show trends.

Understanding social studies materials requires calculations to analyze data or statistics, so you will do some math on the *GED® Social Studies Test*. This work will include interpreting tables, finding measures of **central tendency**, making **comparisons**, and spotting **trends**. Practice your skills with the table below.

Franklin County Family Finances			
Year	Median income (family of 4)	Average % to taxes	Average % to savings
2009	$40,800	27%	5.2%
2010	$41,500	28%	6.0%
2011	$42,300	29%	5.5%
2012	$44,100	29%	5.1%

▶ What is the average (arithmetic mean) percentage of income that a family of four in Franklin County saved each year between 2009 and 2012?

(1) 5.45 percent
(2) 5.35 percent

Choice **(1)** is correct. To find the *average* percentage saved per year, add up the figures from the column "Average % to Savings" and divide the total by 4, since 2009 to 2012 is four years. Thus, $5.2 + 6 + 5.5 + 5.1 = 21.8$, and dividing that number by 4 gives you 5.45.

Some questions may ask you to use graphs to make comparisons or to identify trends.

GED® TEST TIP

When you need to compute on the GED® Social Studies Test, *a calculator symbol with the word* "Calculator" *will appear on the toolbar at the top of your screen. Click on it to open the online calculator.*

▶ What of the following trends is indicated by the data in the chart?

(1) Between 2003 and 2007, foreign arrivals from overseas grew at a faster pace than foreign arrivals from North America.
(2) Between 2003 and 2007, foreign arrivals from North America grew at a faster pace than foreign arrivals from overseas.

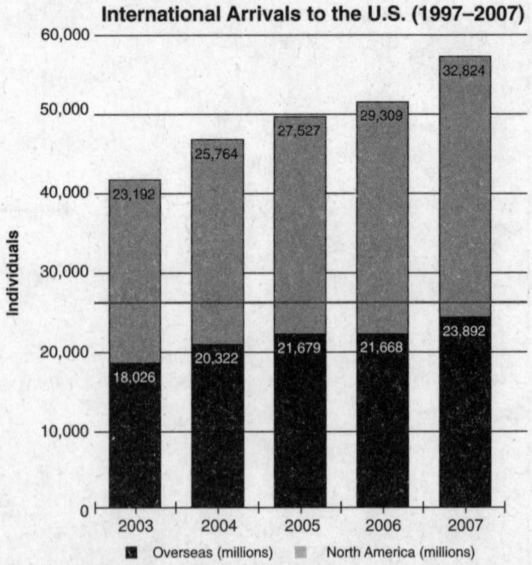

Source: U.S. Department of Commerce, Office of Travel and Tourism Industries

Choice **(2)** is correct here. Foreign arrivals from North America grew from a little over 23 million in 2003 to almost 33 million in 2007, an increase of around 41 percent. Meanwhile, overseas arrivals rose from roughly 18 million in 2003 to just under 24 million, a change of approximately 33 percent growth.

PRACTICE 6

Question 1 is based on the following table.

New Mexico: Population by Age, 2010	
Under 18	518,672
18–19	61,169
20–24	142,370
25–34	267,245
35–49	393,362
50–64	404,106
65 & over	272,255
Total	**2,059,179**

Adapted from U.S. Census Bureau

1. Which of the following could have been the median age in New Mexico in 2010?

   A. 30
   B. 32
   C. 34
   D. 36

Question 2 is based on the following line graph.

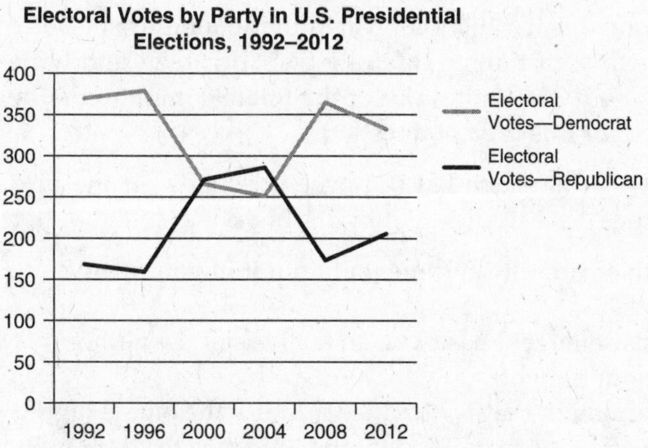

2. The information in the graph supports the conclusion that in the presidential elections from 1992 to 2012,

   A. Democrats and Republicans won the presidency an equal number of times
   B. the average margin of victory was higher in years when a Democrat won than in years when a Republican won
   C. the average margin of victory was higher in years when a Republican won than in years when a Democrat won
   D. more electoral votes were cast in the 2008 presidential election than were cast in the 1996 presidential election

Questions 3 and 4 are based on the following chart.

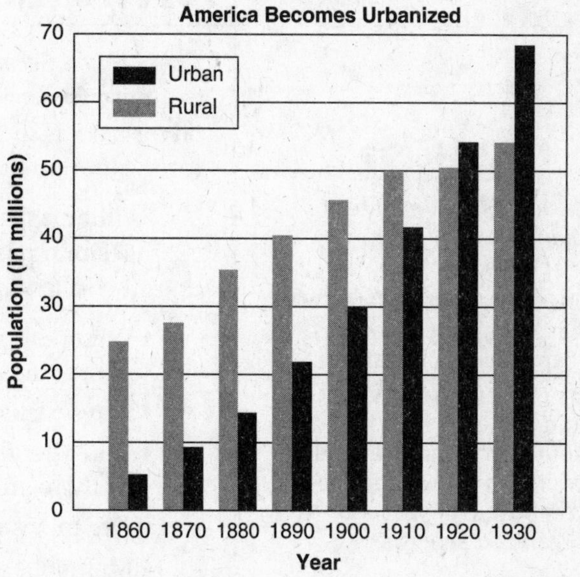

Source: U.S. Census (adapted)

3. According to the bar graph, in what year were there approximately as many Americans living in rural locations as there were in urban settings?

   A. 1860
   B. 1910
   C. 1920
   D. 1930

4. Approximately how much larger was the range of the urban population than the range of the rural population in the United States between 1860 and 1930?

   A. 10 million
   B. 23 million
   C. 34 million
   D. 43 million

Answers and explanations start on page 103.

LESSON

7

Social Studies Practices

Write an Extended Response

Key Ideas

- Take about 25 minutes to plan and write your response.
- Develop a thesis statement based on a well-reasoned response to the material.
- Use specific details, facts, and evidence from the source materials—as well as your own knowledge—to compose a logical and organized analysis.

GED® TEST TIP

If you are presented with two passages or a passage and a graphic, be sure that your response draws from both source materials.

The *GED® Social Studies Test* will require you to compose a written response to a passage, graphic, or combination of the two. *About the Test* on pages 21–25 includes more information about the format and criteria for evaluation of your response of the extended response question.

You will be asked to write a response to a question based on one or two passages or a passage and a graphic. A response that receives a high score does the following:

- Presents a well-supported argument that cites three or more pieces of specific evidence from the text or graphic
- Stays focused on the question prompt throughout the piece
- Consistently links either (a) the two texts or (b) the text and graphic (if there are two passages or a passage and graphic)
- Organizes ideas logically and demonstrates a progression of ideas
- Maintains a formal style (no slang) and objective (unbiased) tone
- Demonstrates limited errors in sentence structure, grammar, spelling, and punctuation

Since the extended response is worth more than individual multiple-choice questions, it is well worth your time to carefully plan, organize, and write it. You should budget about 25 minutes out of the total 90 minutes on the *GED® Social Studies Test* for this type of question.

Practice this process with the extended-response questions on the next page and throughout the social studies unit in this book.

1. Read the question carefully and mentally put it in your own words.
2. Develop a thesis statement based on an analysis of the author's point of view or argument.
3. Reread the information that is provided and use the online highlighter to emphasize the facts, details, and evidence that you will use in your response.
4. Use the provided wipe-off board to organize your response.
5. Compose a clear multi-paragraph response with the following:
   a. Introduction that lays out your thesis statement
   b. Supporting paragraphs based on the evidence from the piece
   c. Conclusion that summarizes your main point
6. Use the online editing tools (cut, copy, paste, undo, and redo) to improve your writing.

PRACTICE 7

Directions: Use 25 minutes to read, plan, and write an analysis of the two quotes below. Incorporate evidence from both materials and your own knowledge in your response. Compose your answer on a computer if one is available, or write your answer on a separate sheet of paper.

Quote A

A decade before assuming office as the second president of the United States, John Adams wrote the following in his *Defence of the Constitutions of Government of the United States of America:*

"If a majority are capable of preferring their own private interest, or that of their families, counties, and party, to that of the nation collectively, some provision must be made in the constitution, in favor of justice, to compel all to respect the common right, the public good, the universal law, in preference to all private and partial considerations. [. . .]

"And that the desires of the majority of the people are often for injustice and inhumanity against the minority, is demonstrated by every page of history of the whole world."

—**John Adams**, *A Defence of the Constitutions of Government of the United States of America*

Quote B

After touring the United States for nine months in 1831–1832, Frenchman Alexis de Tocqueville published his observations from and reflections on his visit in a two-volume work, *Democracy in America,* including this excerpt:

"A majority taken collectively is only an individual, whose opinions, and frequently whose interests, are opposed to those of another individual, who is styled a minority. If it be admitted that a man possessing absolute power may misuse that power by wronging his adversaries, why should not a majority be liable to the same reproach? Men do not change their characters by uniting with each other; nor does their patience in the presence of obstacles increase with their strength. For my own part, I cannot believe it; the power to do everything, which I should refuse to one of my equals, I will never grant to any number of them."

—**Alexis de Tocqueville**, *Democracy in America*

In your response, develop an argument about how both President Adams and Alexis de Tocqueville discuss the tension between the will of the majority and the enduring issue of protection of the minority in a democracy. Incorporate relevant and specific evidence from the quotes and your own knowledge of the United States government.

Refer to the *Social Studies Extended Response Evaluation Guide* on page 135 to evaluate your response.

Social Studies Practices Practice Questions

<u>Questions 1 and 2</u> are based on the following line graph and timeline.

Unemployment Rates During the New Deal : Percentage of Jobless Nonfarm Workers, 1926–1946

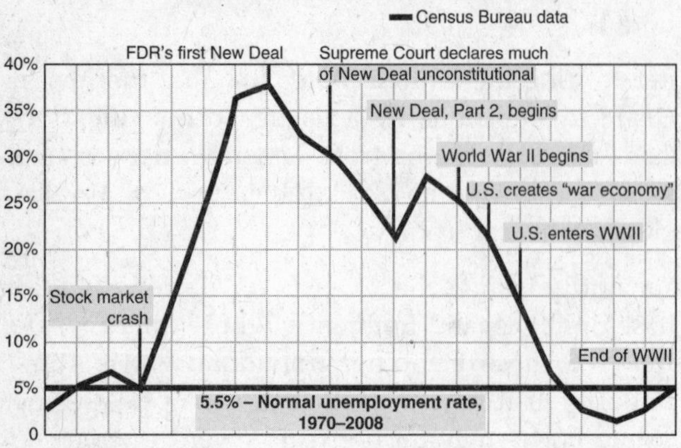

Source: U.S. Census Bureau, Bureau of Labor Statistics, Global insifht.

1. According to the Census Bureau's data on the graph, it can be concluded that the onset of World War II contributed to which change in the U.S. unemployment rate?
   A. The unemployment rate stabilized at the beginning of World War II and remained stable until the war's end.
   B. The unemployment rate declined consistently until shortly before the war's end.
   C. The unemployment rate decreased during World War II but remained above the normal rate throughout the war.
   D. The unemployment rate increased gradually throughout the war.

2. According to the graph, the most significant and uninterrupted change in the U.S. unemployment rate between 1926 and 1946 occurred immediately after
   A. the stock market crash
   B. FDR's first New Deal
   C. New Deal, Part 2, began
   D. the U.S. enters World War II

<u>Questions 3 and 4</u> are based on the following passage.

The women's rights movement in the United States gained strength with the 1848 Seneca Falls Convention. The defining document of this gathering was the Declaration of Sentiments, which was patterned after the Declaration of Independence but focused on the fact that women lacked basic freedoms that men enjoyed. The revolutionary nature of the Seneca Falls Convention was apparent in the public's response to the event. One newspaper described Seneca Falls as "the most shocking and unnatural event ever recorded in the history of womanity."

3. Which of the following statements based on the passage is an opinion, not a fact?
   A. The Seneca Falls Convention helped the women's rights movement gain strength.
   B. The Declaration of Sentiments was modeled on the Declaration of Independence.
   C. The Declaration of Sentiments described how women's rights were limited.
   D. The Seneca Falls Convention was a shocking and unnatural event that undermined the nature of women.

4. Which of the following states the main idea of the passage above?
   A. Women lacked basic freedoms that men had, and they were angry.
   B. The Seneca Falls Convention was open to both men and women.
   C. The women's rights movement was stronger in Seneca Falls than in the rest of the United States.
   D. The Seneca Falls Convention was important in the fight for women's rights.

Questions 5 and 6 refer to the following map.

Reported Cases of Human Plague—United States, 1970–2010

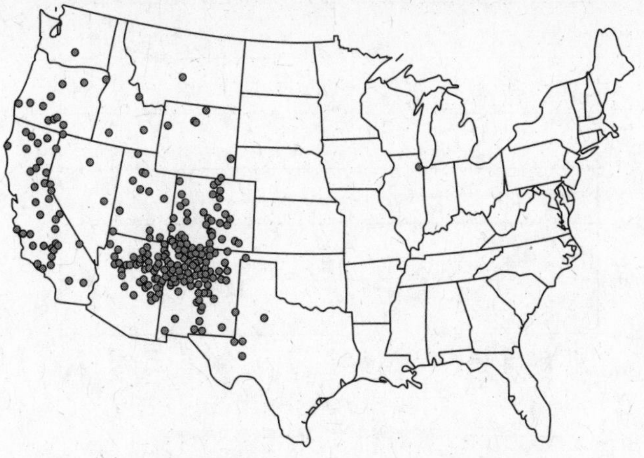

1 dot placed in county of exposure for each plague case

Source: Centers for Disease Control

5. Which of the following conclusions is supported by this map?
   A. More than half of the reported cases of human plague in the United States between 1970 and 2010 were reported in four states.
   B. More than 99 percent of diphtheria-related deaths in the United States between 1970 and 2010 occurred in the western half of the United States.
   C. The majority of reported cases of plague in the American Southwest spread from one infected person.
   D. In the United States, human plague most frequently occurs within larger cities, where the risk of contagion is greatest.

6. The map above could be used to disprove which of the following claims?
   A. There were more cases of plague in the United States between 2000 and 2010 than there were between 1990 and 2000.
   B. Although many cases of plague have been reported in the United States since 1970, no deaths have been reported.
   C. Several cases of plague were reported on the East Coast of the United States between 1970 and 2010.
   D. Plague is less virulent in colder climates than it is in warmer climates.

Questions 7 and 8 are based on the following passage and chart.

The invention of the cotton gin by Eli Whitney in 1784 revolutionized the cotton industry in the American South. The separation of the cotton seeds and fibers, once a painstaking task that slaves performed by hand, could now be done quickly by machine. This made cotton goods more affordable, thereby increasing international demand for these goods and, consequently, the profits of cotton farmers. Ironically, however, the cotton gin did not reduce the South's reliance on slavery. In fact, with the boom of the cotton industry, more slaves were used to pick the cotton at a faster rate to keep up with the increasing demand for cotton.

Growth of Slavery and Cotton in America

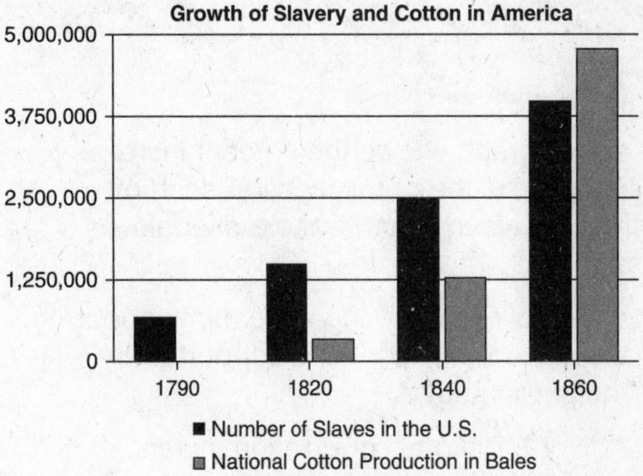

7. Which of the following conclusions is supported by the passage?
   A. Eli Whitney invented the cotton gin with the hope that it would reduce slavery.
   B. The cotton gin had little impact on the cotton industry in the South.
   C. After the invention of the cotton gin, many plantation owners found that they needed fewer slaves.
   D. The effects of the cotton gin on the cotton industry actually led to an increased demand for slaves in the South.

8. According to the graph, approximately how much greater was the increase in the number of cotton bales produced between 1840 and 1860 than the increase in the number of slaves during the same interval?
   A. 750,000
   B. 1,500,000
   C. 2,000,000
   D. 4,000,000

Directions: You MAY use your calculator to answer the following questions.

Questions 9 and 10 are based on the following graph:

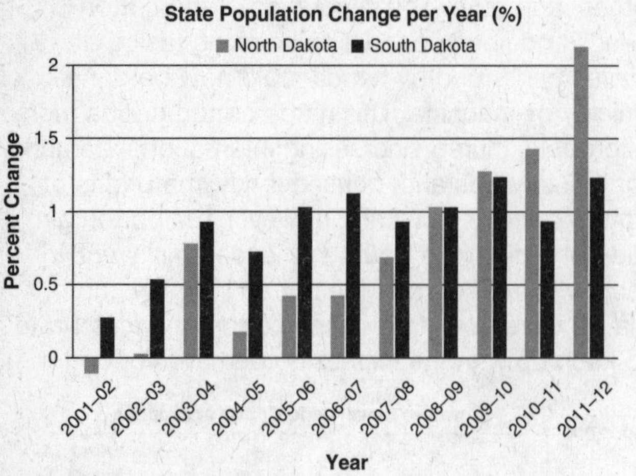

Source: United States Census Bureau

The above graph shows the percent increase, year by year, in the populations of each of North Dakota and South Dakota over eleven years.

9. Which of the following statements about the eleven-year period is supported by the graph above?

   A. North Dakota's population increased every year, while South Dakota's stayed the same.
   B. The population of South Dakota was originally greater than that of North Dakota, but in 2012, the population of North Dakota was greater than that of South Dakota.
   C. In most years, the percent population increase in South Dakota was greater than that in North Dakota.
   D. In most years, the percent population increase in North Dakota was greater than that in South Dakota.

10. Based on the graph above, the average percent increase in population per year for North Dakota was [Select...] the average percent increase in population per year for South Dakota for the period shown.

   - greater than
   - equal to
   - less than

Question 11 is based on the following graphic.

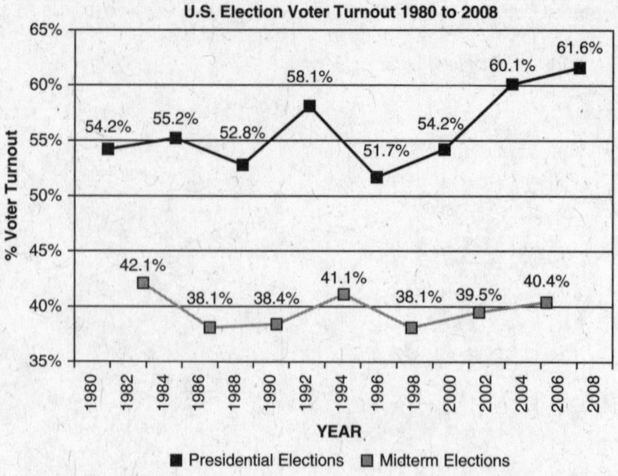

Source: weathertrends360.com

The chart above shows the percentage of registered voters who voted in presidential and midterm elections from 1980 to 2008.

11. The average voter turnout for midterm elections is approximately [Select...] of the average voter turnout for presidential elections.

   - 10 percent
   - 25 percent
   - 50 percent
   - 70 percent

Question 12 is based on the following chart.

Average Federal Tax Rates for All Households, by Household Income Quintile, 2005–2009

Year	Lowest Quintile	Second Quintile	Middle Quintile	Fourth Quintile	Highest Quintile
2005	5.4	9.9	13.8	17.6	25.4
2006	5.7	9.9	13.9	17.7	25.4
2007	5.1	10.3	14.0	17.5	24.7
2008	1.5	7.3	11.6	15.6	23.6
2009	1.0	6.8	11.1	15.1	23.2

12. According to the chart, from 2005 to 2009, the median tax rate for households in the middle income quintile was

   A. 11.6 percent
   B. 12.8 percent
   C. 13.8 percent
   D. 14.0 percent

Answers and explanations start on page 104.

13. **Directions: Use 25 minutes to read, plan, and write an analysis of the two speech excerpts below. Incorporate evidence from both materials and your own knowledge in your response. Compose your answer on a computer if one is available, or write your answer on a separate sheet of paper.**

In this 1821 speech, Secretary of State John Quincy Adams spoke to the U.S. House of Representatives in celebration of the anniversary of Independence Day. In this speech, he touched on his ideal role for America in foreign affairs.

SPEECH EXCERPT

[America] goes not abroad, in search of monsters to destroy. She is the well-wisher to the freedom and independence of all. She is the champion and vindicator only of her own. She will commend the general cause by the countenance of her voice, and the benign sympathy of her example. She well knows that by once enlisting under other banners than her own, were they even the banners of foreign independence; she would involve herself beyond the power of extrication, in all the wars of interest and intrigue, of envy, and ambition, which assume the colors and usurp the standard of freedom. The fundamental maxims of her policy would insensibly change from liberty to force. She might become the dictatress of the world. She would be no longer the ruler of her own spirit.

—John Quincy Adams, July 1821

In the following speech, "The March of the Flag," Senator Albert Beveridge spoke of American imperialism as part of his 1898 campaign. His campaign followed President McKinley's success in the Spanish-American War and the American acquisition of Cuba, Puerto Rico, and Guam from the Spanish. At the time of this speech, the status of these newly acquired territories remained an open issue.

SPEECH EXCERPT

Therefore, in this campaign, the question is larger than a party question. It is an American question. It is a world question. Shall the American people continue their march toward the commercial supremacy of the world?

Shall free institutions broaden their blessed reign as the children of liberty wax in strength, until the empire of our principles is established over the hearts of all mankind?

. . .

Shall we be as the man who had one talent and hid it, or as he who had ten talents and used them until they grew to riches? And shall we reap the reward that waits on our discharge of our high duty; shall we occupy new markets for what our farmers raise, our factories make, our merchants sell—aye, and, please God, new markets for what our ships shall carry?

Hawaii is ours; [Puerto Rico] is to be ours; at the prayer of her people, Cuba finally will be ours.

. . .

. . .

The Opposition tells us that we ought not to govern a people without their consent. I answer: The rule of liberty that all just government derives its authority from the consent of the governed, applies only to those who are capable of self-government. We govern the Indians without their consent, we govern our territories without their consent, we govern our children without their consent. How do they know that our government would be without their consent?

—Albert Beveridge, September 1898

In your response, develop an argument comparing and contrasting John Quincy Adams's and Senator Beveridge's views of the role of America in foreign affairs. Discuss how these speeches may or may not apply to America and the world today. Incorporate relevant and specific evidence from the speeches and from your own knowledge.

Refer to the *Social Studies Extended Response Evaluation Guide* on page 135 to evaluate your response.

LESSON

1

U.S. HISTORY

Exploration, Colonialism, and the American Revolution

Key Ideas

- European explorers sought wealth and conquest in the New World from the 1400s to the 1600s.
- The Thirteen Colonies declared independence from England in 1776.
- America won its independence in 1783 and ratified the U.S. Constitution in 1788.

GED® TEST TIP

Reviewing key vocabulary can help you prepare for the GED® Test. As you review, look up any words that you do not understand. Pay special attention to the words in ***bold*** *type.*

The first Americans traveled from Asia across the Bering Strait into North America and, over many generations, down to South America. Called **Native Americans**, they established extensive tribal cultures and several advanced civilizations.

In the late 1400s, **explorers** from Europe searched for a sea route to Asia so they could trade for Asian gold and spices. They traveled around the tip of Africa. However, in 1492 Christopher Columbus convinced Spain to finance a trip west, across the Atlantic Ocean. When he reached land, he thought he had found India and called the inhabitants Indians. Later explorers realized that they had found a "New World," and many European nations set out to establish **colonies** there. The first explorers were searching for valuable resources and for the glory of conquest. This colonization led to tragedy for many Native Americans who died from diseases or were killed, enslaved, or forced off their lands.

In the 1500s and 1600s, European nations, including Spain, France, England, and the Netherlands, established settlements in North America. Settlements were established to gain power and wealth or to provide colonists a place for permanent residence. The first permanent English settlement was established in Jamestown, Virginia, in 1607. In 1620, the **Pilgrims** sailed to the Americas aboard the *Mayflower* and established a second English colony in Massachusetts. Beginning about 1675, colonists began importing a large number of slaves who had been forcibly taken from Africa. Many were put to work on the plantation system in the Southern colonies.

The colonies grew rapidly in the early 1700s. When England defeated France in the French and Indian War (1754–1763), England acquired many of France's American colonies. After the war, England sought to regain more control over the Thirteen Colonies. It also sought to recover economically from the debts caused by the costly war. New British taxes and policies troubled the colonists; however, it was not until 1775 that a war for independence seemed inevitable. After a series of skirmishes, the **Continental Congress** assigned George Washington to lead the Continental Army and ordered publication of the **Declaration of Independence** on July 4, 1776.

Despite the superiority of the well-trained British forces, the Americans had the advantage of defending their own land and eventually forged a fighting force with strong military leaders. The **American Revolution** lasted until the surrender of the British at Yorktown in 1781. In 1783, the final treaty to end the war resulted in the recognition of American independence. The new nation initially formed a weak national government through the **Articles of Confederation**. This first effort stressed a loose confederation of the states with strong local control. Over time, many colonial leaders recognized the need for a centralized government. The principles of this government were established in the **U.S. Constitution**, which was ratified in 1788. To counter fears of an overly powerful government, the first ten amendments to the Constitution, the **Bill of Rights**, promised many individual freedoms, such as freedom of speech and assembly.

PRACTICE 1

<u>Questions 1 and 2</u> **refer to the following map.**

European Colonial Settlements, 1650

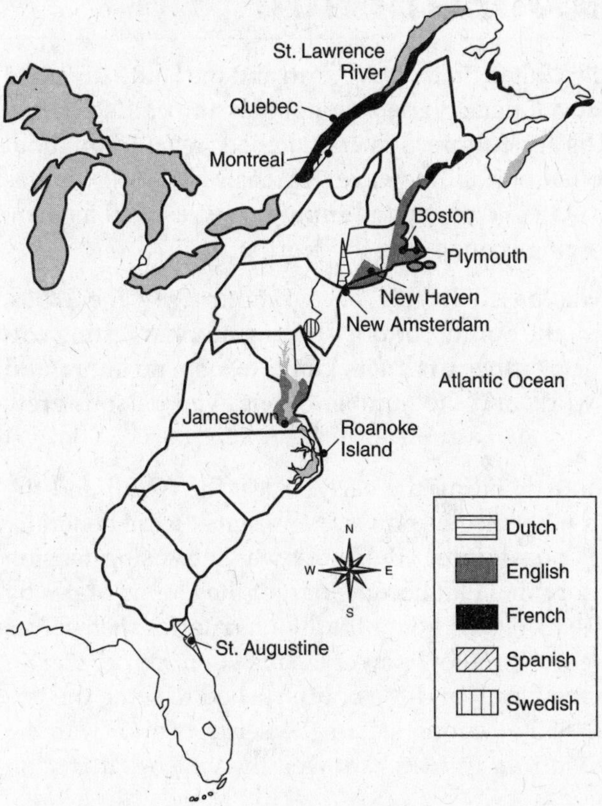

1. Choose the correct phrase that would fill in the blank.
Based on the map, [Select...] had the southernmost colony in 1650.

- the Dutch
- the English
- the Spanish
- the Swedish

2. Which of the following conclusions is supported by the map?

A. By 1650, Spain had conquered most of North America.
B. The English established several colonies in the New World.
C. The Dutch established their colonies in the western part of North America.
D. French colonies extended along the East Coast between Boston and Jamestown.

3. Some of the early colonists did not come to the New World to gain power and wealth. These groups came seeking freedom from persecution.

Which immigrant group is most similar to those early colonists?

A. African slaves who were involuntarily brought to work on plantations
B. Mexican workers who came to the United States to earn better wages than they could at home
C. British businessmen who visited the United States to invest in media companies
D. Haitian refugees who fled to the United States to escape a dictatorship

4. According to the information on page 46, which of the following was a cause of the American Revolution?

A. France's defeat in the French and Indian War
B. increased British taxes and restrictions on the colonies
C. Britain's acquisition of France's colonies in North America
D. the publication of the Declaration of Independence

5. The first amendment to the U.S. Constitution states: "Congress shall make no law abridging the right of the people peaceably to assemble, and to petition the government for a redress of grievances."

Based on the passage on page 46, what is the most likely reason the framers of the Constitution included these guarantees?

A. They were planning to organize assemblies.
B. They were concerned about the government becoming tyrannical.
C. They were hoping to petition the government.
D. They were attempting to prevent a redress of grievances.

Answers and explanations start on page 105.

LESSON

2

U.S. HISTORY

Westward Expansion, the Civil War, and Reconstruction

Key Ideas

- The economy of the South was based on slavery. The Northern economy was based on paid labor.
- Conflict over whether slavery should be allowed in the nation's new western territories led to the Civil War.
- The North won the war and ended slavery. During Reconstruction, the South was rebuilt.

GED® TEST TIP

As you study for the GED® Social Studies Test, *focus on analyzing events to understand causes and effects, rather than memorizing names and dates.*

Early on in the history of the United States, the North and the South diverged economically. The North developed a varied economy that included industry and commerce as well as agriculture. Slavery had been legal throughout the North during the colonial period. However, by the early 1800s, it was **abolished** in all Northern states. Women and **immigrants**, as well as men, provided labor for the growing economy in the North.

The Southern economy was based largely on agriculture. By the 1800s, there was one major crop in the South: cotton. Planting and harvesting cotton required a lot of labor. Southern farmers came to depend more and more on slaves to do the work, and the number of enslaved persons grew in the South.

As the United States expanded during the early 1800s, the North and the South worked to maintain a balance of power. New states were generally added in pairs, one slave and one free. But there was increasing tension over the vast western territory that had become part of the United States by the mid-1800s. In the 1850s, Congress voted that the territories themselves should decide whether or not to allow slavery. This soon led to war in Kansas. People from both the North and the South rushed to settle the territory. Voter fraud in the 1855 elections led to the setup of two warring governments. The violence in Kansas foreshadowed the violence that soon tore up the nation.

In the late 1850s, political parties fractured over the slavery issue. Four candidates ran for president in 1860. Abraham Lincoln, who promised to halt the spread of slavery (although not abolish it where it already existed) won. Opposed to Lincoln's policies, most slave states **seceded** from the United States. They set up their own government, called the **Confederacy**. By April 1861, the United States (called the **Union**) and the Confederacy were at war.

At first it seemed as if the Confederacy might win. They had well-trained military leaders and soldiers who were willing to fight hard to hold onto their way of life, so the Confederacy won many early battles. However, by the summer of 1863, the Confederacy began to wear down. Ammunition, uniforms, and shoes were in short supply for Confederate soldiers because the South lacked industry. There were food shortages for soldiers and civilians alike. The war was fought mostly in the South, and the destruction was terrible. After four long years, in 1865, Confederate general Robert E. Lee surrendered to Union general Ulysses S. Grant. The Civil War ended.

For the next 12 years, federal troops oversaw the rebuilding of the South. This period was called **Reconstruction**. Schools were established for former slaves, who were all freed when the war ended. However, the **sharecropping** system, which kept black farmers enslaved economically, soon came into being. Whites who came back to power as Reconstruction ended in the South in the 1870s prevented African Americans from exercising their right to vote. The Civil War ended slavery, but it did not end racism.

PRACTICE 2

1. Based on the passage on page 48, which of the following disagreements was a main cause of the Civil War?

   A. whether cotton should be the main crop in the South
   B. whether slavery should continue to exist
   C. whether the United States should expand westward
   D. whether slavery should be permitted in territories in the West

2. In 1820, Missouri proposed to enter the Union as a slave state. Based on the passage, what do you think was the response of Northerners in Congress?

   A. They supported having another slave state join the Union.
   B. They lobbied against having Missouri join the Union at all.
   C. To balance the admission of Missouri, they agreed to a compromise in which Maine was admitted as a free state.
   D. They started a war to prevent Missouri from attaining statehood.

---

3. In the mid-1950s, the country of Vietnam was divided. There was a communist government in the North and a noncommunist government in the South. The two fought for control of Vietnam. In 1975, the communists won. Vietnam was united under this form of government.

   Because both wars [Select...], the Vietnam War and the U.S. Civil War can be said to share some similarities.

   - involved racial conflict
   - saw the addition of new territory upset the balance of power
   - concluded with the formation of new nations
   - concluded with the reunification of the nation

Questions 4 and 5 refer to the following photographs of people who served in South Carolina's state government in 1868.

Photography by Katherine Wetzel. Reprinted with the permission of The Museum of the Confederacy, Richmond, Virginia.

4. Which of the following is a fact confirmed by information in the photographs?

   A. Southern Democrats were treated very well during Reconstruction.
   B. It was unfair that former Confederate soldiers could vote during Reconstruction.
   C. In 1868, many African Americans served in the government of South Carolina.
   D. The most qualified leaders in South Carolina government in 1868 were African Americans.

5. Which of the following conclusions is supported by the photographs and the passage on page 48?

   A. Over the course of Reconstruction, African Americans in the South gained and then lost political power.
   B. Over the course of Reconstruction, African Americans in the South lost and then gained political power.
   C. Over the course of Reconstruction, whites in the South gained and then lost political power.
   D. In the early years of Reconstruction, African Americans served in government in each Southern state.

Answers and explanations start on page 105.

LESSON

3

U.S. HISTORY

Industrialization, Immigration, and the Progressive Era

Key Ideas

- The U.S. underwent rapid industrialization starting in the mid-1800s.
- Immigrants came from many places to work in the expanding American industries.
- Rapid industrialization brought problems, which labor unions and reformers tried to solve, especially during the Progressive Era.

In the mid-1800s, American industries, which had been growing steadily since the late 1700s, began a period of extremely fast growth. This rapid **industrialization** occurred for several interconnected reasons. With the addition of the vast western territories, the United States gained plentiful **natural resources**. Among these resources were materials, such as metals, needed to manufacture new products and machines, and fuels, such as coal, needed to run these machines. Another reason for rapid industrialization was the invention of many new machines and new industrial processes. With these new inventions and processes, manufactured goods could be produced more easily, more efficiently, and less expensively. A third reason for the rapid industrialization was the nation's booming population. The U.S. population more than doubled in the last 40 years of the 1800s. There were more people to buy more goods, spurring commerce and further industrial growth.

Rapid industrialization meant that many new factories were built in the mid- and late-1800s. Most were built in or near the nation's large cities, including New York, Boston, Chicago, Philadelphia, and Pittsburgh. These urban centers had large groups of people who could work in the factories and large groups of people who would buy the goods the factories produced.

U.S. factory jobs drew many **immigrants** to American cities. Although the United States has always been a "nation of immigrants," the late 1800s saw a sharp rise in the number of people moving here from foreign countries. The majority came from Europe, including Germany, Italy, Russia, and Eastern European countries. Many also came from Mexico and Central America. Asian immigration was declining because the government had passed laws barring Chinese from moving to the United States. However, thousands of Japanese came to this country, taking jobs in farm fields and mines.

ON THE GED® TEST

The GED® Social Studies Test *examines your ability to interpret graphs, charts, maps, and other visual sources of information.*

America's factory workers, whether native- or foreign-born, worked very hard at grueling, dangerous work. Many received low pay for long hours on the job. Over time, workers began to unionize. By joining a **union**, workers pledged to work together for better and safer working conditions and higher wages. They called **strikes** when their employers cut their pay or refused to grant raises. Many of the laws we have today, including the eight-hour workday and the five-day workweek, came about through the bitter struggles for better working conditions that unions waged in the late 1800s and the early 1900s.

Unions weren't the only groups working to solve problems brought on by America's rapid industrialization. Some reformers worked to clean up slums, improve health care, and stop child labor. Others worked to preserve the nation's natural beauty by creating national parks. Still others worked to give more people a voice in government. For example, many women lobbied to gain the right to vote. In the early 1900s, groups were working toward so many sweeping social and political improvements that the time is called the **Progressive Era**.

PRACTICE 3

Questions 1 through 4 are based on the information on page 50.

1. Which of the following always occurs during a period of rapid industrialization?

   A. the annexation of new territory
   B. an increase in manufacturing
   C. an increase in population
   D. an increase in immigration

2. Which event directly contributed to the growth of American industries in the mid-1800s?

   A. the passage of the Chinese Exclusion Act, which banned Chinese immigration
   B. the passage of the Sherman Antitrust Act, which helped prevent businesses from forming monopolies
   C. the development of the Bessemer process, which made it easier to produce steel
   D. the development of settlement houses to aid impoverished immigrants and city dwellers

3. Based on the passage, which of the following would early union workers have valued the most?

   A. productivity in the workplace
   B. contact with people of all different backgrounds
   C. cooperation with others to improve worker safety
   D. the freedom to work whenever they pleased

4. What was a strong ideal held by people working toward reforms during the Progressive Era?

   A. efficiency
   B. wealth
   C. artistic beauty
   D. fairness

Questions 5 and 6 refer to the following graphs.

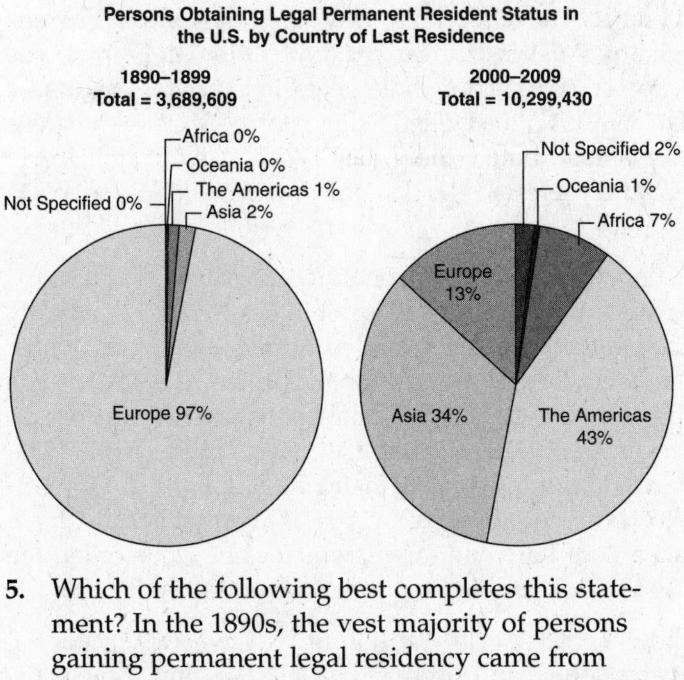

5. Which of the following best completes this statement? In the 1890s, the vest majority of persons gaining permanent legal residency came from Europe, whereas in the early 2000s, a majority of such persons came from Select... .

   - Europe and Asia
   - Asia and the Americas
   - Africa, Oceania, and Europe

6. **You MAY use your calculator to answer this question.**
   Based on the graphs, which of the following is true of the number of persons who came from Europe and gained legal permanent resident status?

   A. In the 1890s, that number was roughly seven times what it was in the period of 2000–2009.
   B. In the 1890s, that number was less than what it was in the period of 2000–2009.
   C. In the 1890s, that number was roughly three times what it was in the period of 2000–2009.
   D. In the 1890s, that number was the same as what it was in the period of 2000–2009.

Answers and explanations start on page 105.

LESSON

4

U.S. HISTORY

The United States as an Emerging World Power

Key Ideas

- Industrialization spurred U.S. interest in gaining access to the raw materials and markets of other countries.
- The U.S. pursued imperialist policies in the late 1800s.
- The U.S. entered both WWI and WWII on the side of the Allies and contributed to their winning both wars.

The expansion of U.S. industries in the mid-1800s had an effect not only on the nation's economy but also on its politics. Business and government leaders wanted access to more natural resources, which industries needed to continue growing. They also wanted to be able to sell more goods overseas. Regions in Africa, Asia, and Latin America had rich natural resources. People in these regions might buy what Americans wanted to sell. To promote industrial growth and increase its power, the United States became imperialistic. **Imperialism** is the policy by which a stronger nation extends economic, military, and/or political control over a weaker nation or region.

European nations had been engaging in imperialism for many centuries. In the late 1800s, the United States joined in. In 1898, the United States fought the Spanish-American War. Ostensibly, the United States declared war on Spain because of Spain's mistreatment of Cuba, which was a Spanish colony. Yet, after winning the war, the United States took over Spain's colonies of Cuba, Puerto Rico, the Philippines, and Guam. It granted independence to none of them.

The next war the United States was involved in was World War I, which began in Europe in 1913. It pitted two groups of nations against each other. One group was called the **Allies;** the leading Allied nations included Great Britain, Russia, and France. The other group was called the **Central Powers,** which included Germany, Austria-Hungary, and the Ottoman Empire. The Allies and Central Powers fought for three years in what fast became a deadly stalemate. Then, in 1917, the United States, alarmed over Germany's sinking of American ships, joined the Allies. With American help, in November 1918 the Allies defeated the Central Powers, and World War I ended.

GED® TEST TIP

When weighing answer choices, immediately eliminate ones that are directly contradicted by information in the passage or graphic.

Because the destruction was so terrible, some people called World War I "the war to end all wars." However, this was not to be. Within 12 years, by 1929, the world had fallen into a serious economic downturn, which Americans called the **Great Depression**. Economic problems aided the rise of **fascism** in Europe and elsewhere. Fascist nations squelched democracy and advocated the takeover of other nations. Germany, led by fascist dictator Adolf Hitler, started attacking smaller nations in Europe in the mid-1930s. Italy fought to take over Ethiopia, in Africa. Japan attacked China. Hitler built an alliance with Italy and Japan, which came to be called the **Axis**. By 1939, war again broke out between the Axis and the Allies.

The United States did not enter World War II until 1941, when the Japanese bombed the U.S. naval base at Pearl Harbor in Hawaii. This time, Americans fought not only in Europe but also in Africa and Asia as well. With its horrific battles, the fire-bombing of cities, the **Holocaust**, and the dropping of two atomic bombs on Japan, World War II led to massive destruction. The United States, which played a major part in the Allied victory in World War II in 1945, also played a major part in helping to rebuild war-scourged nations after the war was over.

PRACTICE 4

Question 1 refers to the following chart.

Factors Related to the Growth of Imperialism

Economic	Desire for greater access to natural resources or new markets
Military	Desire for control of ports that could serve as refueling stations for long sea voyages or air flights
Political	Desire to spread the institutions of democracy or other political systems
Religious	Desire to spread Christianity or other faith
Cultural/Racial	Lack of respect for different cultures or races

1. Cuba lies about 90 miles off the coast of Florida. After the United States freed Cuba from Spanish rule in 1898, the U.S. Navy built an important base there.

Circle the factor in the chart above that best explains the situation in Cuba after 1898.

2. What assumption do you need to make to fully understand the last sentence in paragraph 4 on page 52?

A. In World War I, the Allies fought the Central Powers.
B. In World War II, the Allies included England, France, and Russia.
C. In World War II, the Allies included the Germans, Austrians, and Ottoman Turks.
D. In World War II, the Axis included Germany, Italy, and Japan.

3. Franklin D. Roosevelt became president during the height of the Great Depression, in 1933. He soon instituted a set of federal programs called the New Deal to try to lower unemployment.

Which conclusion about the effectiveness of New Deal programs does the text on page 52 and graph below support?

U.S. Unemployment Rate, 1929–1944

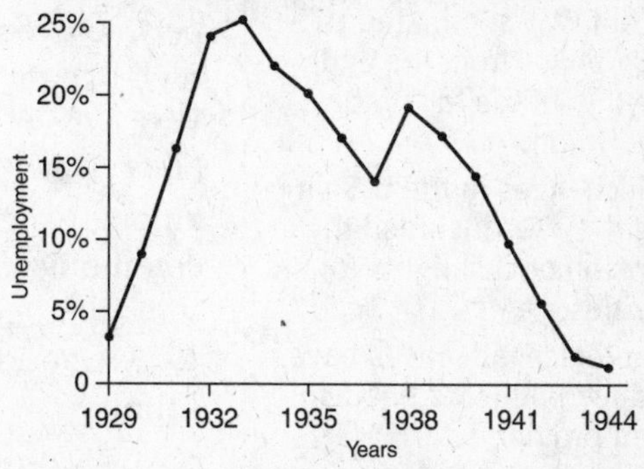

Source: *Historical Statistics of the United States*

A. Within a year, the New Deal had raised unemployment to its pre-Depression level.
B. Within a year, the New Deal had lowered unemployment to its pre-Depression level.
C. Unemployment fell after the start of the New Deal and continued to fall sharply as the United States entered World War II.
D. The New Deal lowered unemployment, but Allied victory in World War II lowered it further.

4. Which statement best summarizes the main idea of paragraph 5 on page 52?

A. America entered World War II in 1941.
B. Americans fought in Europe, Africa, and Asia.
C. World War II involved more nations than any other war ever fought.
D. America took a strong leadership role during and after World War II.

Answers and explanations start on page 106.

LESSON

5

U.S. HISTORY

The Cold War and the Civil Rights Era

Key Ideas

- The Cold War dominated U.S. foreign policy from the end of WWII until the fall of the Soviet Union.
- Social changes in the U.S. in the mid-1900s included the expansion of civil rights for minorities.
- Technological advances have introduced benefits but also caused problems.

ON THE GED® TEST

The GED® Social Studies Test *will include some questions that focus on the role of the United States in the world.*

After World War II ended, the capitalist and communist nations soon began engaging in a power struggle called the **Cold War**. Leading the capitalist nations was the United States; leading the communist nations was the Soviet Union. The Cold War never led to direct fighting between these two superpowers, although there was a constant threat of nuclear war. Clashes between communism and capitalism did lead to numerous smaller conflicts. These included the Korean War of the early 1950s and the Vietnam War, which lasted from 1954 to 1975. The United States sent soldiers to both. The Vietnam War was long and difficult and caused deep division among Americans. The United States sent massive military aid to the non-communist South Vietnamese, but they kept losing to the communist North Vietnamese. Although a few Americans wanted to continue fighting, in 1973 America pulled out of Vietnam. In 1975, the communists took over the country.

The Cold War ended in 1991 with the breakup of the Soviet Union and the end of communism there. In the late 1980s, Soviet leader Mikhail Gorbachev had tried to reform the communist government. But the loosening of Soviet control had led to the collapse of many communist governments of Eastern Europe. The Berlin Wall, which had separated East and West Germany, was torn down. With communism no longer so threatening, world politics became less tense but also more unpredictable.

During the second half of the 20th century, the United States continued to face many challenges. In the 1950s, African American leaders launched the **civil rights movement** to try to end segregation and discrimination in the United States. Among their victories included the integration of public schools and other public facilities, the passage of laws protecting the voting rights of minorities, and the striking down of laws that permitted overt discrimination based on race or cultural background. However, minority groups and people of all backgrounds concerned about fair application of the law have continued to be vigilant in insisting that civil rights laws be upheld.

Another area of challenge in recent decades has been **technology**. Technology has led to many advances in science, medicine, and our personal lives. Computers, for instance, make many jobs easier and more productive. They allow almost instantaneous communication with co-workers, family, and friends. Furthermore, they allow people from around the world to share information quickly and easily, giving us the sense that we live in a "global village." However, our reliance on the use of technology has led us to pollute the air with exhaust from a growing number of cars. It has led us to pollute the water with acid rain, resulting from burning coal to generate increased electricity. It has led us to pollute our land with mountains of trash and tons of hazardous wastes.

PRACTICE 5

1. The conflict during the second half of the twentieth century between the United States and the Soviet Union was called the Cold War because it involved (1) [Select...]. In 1991, the (2) [Select...] finally brought the Cold War to an end.

Select (1)	Select (2)
• communists and capitalists	• destruction of the Berlin Wall
• two countries at the far north of Earth	• dissolution of the Soviet Union
• the threat of nuclear war	• separation of East and West Germany
• no direct combat	• death of Mikhail Gorbachev

2. Which of the following best summarizes the message of the cartoon below?

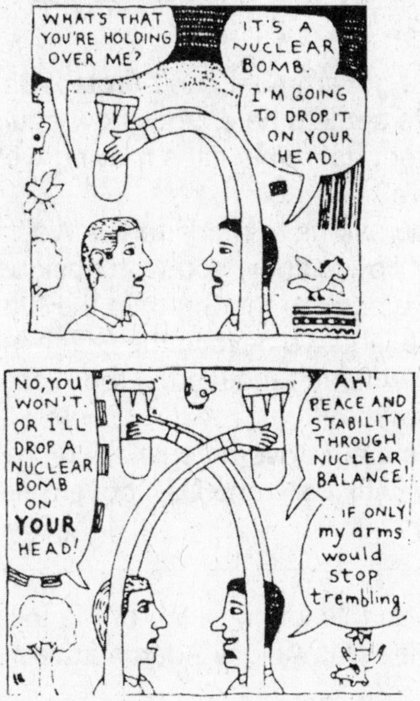

A. Nuclear bombs are extremely destructive.
B. Expanding U.S. nuclear capabilities is a good idea.
C. The buildup of nuclear arms increases fear and instability, not peace.
D. The threat of nuclear war is lessened if both superpowers have equally powerful weapons.

3. Which of the following statements about the Vietnam War is a false generalization?

A. Some Americans served in both Korea and Vietnam.
B. The United States sent massive military aid to South Vietnam.
C. Americans were in complete agreement about pulling out of Vietnam.
D. The Vietnam War lasted much longer than the Korean War.

4. Which of the following goals would a civil rights activist be most likely to pursue?

A. getting Congress to enact laws to restrict the sale of firearms
B. petition for a city ordinance requiring those selling real estate to select a buyer without regard to race
C. getting local companies to stop polluting the environment
D. working with local clergy to publicize a worship service open to people of all religions

5. Which of the following is a conclusion about technology rather than a supporting detail?

A. Reliance on technology has increased pollution.
B. Cars cause air pollution.
C. Coal-generating power plants cause acid-rain pollution.
D. The ease of manufacturing disposable items has led to land pollution at landfill sites.

Answers and explanations start on page 106.

U.S. History Practice Questions

Questions 1 and 2 refer to the timeline below.

Important Events in Early Cherokee History

~800	1540	1700	1800	1820	1838
Cherokee adopt agriculture, with corn as major crop	Europeans first visit Cherokee villages; spread deadly disease, smallpox	White settlers begin to clash with Cherokee over possession of land in the South	Cherokee adopt white farming methods, religion, and life style	Cherokee develop a written language used to this day	Cherokee forced to give up their lands in the South and move to the West

1. Which of the following is a conclusion based on multiple details in the timeline?

   A. The Cherokee had begun farming around 800, before Europeans came to America.
   B. Although the Cherokee adopted many aspects of white culture, they were driven off their ancestral lands.
   C. The Cherokee traditionally considered land ownership to be a tribal matter rather than a right of individuals acting on their own.
   D. The Bible was one of the first books the Cherokee translated into their written language.

2. When President Andrew Jackson mandated that the Cherokee move west in 1830, he claimed that the U.S. government would be better able to protect the Cherokee from whites who might try to get their new land in the West. The Cherokee considered this to be illogical.

   Which of the following summarizes the logical fallacy?

   A. If the government can't protect us from white settlers here, now, how could it protect us from whites moving west in the future?
   B. If you ask us to move to the West now, how do we know you won't ask us to move back to the South in the future?
   C. If the land we have in the South is good, why wouldn't the land in the West be better?
   D. If the state governments are protecting us now, why can't the U.S. government help later?

3. In the late 1700s, Abigail Adams—wife of John Adams, who was our nation's second president—wrote the following in a letter to her sister:

   I will never consent to have our sex considered in an inferior point of light. Let each planet shine in their [its] own orbit . . . if man is Lord, woman is *Lordess*—that is what I contend for.

   Based on this letter, which of the following principles was Abigail Adams advocating?

   A. the separation of church and state
   B. the abolition of slavery
   C. the promotion of scientific learning
   D. equal rights and opportunities for women

Questions 4 and 5 refer to the following map.

The Union and the Confederacy

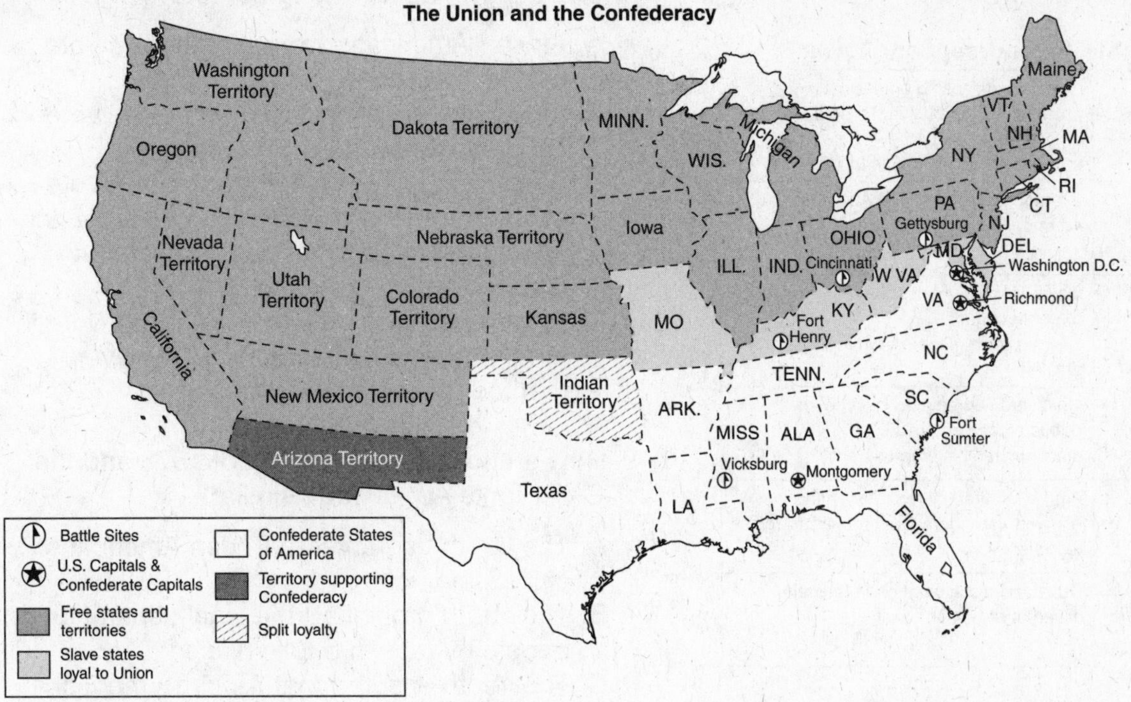

4. List four states that permitted slavery but did not join the Confederacy.

____

____

____

____

5. The loyalty of Maryland was of crucial importance to the Union. Based on the map, which statement best explains why this was so?

A. The nation's capital was located nearby.
B. The Confederate capital was located there.
C. It was close to Fort Sumter, where the Civil War began.
D. Important rail lines ran through Baltimore, Maryland.

---

6. In the Emancipation Proclamation, issued in 1863, President Lincoln freed all people enslaved in the states that had seceded from the Union. This proclamation was explicitly not to be put into effect in slave states that had remained in the Union. The proclamation went on to say:

I hereby enjoin upon the people so declared to be free to abstain from all violence . . . and make known that such persons of suitable condition will be received into the armed services of the United States to garrison forts, positions, stations, and other places, and to man vessels of all sorts.

Based on the information given about the Emancipation Proclamation and the text of the order itself, which of the following was a major reason Lincoln issued the proclamation?

A. to encourage states to secede from the Union
B. to punish slaveholders throughout the South
C. to weaken the North by enlisting former slaves in the Confederate army
D. to weaken the South by enlisting former slaves in the Union army

Questions 7 through 9 refer to the following chart.

Civil Rights Amendment and Laws

14th Amendment (1868)	Granted citizenship and equal protection of the law to all persons born in the United States (not applied to American Indians)
15th Amendment (1870)	Granted voting rights to African Americans
Civil Rights Act of 1875	Gave African Americans the right to serve on juries Banned racial segregation in public places
Civil Rights Act of 1964	Outlawed segregation by race in public places and racial discrimination in employment
Voting Rights Act of 1965	Prohibited literacy tests for voting Allowed the federal government to register voters
Civil Rights Act of 1968	Outlawed discrimination in the sale or rental of homes

7. An Asian American registers to vote and is given a reading test. Place a dot in the cell from the chart above containing the civil rights amendment or law relevant to this situation.

8. Which statement best summarizes what this chart shows about voting rights?

   A. African Americans were granted the vote five years after the Civil War ended.
   B. African Americans were granted the vote 100 years after the Civil War ended.
   C. African Americans were granted the vote soon after the Civil War, but laws enforcing these rights had to be passed a century later.
   D. African Americans were granted the vote in 1870 but American Indians were never granted these same rights.

9. How are the Civil Rights Act of 1875 and the Civil Rights Act of 1964 similar?

   A. They both guaranteed African Americans citizenship rights.
   B. They both prohibited the legal separation of people by race in public places.
   C. They both ensured that African Americans could serve on juries.
   D. They both make job discrimination illegal.

10. Alexander Graham Bell invented the telephone in the spring of 1876. In the fall, he exhibited it at an exposition in Philadelphia. When leading scientists saw Bell's invention, they said, "Here is the greatest marvel ever achieved in electrical science."

    Which of the following statements related to the passage is an opinion, not a fact?

    A. Bell invented the telephone in 1876.
    B. Bell exhibited the telephone at an exposition in Philadelphia.
    C. Scientists admired Bell's invention.
    D. The telephone was the greatest electrical invention ever.

Questions 11 through 13 are based on the paragraph and the political cartoon below.

In 1974, President Richard Nixon resigned from office. He had been involved in a scandal known as Watergate. The Watergate scandal implicated Nixon in covering up crimes committed by members of his reelection committee. These crimes ranged from illegally harassing political opponents to burglary and bribery. With Congress investigating him, he was sure to be impeached. This cartoon was published before Nixon resigned to avoid impeachment.

Hey guys, do you really think we need that clause about impeachment in there?

Cartoon by Robert Lawlor. Reprinted with permission of the *Philadelphia Daily News*.

11. In this cartoon, whom is Nixon addressing?

A. the writers of the Declaration of Independence
B. the framers of the U.S. Constitution
C. the past presidents of the United States
D. the present session of Congress

12. Which value was Congress furthering by investigating Nixon and Watergate?

A. the pursuit of justice
B. the duty of obedience
C. loyalty to a friend
D. love of mercy

13. About Watergate, one historian has written, "In a society in which distrust of leaders and institutions of authority was already widespread, the fall of Richard Nixon seemed to confirm the most cynical assumptions about the character of American public life."

Based on the information on page 54, which of the following was most likely a reason for Americans' growing distrust of their government in the years just prior to Watergate?

A. mismanagement of the New Deal
B. the beginning of rock music
C. the escalation and failure of the Vietnam War
D. the scandals of previous presidents, including John Kennedy and Bill Clinton

Questions 14 and 15 refer to the graph below.

Hispanic Population by Nationality, 1990

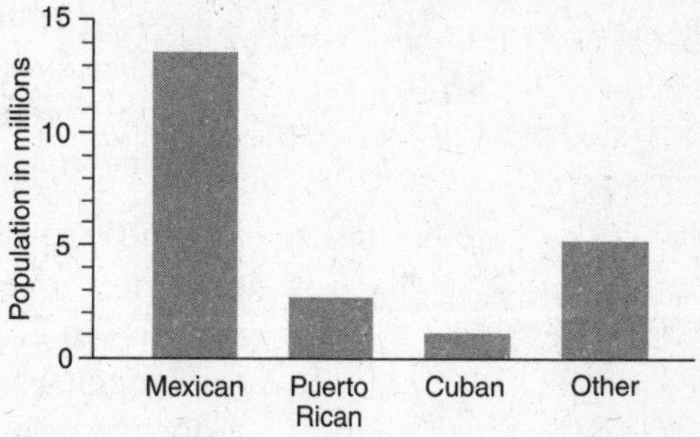

Source: U.S. Census Bureau

14. In 1990, approximately how many people of Cuban nationality lived in the United States?

A. 100
B. 100,000
C. 1,000,000
D. 5,000,000

15. A Hispanic family moved into an apartment next door to yours in 1990. Based solely on the bar graph, which place was the family most likely to be from?

A. Cuba
B. Mexico
C. Puerto Rico
D. Spain

Answers and explanations start on page 106.

LESSON

1

Civics and Government

Historic Basis for U.S. System

Key Ideas

- The idea of democracy originated with the Ancient Greeks who spoke of the 'rule of the people.'
- The historic basis of the U.S. government came from the British system that limited the king's powers and protected individual rights.
- The U.S. system evolved from the British idea of a parliamentary democracy to a representative democracy.

ON THE GED® TEST

While you will not need to memorize dates, it will be helpful to be familiar with key terms, such as the ones in ***bold*** *type.*

The system of government in the United States is known as **representative democracy**. In this form of government, the citizens vote to elect representatives who make and execute laws. To understand this form of democracy, it is helpful to first distinguish democracy from other types of government. Then, you can trace the historical development of democracy and see how representative democracy differs from other types of democracy employed over time and around the globe.

The origins of **democracy** are ancient. The term *democracy,* which means "rule of the people" in Greek, arose in approximately 500 BCE in the Greek city-state of Athens. This distinguishes democracy from **monarchy**, the "rule of one person" (such as a king or queen); **aristocracy**, the "rule of an elite class" (lords or barons, for example); **theocracy**, the "rule of the church"; and **anarchy**, the "rule of the mob" (arguably not a form of government at all). Democracy is also distinct from forms of **authoritarian rule**, such as dictatorship, military rule, and fascism.

In ancient Athenian democracy, laws were voted upon by a council of all citizens, a system known as **direct democracy**. In ancient Athens, however, a "citizen" was defined as a free male landowner over the age of 20. Women, foreigners, slaves, non-landowners, and minors were excluded from the vote.

For the eventual development of democracy in the U.S., one of the most important events was the signing of the **Magna Carta** (Latin for Great Charter) in England in 1215. England was a monarchy, but some protested the king's absolute power. The result was the signing of the Magna Carta, a document limiting the king's rule and subjecting his decisions to review. This same period also saw the development of the legal doctrine of **habeas corpus**, which made it illegal for the government to hold or imprison individuals without granting them trials.

Over time, the group allowed by the Magna Carta to review the king's decisions developed into a **parliament** of lawmakers appointed by title and/or elected by citizens. As the power of the parliament grew, England transformed into a **parliamentary democracy**. In this system, a government is formed by the party holding a majority of seats in the parliament. In most parliamentary democracies, the majority party appoints or authorizes the chief executive, such as the president.

Known as the Age of Enlightenment, the 17th and 18th centuries saw the spread of democracy to many other European countries. England, France, Holland, and other European powers also adopted **bills of rights** for individuals during this period. The philosophies dominant in this era emphasized reason and individual rights and encouraged government by the people. Enlightenment philosophers such as Adam Smith, John Locke, and Voltaire strongly influenced the founders of the United States.

PRACTICE 1

<u>Questions 1 through 5</u> **are based on the information on page 60.**

Directions: Match each choice in the box corresponding to the form of government that best matches the description.

1.

Direct democracy	
Monarchy	
Representative democracy	
Aristocracy	

Choices:

In <u>Country A</u>, laws are made and administered by lords who inherit their lands and titles.
In <u>Country B</u>, laws are made by a sovereign king and are subject to no review.
In <u>Country C</u>, laws are made by Congress, an elected group of representatives.
In <u>Country D</u>, laws are made by the vote of all citizens.

Directions: For <u>Questions 2 through 5</u>, choose the <u>one best answer</u> to each question.

2. Which of following can be inferred about the Founding Fathers of the United States?

   A. They sought to establish the power of the king of England in the United States.
   B. They were concerned about protecting the rights of individuals.
   C. They argued that the United States should adopt a system of direct democracy.
   D. They thought representatives from the United States should sit in Parliament.

3. In the United States, laws are enacted by Congress, a group of representatives elected by the people. Which of the following was most likely the chief historical model for the U.S. Congress?

   A. Athenian council of citizens
   B. Magna Carta
   C. Parliament of England
   D. Declaration of the Rights of Man and the Citizen adopted in France in 1789

4. Some nations have been ruled by a form of government known as constitutional monarchy. While a king or queen is the single, sovereign ruler of the country, his or her power is limited by a constitution, a formal document outlining which of the monarch's decisions are subject to review or may be overruled by a court of law.

   Which of the following was most likely a constitutional monarchy?

   A. the ancient city-state of Athens
   B. any country ruled by fascism
   C. the United States at the time of its founding
   D. England during the Age of Enlightenment

5. If the United States were a parliamentary democracy, which of the following would be most likely to occur?

   A. The office of the president would decrease in power.
   B. The office of the president would increase in power.
   C. The president would be elected by a majority vote of all citizens.
   D. The president would be appointed by the majority party in parliament.

Answers and explanations start on page 107.

LESSON

2

CIVICS AND GOVERNMENT

Constitutional Government

Key Ideas

- The U.S. Constitution is the basis for our government structure and legal system.
- The Bill of Rights—the first ten constitutional amendments—define the rights of citizens.
- Amendments to the Constitution require wide support, but many important amendments have gained enough support to be ratified.

ON THE GED® TEST

The GED® Social Studies Test *may include an excerpt from or a reference to one of the following U.S. historical documents:*

- *Declaration of Independence*
- *U.S. Constitution, including the Bill of Rights and other amendments*
- *Landmark Supreme Court cases*

The Constitution of the United States is the foundation of our national government and legal system. The United States is a **republic**, a form of government in which citizens elect the people who will govern them. A republic is very different from a government system in which citizens do not choose their political leaders, such as a **monarchy** or **dictatorship**.

The people who wrote the Constitution set particular goals for the new nation, which they stated in the **preamble**, or introduction. They wanted to unite the states under one government, establish a nation where people could live peacefully and safely under the rule of law, and make prosperity and freedom possible for all citizens.

Following the preamble are the original seven **articles** of the U.S. Constitution. These articles provide for the three branches of government (see page 64), establish the rights of states, and set forth procedures for ratifying and amending the Constitution. Article 6 states that all government officials must uphold the Constitution as "the supreme law of the land" and that no other laws can contradict any part of the Constitution.

According to Article 5, a constitutional **amendment** can be proposed by Congress if it is supported by two-thirds majorities in both the House and Senate. The proposed amendment then must be ratified by three-fourths of the states. This process ensures that amendments have very broad national support.

The original Constitution did not specifically describe citizens' rights. Even as the Constitution was being written, some political leaders insisted that a bill of rights was needed to help develop citizens' trust in the new government. However, they agreed to wait to make amendments to the Constitution until after it was **ratified**. As a result of this compromise, the first ten amendments to the U.S. Constitution, passed in 1791, became the **Bill of Rights**. These rights are well known to many Americans. The First Amendment, for example, guarantees freedom of religion, freedom of speech, and freedom of the press. The Sixth and Seventh Amendments guarantee citizens' rights to trial by jury.

As Americans' ideas about citizenship and government have evolved, the amendment process has allowed the Constitution to evolve as well. The Thirteenth Amendment (1865) outlawed slavery; the Fifteenth Amendment (1870) established that the rights of citizens "shall not be denied or abridged ... on account of race, color, or previous condition of servitude."

A number of constitutional amendments have extended voting rights to citizens. The Nineteenth Amendment (1920) gave women the right to vote. The Twenty-fourth Amendment (1964) banned poll taxes, which some states were using to prevent African Americans from voting. The Twenty-sixth Amendment (1971) lowered the voting age to 18.

PRACTICE 2

1. Based on the information on page 62, which of the following is the main characteristic of a republic?

   A. voting rights extended to few adult citizens
   B. elected representatives exercising government power on behalf of citizens
   C. people governing themselves by voting directly on all issues
   D. power concentrated among a small group

2. The Constitution is a relatively brief document containing only about seven thousand words. It establishes the structure and powers of the U.S. government but does not give many specifics.

   What assumption were the drafters of the Constitution working under as they kept the document general and brief?

   A. There was not enough time to draft a long, detailed document before the states had to ratify it.
   B. Most of the power of the federal government would be reserved to the president, who could govern as he saw fit.
   C. The details of government would be worked out in the future, as the need arose, within the framework of the Constitution.
   D. Written constitutions were an untested basis for democratic government, so it was better to keep such a document brief.

3. Franklin Delano Roosevelt was elected to the presidency four times between 1933 and 1945. In reaction to this, the Twenty-second Amendment, ratified in 1951, allowed presidents a maximum of two terms in office.

   People who favored presidential term limits would most likely have valued which of the following?

   A. responsibility but no authority
   B. authority but no responsibility
   C. the power of an office, not an individual
   D. the power of an individual, not an office

4. The third paragraph of the passage on page 62 includes a summary of Article 6 of the Constitution, also called the supremacy clause.

   ____________ is an example of the supremacy clause in action.

   - Congress voting to appropriate $2 billion for a federal highways program
   - The Environmental Protection Agency issuing new regulations on a pollutant
   - The U.S. Supreme Court refusing to hear a case
   - The U.S. Supreme Court declaring an Illinois state law unconstitutional

Question 5 refers to the following chart.

Methods of Amending the Constitution

Proposal	Ratification Method	When Used
Two-thirds vote in both houses of Congress to propose an amendment	By three-quarters of the state legislatures	For every amendment except one
	By special conventions in three-fourths of the states	Twenty-first Amendment (repealing Prohibition)
Two-thirds of states request Congress to call a constitutional convention to consider an amendment	By three-quarters of the state legislatures	Never used
	By special conventions in three-fourths of the states	Never used

5. Which of the following would best explain why the third and fourth methods of amending the Constitution have never been used?

   A. State governments do not usually act together.
   B. Only Congress can propose amendments.
   C. State legislatures can vote on an amendment.
   D. Conventions meet more frequently than Congress and state legislatures do.

Answers and explanations start on page 107.

LESSON

3

CIVICS AND GOVERNMENT

Levels and Branches of Government

Key Ideas

- Under our Constitution, the federal government must share power with the states.
- The federal government has three major branches—executive, legislative, and judicial.
- The three branches of the government balance each other's power.

ON THE GED® TEST

Editorial cartoons like the one on page 65 use pictures and humor to make a political point.

The U.S. government works in layers with different responsibilities at the national, or **federal**, level; the state level; and local levels, including cities, villages, and counties. The federal government works across all 50 states, and its decisions and actions affect everyone. States have their own constitutions, similar to the U.S. Constitution. State governments also are quite powerful in shaping the lives of people in their states.

Federalism, which is a basic principle of the U.S. Constitution, means that power is shared between the national and state levels of government. Dividing power between federal and state government protects the rights of individual states, but also allows our national government to enforce certain rights of citizenship. The Constitution gives some powers only to the national government, some only to state government, and some to both. For example, only the federal government can declare war. States are given the power to establish schools. Both federal and state governments can levy taxes and set up court systems.

There are three branches of government at the federal level, each with different roles to play. The powers of each branch are described in the Constitution. The **executive branch** consists of the president and various advisors (including the president's cabinet) and government departments. The executive branch enforces the nation's laws and provides national leadership, setting goals and policies. The **legislative branch** consists of two houses of **Congress**: the **Senate** and the **House of Representatives**. Congress is responsible for making laws that all citizens, organizations, and businesses must follow. The **judicial branch**, made up of the federal court system including the Supreme Court, decides disputes related to laws, including the U.S. Constitution.

U.S. citizens vote for the president and all members of Congress. As a result, these politicians have a responsibility to represent and serve their **constituents**—the people who elected them. The president may be elected to only two terms of four years each. Representatives are elected for two years and Senators for six years; these members of Congress may be reelected for any number of terms.

Federal judges, in contrast, are appointed by the president and **confirmed** by the Senate. They can serve in these positions for life. As citizens, we have a right to expect our federal judges to make **impartial** decisions based on the Constitution and the laws of the United States.

The people who wrote the U.S. Constitution were afraid to give any government body too much power. Therefore, the Constitution limits the power of each branch of the federal government. Each branch has separate powers. Each branch also has the power to act in ways that affect the other branches, in a system called **checks and balances**. For example, the president can **veto** laws made by Congress. Congress can override a presidential veto by repassing the law with a two-thirds majority. The Constitution is also now interpreted to mean that judges can review laws and declare them **unconstitutional**.

PRACTICE 3

<u>Questions 1 through 4</u> **are based on the information on page 64.**

1. What is the key characteristic of federalism?

   A. division of power between national and state governments
   B. concentration of power in one government
   C. concentration of power at the local level
   D. a judicial system with trial, appellate, and supreme courts

2. Which of the following is an example of a government entity that is part of the executive branch?

   A. the Democratic National Committee
   B. Congress's House Rules Committee
   C. the U.S. Court of Appeals
   D. the State Department

3. Why do lifetime appointments help ensure that federal judges rule impartially on legal issues?

   A. Federal judges need not worry about pleasing their constituents in order to be reelected.
   B. Only people who demonstrate loyalty to the ruling political party are appointed.
   C. Lifetime appointments mean that federal judges acquire a great deal of experience.
   D. A federal judge must be impartial or he or she will not be reelected.

4. Match each of the following definitions to the matching term.

Terms

Checks and balances	
Veto	
Senators	
Constituents	
Representatives	

Definitions

Limits that one branch of government can place on the other branches
The people whom political leaders represent
The president's power to strike down a law
Legislators who serve two-year terms
Legislators who serve six-year terms

<u>Question 5</u> **refers to the following cartoon.**

"Let's never forget that the constitution provides for three equally important branches of government: the legislative and the other two."

5. Which of the following people is most likely depicted in the cartoon?

   A. the president
   B. a member of Congress
   C. the head of a government department
   D. a federal judge

6. Although the states have the power to make their own laws in many areas, in practice they cooperate with one another to a great extent. For example, when a person travels, his or her driver's license, which was issued by one state, will be honored in other states.

   On which of the following principles is this type of cooperation based?

   A. mutual respect and convenience
   B. centralization of authority
   C. common law
   D. division of power

Answers and explanations start on page 107.

LESSON

4

CIVICS AND GOVERNMENT

The Electoral System

Key Ideas

- U.S. politics are dominated by the Democratic and Republican parties.
- Political parties hold primaries to select candidates for the general election.
- Political campaigns are very expensive, and many people believe that we must reform our campaign finance laws.

GED® TEST TIP

When you are asked a question about a circle graph, remember that it represents a whole, or 100%.

At the national level in particular, two **political parties** dominate the political arena in the United States: the **Democrats** and the **Republicans**. These parties represent different ideas about the role of government in our nation. In each election season, the parties and candidates work to promote their views, or **platforms**—their positions on issues like tax reform, Social Security, education spending, environmental protection, and so on.

The political parties have developed large organizations for raising money and getting their candidates elected. Each party runs its own **primary** election, in which candidates within the party compete with each other for the party's **nomination**. After the primary elections, the winners from each party's primary face off in the general election. In presidential elections, the primary season ends with a party **convention**, where delegates from each state gather to select the party's candidate. Citizens vote in a general election, and the results are tallied by state. Following the general election, electors from each state cast their state's votes in the **Electoral College**. The electors generally must cast their votes for the candidate who won the general election in their state. The candidate who wins the greatest number of electoral votes becomes president.

Although Democrats and Republicans are by far the largest political parties, there are small parties as well. At times, a "third-party candidate" like Ralph Nader or Ross Perot attracts enough support to influence the outcome of the national election. Even when small parties offer interesting new ideas or solutions to problems, they have great difficulty attracting money and public attention because the Democratic and Republican parties are so well established.

Although many voters consider themselves to be either Republicans or Democrats, many others are **independent**. Candidates and their political parties rely heavily on **opinion polls** to find out what voters think; they try to tailor their campaign messages to appeal to large numbers of voters. Groups of voters who might "swing" an election one way or another are particularly important targets for political campaigns. Sometimes opposing candidates participate in public **debates**.

Political campaigns can be very expensive, and the higher the office, the more expensive the campaign. To reach the public, candidates pay for mailings, TV ads, and events, including personal appearances; they need campaign staff and offices; they must pay for travel expenses. As a result, fund-raising has become a very important part of running for office.

In recent decades, Americans have become more and more concerned about the high cost of running for office. Many Americans believe that a candidate should not have to be wealthy to begin with, or be overly obligated to contributors, in order to gain political office. We now have laws that restrict the size of campaign contributions. We also have restrictions on how **Political Action Committees** (PACs) operate. However, many people believe that more reforms are needed.

PRACTICE 4

<u>Questions 1 through 3</u> **are based on the information on page 66.**

1. Which of the following is necessary for a candidate to win the presidency?

   A. earning a majority of primary wins
   B. receiving a majority of the popular vote
   C. receiving a majority in the Electoral College
   D. having no third-party opponent

2. An exit poll is one that surveys people as they leave a voting location. Instead of waiting for votes to be counted, the media often announce the winners of elections based on exit polls.

   Which of the following is an important drawback of using exit polls?

   A. Exit polls may be inaccurate if the people polled are not representative of the political unit as a whole or if the election is very close.
   B. Exit polls allow the media to present election results during prime time on election night instead of waiting until later in the evening.
   C. Exit polls have undue influence on the way politicians running for office conduct their campaigns.
   D. Exit polls are likely to be unreliable when there is a wide margin between the candidates.

3. Which of the following is an example of a primary election?

   A. A Democrat and a Republican oppose one another in a race for the U.S. Senate.
   B. A Republican and an independent candidate oppose one another in a race for the state senate.
   C. Once presidential candidates are chosen, they select their running mates.
   D. Two city council members are on a ballot to determine which one will run for mayor as a Democrat.

<u>Questions 4 and 5</u> **refer to the following graphs.**

2010 Election

Senate Candidates' Funds $597,600,000

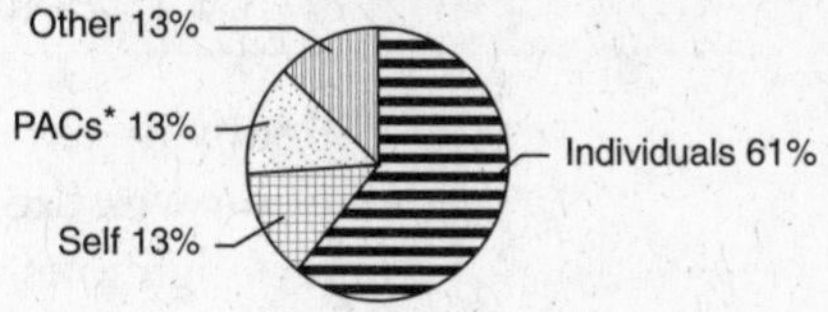

House Candidates' Funds $949,300,000

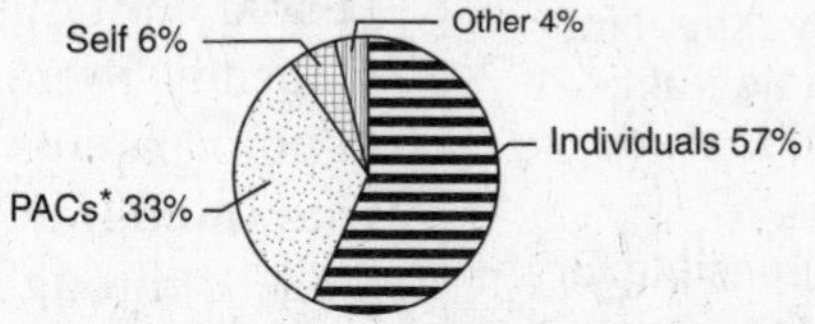

*PACs are Political Action Committees – groups that raise money for candidates.

Source: Federal Election Commission.

4. How do the campaign funding sources of Senate and House candidates compare?

   A. Individual donations provided a larger percentage of funds raised by House candidates than of those raised by Senate candidates.
   B. In total, individuals contributed a greater dollar amount to House candidates than they did to Senate candidates.
   C. Political parties provided a greater percentage of the funds raised by House candidates than they did of funds raised by Senate candidates.
   D. On average, Senate candidates received a greater percentage of their funds from PACs than did House candidates.

5. Which of the following statements is supported by the graphs?

   A. In 2010, self-funding was a larger source of funds for Senate candidates than it was for House candidates.
   B. In 2010, individual donations were the largest source of funds for Senate candidates but not for House candidates.
   C. In 2010, PACs were the largest source of funds for House candidates but not for Senate candidates.
   D. Fund-raising accounts for most of the work on a congressional campaign.

Answers and explanations start on page 108.

LESSON 5

CIVICS AND GOVERNMENT

The Role of the Citizen

Key Ideas

- U.S. citizens have the right to vote and to hold public office, as well as to enjoy many freedoms.
- Citizens are responsible for contributing to the general welfare of the nation.
- In our court system, citizens serve on juries in order to protect the rights of other citizens.

ON THE GED® TEST

The GED® Social Studies Test *will include questions about "practical documents," which may include voter registration or election information.*

Citizenship is a special relationship between a person and a nation: the nation owes the person certain rights and guarantees; the person has certain obligations to the nation. Thus citizens of the United States have both rights and responsibilities.

People born in the United States, no matter what the circumstances, automatically become U.S. citizens. Regardless of where you were born, if one of your parents was a U.S. citizen, then you are also a U.S. citizen. People who **immigrate** to the United States from other countries can become U.S. citizens through a legal process called **naturalization**; underage children are naturalized along with their parents.

Our rights of citizenship are established in the first ten amendments to the U.S. Constitution—the Bill of Rights (see page 62)—and in other sections of the Constitution. One of the most fundamental rights of U.S. citizens is our right to participate in our nation's political life. We are eligible to vote and to hold public office, and we elect representatives to govern us. In a famous phrase in the Gettysburg Address, Abraham Lincoln said that we have a government "of the people, by the people, and for the people."

As Lincoln's famous remark implies, a government "by the people" requires that citizens take responsibility. First and foremost, we must uphold the laws of our country. As citizens, we also make contributions to the national welfare. Our taxes pay for services that the government provides to benefit everyone. By voting, we not only choose our government representatives, but we also help to make the political process meaningful for everyone. Through national service—such as military service, holding public office, or participating in intensive volunteer programs like Teach for America—citizens may devote years of their lives to the responsibilities of citizenship.

Our **jury** system is an important example of the give-and-take of citizenship. Each of us is guaranteed the right to a fair and speedy trial, heard by "a jury of peers," if we are accused of a crime. However, we are also obligated to serve on juries or as **witnesses** when we are called by the court system. The fairness of our legal system depends on citizens participating in that system. Therefore, our employers are obligated to release us from work at the request of the courts.

In addition to the rights and responsibilities established by law, many citizens contribute their time and money in other ways that serve society as a whole. People volunteer to serve organizations in their communities or within their professions—serving meals in shelters, fund-raising for schools, offering free medical services, etc. People also give money to causes they think are important, from political campaigns to food pantries to environmental organizations. Many citizens also work hard to conduct their daily lives in ways that contribute to the general welfare: by recycling, cleaning up trash, and looking out for their neighbors and family members.

PRACTICE 5

Question 1 is based on the information on page 68.

1. ________________ outlines the rights of U.S. citizens.

- The Declaration of Independence
- The U.S. Constitution
- A U.S. passport
- A person's naturalization papers.

Questions 2 and 3 refer to the following information.

Noncitizens can be classified into five groups:

Resident alien: A foreigner who has established permanent residence in the United States.

Nonresident alien: A foreigner who is staying in the United States for a brief, specified period.

Enemy alien: A foreigner who is a citizen of a nation at war with the United States.

Refugee: A foreigner fleeing his or her country to escape persecution or danger.

Illegal alien: A foreigner who comes to the United States without legal documentation.

2. Louvina married an American and moved to the United States from Trinidad in 2010. Three years later, she filed a legal petition requesting U.S. citizenship. In what category of alien does Louvina belong?

A. resident alien
B. nonresident alien
C. enemy alien
D. refugee

3. What would happen to the legal status of noncitizens living in the United States if their country declares war on the United States?

A. They would become nonresident aliens.
B. They would become resident aliens.
C. They would become enemy aliens.
D. They would become refugees.

4. The United States must balance the right of society to protect itself against the rights of an accused criminal. One aspect of this tension is the Fourth Amendment guarantee of "the right of people to be secure in their persons, houses, papers, and effects, against unreasonable searches and seizures."

Which of the following values is supported by the Fourth Amendment?

A. free speech
B. privacy
C. civic duty
D. volunteerism

Question 5 refers to the following graph.

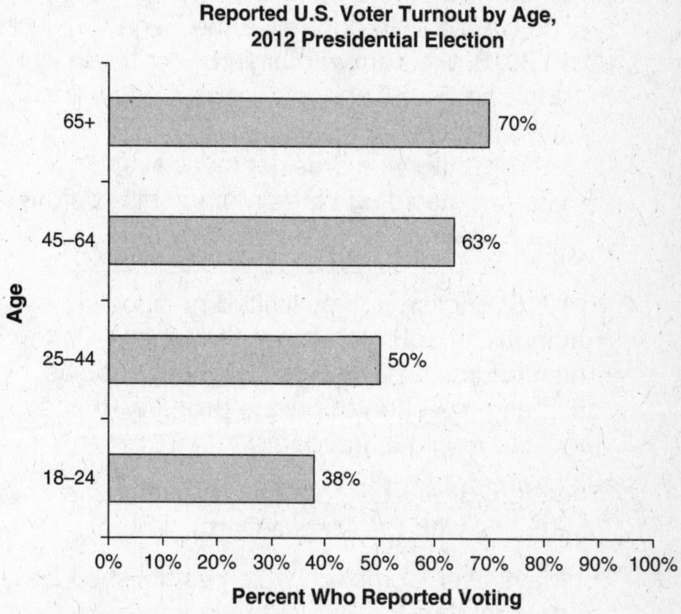

Source: United States Census Bureau

5. Which of the following is a conclusion based on the graph rather than a detail of the graph?

A. About 63 percent of people aged 45 to 64 reported voting in the 2012 presidential election.
B. Those aged 65+ reported the highest voter turnout in the 2012 presidential election, at 70 percent.
C. If the 2012 presidential election is representative of elections generally in the United States, voter turnout increases with age.
D. Only about 38 percent of young people reported voting in the 2012 presidential election.

Answers and explanations start on page 108.

Civics and Government Practice Questions

Question 1 refers to the following chart.

Political Divisions in the 113th Congress, 2013

Party	House	Senate
Republicans	234	45
Democrats	201	53
Others	—	2 (In case of a tie, Vice President Joe Biden (D) would vote.)
Vacant	—	—

1. Which of the following is the best summary of the chart above?

   A. Congress is made up of the House and the Senate.
   B. In 2013, a different major party controlled the House than controlled the Senate.
   C. In 2013, the narrow margin of control in each body of Congress made it difficult to pass legislation.
   D. In 2013, the vice president was likely to cast the deciding vote on many bills before the Senate.

---

2. In 1215, English nobles limited royal power by forcing King John to accept the Magna Carta. This document gave certain rights to nobles, such as protection of private property, trial by jury, and religious freedoms.

   Therefore, the [Select...] shares essential characteristics with the Magna Carta.

   - Mayflower Compact, which established a government for Plymouth colony,
   - Bill of Rights of the U.S. Constitution, which guarantees citizens certain rights,
   - Albany Plan of Union, which called for a colonial confederation,
   - *Federalist Papers*, which encouraged ratification of the U.S. Constitution,

Questions 3 and 4 refer to the following passage.

In 1979, Congress passed legislation to allow political parties to raise unlimited amounts of general-purpose money not designated for particular candidates. In 1991, a lawsuit forced disclosure of such "soft money" contributions, and concern grew about the size of individual donations, the extent of total donations, and the ways in which the money was being spent. During the presidential elections of 1996 and 2000, campaign fund-raising, especially the raising and spending of soft money, was an issue, with the candidates promising reform. Finally, in 2001, after several years of hearings, the Senate passed the McCain-Feingold bill, which would eliminate the unregulated soft money contributions that make up a large proportion of the parties' budgets.

3. Which of the following is an example of a soft money contribution?

   A. a $250 ticket to a fund-raising dinner-dance to benefit a mayoral candidate
   B. a $3,000 donation to the campaign fund of an incumbent senator
   C. a $3,000 contribution to a party fund for TV ads on political issues
   D. a $1,000 gift to a senator's campaign fund in response to a direct mail solicitation

4. Which of the following is the most likely reason soft money was not a major issue in the 1980s?

   A. People were less aware of soft money because disclosure was not required at that time.
   B. Political campaigns were publicly financed, so soft money was not needed.
   C. Most candidates spent part of their campaign funds on television ads.
   D. McCain and Feingold had not submitted their campaign finance reform bill.

Questions 5 and 6 refer to the following paragraph and graphs.

In order to win a presidential election, a candidate must win a majority of the vote in the Electoral College. Each state has as many electors as it has senators and representatives in Congress. In most states, the winner of the popular vote gets all the electoral votes of the state. These graphs show the popular and Electoral College votes in the election of 2012.

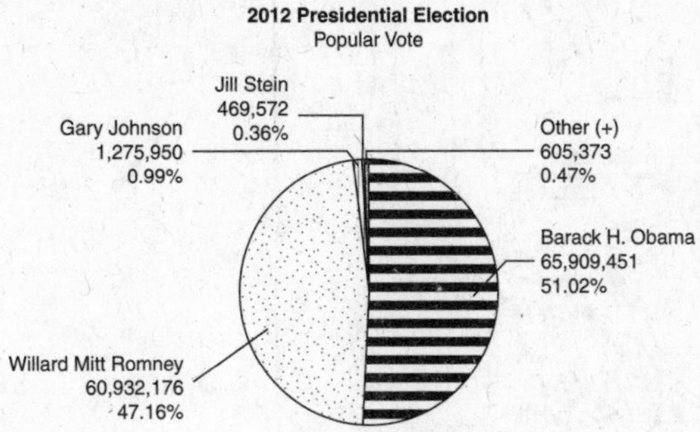

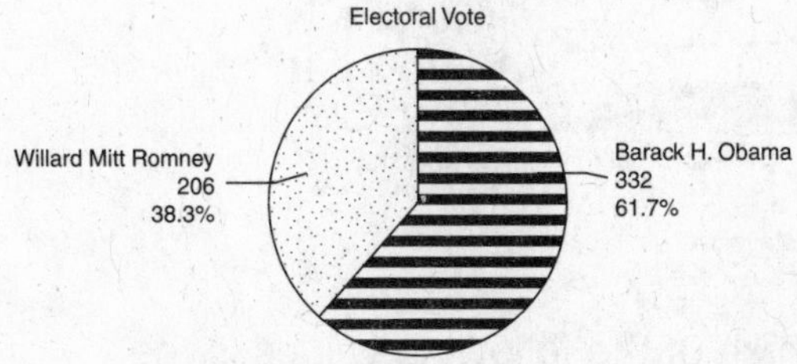

5. Which one of the following statements is supported by the information in the paragraph and the graphs?

   A. A presidential candidate will receive the same percentage of electoral votes as he or she received of the popular vote.
   B. Romney won a greater percentage of the electoral vote than of the popular vote in 2012.
   C. Jill Stein won a greater percentage of the popular vote than of the electoral vote in 2012.
   D. The total of popular votes cast for all candidates other than Barack Obama was greater than the total of those cast for Barack Obama.

6. Which of the following would be the best title for the paragraph and the graphs?

   A. 2012 Presidential Election: How Obama Defeated Romney
   B. 2012 Presidential Election: Third-Party Influence
   C. 2012 Presidential Election: Winning the Electoral College
   D. 2012 Presidential Election: Popular and Electoral Votes

Question 7 refers to the following passage.

Where do I vote? Your voting district is determined by your place of residence. Watch your local newspaper for an announcement indicating polling locations and times, or contact your local board of election to determine your voting location.

You may also obtain your polling place location by accessing the website of the Office of the Secretary of State at www.anystate.us. You may also call the Office of the Secretary of State for assistance.

7. Which of the following is assumed but not stated outright in the voter guide above?

   A. The board of election is the county, city, or town office responsible for local voting.
   B. A voter's polling place is determined by his or her address.
   C. A voter can find his or her polling place on the Internet.
   D. A voter can call the Office of the Secretary of State to find out where to vote.

---

8. An interest group is an organization with specific goals that seeks to influence government policies.

   Place a ★ into the box next to each entity that constitutes an interest group. There may be more than one.

The Democratic Party, which nominates candidates and tries to win elections	
The National Association of Manufacturers, which lobbies for businesses	
The Federal Communications Commission, which regulates broadcasters	
The Cabinet, an advisory body for the president	
Public Citizen, a nonprofit consumer rights advocacy group	

Questions 9 and 10 refer to the following cartoon.

WAYNE STAYSKAL
Courtesy Tampa Tribune

9. What is the main idea of this cartoon?
   A. Most voters are working people.
   B. Most registered voters don't vote.
   C. Voters should establish another political party.
   D. A non-voters' party would lose every election.

10. Which of the following values is the cartoonist appealing for?
    A. the work ethic
    B. majority rule
    C. civic duty
    D. national pride

11. An oligarchy is a system of government in which a small group of people holds power.

    Which of the following is an oligarchy?
    A. China, where the top leaders of the communist party control the government
    B. Iraq, when it had a dictator, Saddam Hussein
    C. Great Britain, with a monarch, a prime minister, and an elected parliament
    D. Greece, with a prime minister and an elected parliament

12. Three typical laws from the code of Hammurabi, written about 1700 B.C.E., are "If a son strike his father, his hands shall be hewn off. If a man put out the eye of another man, his eye shall be put out. If he break another man's bone, his bone shall be broken."

    What principle underlies these laws?
    A. retribution
    B. rehabilitation
    C. incarceration
    D. mediation

Questions 13 and 14 refer to the following map and table.

The Death Penalty in the United States, 2013

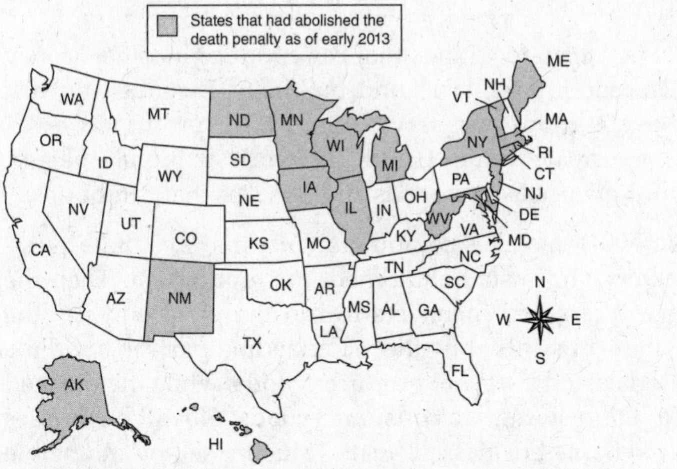

NOTE: By early 2013, Connecticut, Maryland, and New Mexico had abolished the death penalty prospectively. Anyone convicted of a capital offense that occurred prior to abolition of the death penalty in these states may be legally executed.

Homicide Rate per 100,000 Population, 2010

Highest	Lowest
Louisiana, 11.9	Vermont, 1.3
Mississippi, 9.6	New Hampshire, 1.4
Alabama, 8.2	Idaho, 1.5
Maryland, 7.6	Wyoming, 1.6
New Mexico, 7.4	Hawaii, 1.8

Source: National Center for Health Statistics and U.S. Bureau of the Census.

13. How many states have the death penalty?

A. 12
B. 18
C. 32
D. 40

14. People who favor capital punishment usually argue that it prevents serious crimes like homicide. Based on the map and chart, what is a logical flaw with this argument?

A. A life sentence without parole costs taxpayers more than executing an inmate.
B. Some executed inmates turn out to have been innocent based on newly discovered evidence.
C. Two of the five states with the highest per capita homicide rates have abolished the death penalty.
D. Two of the five states with the lowest per capita homicide rates have abolished the death penalty.

15. The U.S. Constitution gives the president the power to make treaties with foreign nations, and it gives the Senate the power to "advise and consent" on all treaties. Thus a two-thirds majority of the Senate must ratify any treaty presented by the president. In 1978, President Jimmy Carter persuaded the Senate to ratify treaties with Panama that transferred control of the Panama Canal from the United States to Panama. Many Americans were outraged and believed that U.S. interests had been given away.

Which of the following is an opinion rather than a statement of fact?

A. Presidents have the power to enter into treaties with foreign nations.
B. A two-thirds majority of the Senate is needed to ratify a treaty.
C. The 1978 Panama treaties sold out U.S. interests to Panama.
D. The 1978 Panama treaties gave control of the Panama Canal to Panama.

16. In the mayor-council form of city government, voters elect both a mayor and a city council. The mayor is the city's chief executive, operating the city on a day-to-day basis and also serving a ceremonial function. The city council is a legislative body, in charge of the city's finances and passing city laws. In the council-manager form of city government, voters elect a city council that makes city policies and laws. The council may elect a mayor who has a largely ceremonial function. It appoints a professionally trained city manager to oversee day-to-day operations.

What is the main similarity between the mayor's role in the mayor-council and in the council-manager forms of city government?

A. The mayor sets policy.
B. The mayor runs day-to-day operations.
C. The mayor is elected by voters.
D. The mayor has ceremonial duties.

Answers and explanations start on page 109.

LESSON

1

ECONOMICS

Basic Economics Concepts

Key Ideas

- Businesses utilize capital, labor, and materials to create goods and services to sell.
- Markets are systems that bring sellers' goods and services to buyers.
- The prices of goods and services are determined in part by supply and demand.

ON THE GED® TEST

Use the direction of lines on line graphs to spot trends and make predictions.

In economics, *capital* is a term for things that can produce income. Money can be capital; so can equipment, land, and buildings. Businesses invest capital in order to create **goods** and **services** to sell for profit. However, capital by itself cannot create value. **Labor**, the work of human beings, transforms capital and materials into goods and services that can be sold.

For example, a business that makes computers must make capital investments to build a factory and install equipment for **production**. Then the business must hire workers and managers to run the plant and use the equipment. The business must also buy the materials and parts to build the computers. The materials and parts are **producer goods**, while the finished computers, ready to sell in stores, are **consumer goods**. Not all businesses make or build objects. Some businesses create value by selling intangible services to their customers—such as an employment agency that offers the service of matching people with jobs.

Markets are established routines and networks for selling and buying goods and services. There are producers' markets for producer goods; there are **retail** and **wholesale** markets for consumer goods; there are markets for **raw materials** such as minerals; there are financial markets for selling stocks and bonds. Some markets are more highly organized than others, and all markets are regulated by law to some extent. But markets, by definition, are not completely under the control of any government or agency.

Goods and services are **distributed** through markets so that they can be **consumed** where they are wanted. Through the market system, sellers and buyers negotiate prices and contracts; they **compete** for the best terms possible in that market. For example, a computer manufacturer might enter the consumer electronics market, competing with other manufacturers to sell its goods at a fair price to retailers. The retailers negotiate contracts specifying how many computers they are willing to buy and distribute to consumers through their stores or catalogs.

How are prices determined in the market system? In economics, price is related to **supply** and **demand**. Sellers need to earn money on the goods they have produced. Buyers want to spend as little as possible. When the supply of something is large, buyers shop around looking for the best price, and sellers lower their prices in order to move their **inventory**. On the other hand, if a product is **scarce**, buyers are less able to shop around, and sellers can raise their prices. When Florida has a hard freeze and fruit growers lose their citrus crops, the price of oranges goes up. That is because there are fewer oranges to buy and fewer sellers to buy them from, so those sellers can charge more.

Supply and demand most clearly influence price in a **free market economy**. The U.S. economy operates primarily, but not completely, as a free market. For example, governmental **price supports** ensure that farmers can sell certain agricultural products at prices that allow them to earn a profit.

PRACTICE 1

Questions 1 through 4 are based on the information on page 74.

1. What is the main role of labor in an economy?

   A. to provide capital to start new businesses
   B. to convert capital and raw materials into products and services
   C. to purchase all the goods and services that are produced
   D. to purchase raw materials in retail and wholesale markets

2. Which of the following is an example of a producer good rather than a consumer good?

   A. a pencil
   B. a can opener
   C. a cell phone
   D. a plastic material

3. When there are very few houses for sale in an area, the real estate market is said to be a seller's market.

   Why is this name appropriate?

   A. When the supply of houses is low and demand is high, sellers can raise their prices.
   B. When the supply of houses is low and demand is high, sellers will accept an offer lower than list price.
   C. Sellers are always at an advantage in the real estate market.
   D. Competition among sellers raises prices.

4. Why might the U.S. government offer price supports to farmers but not to toy manufacturers?

   A. Toy sales vary widely, depending on the appeal of a particular toy.
   B. Toys are not critical to a nation's economic and political well-being.
   C. Toys are sold to adults for use by children.
   D. Toys are distributed through conventional wholesale and retail channels.

Questions 5 and 6 refer to the following graph.

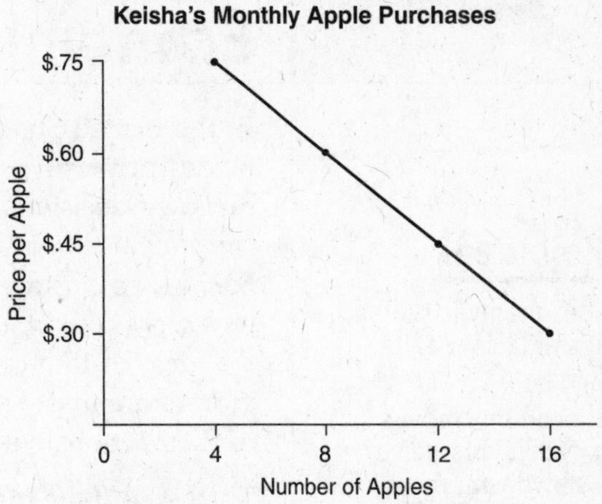

5. When apples cost 30 cents each, how many apples does Keisha buy each month?

   A. 4
   B. 8
   C. 12
   D. 16

6. Which of the following conclusions is supported by the data on the graph?

   A. As the supply of apples rises, Keisha buys fewer apples.
   B. As the supply of apples rises, the demand for apples falls.
   C. As the price of apples rises, Keisha buys fewer apples.
   D. As the price of apples falls, Keisha buys the same number of apples.

7. Place a ★ into the box corresponding to each service business in the list below.

a tool manufacturer	a bicycle repair shop
a paper mill	a microchip factory
a car wash	a beauty salon

Answers and explanations start on page 109.

LESSON

2

ECONOMICS

The U.S. Economic System

Key Ideas

- The U.S. economy is built on principles of laissez-faire capitalism.
- The U.S. economy moves through cyclical phases of growth, slowdown, recession, and recovery.
- Saving and investing contribute to the economy by making money available for businesses to grow.

ON THE GED® TEST

A short reading passage may accompany a graphic, such as a map. Some questions may require you to use information from both the passage and the graphic.

In the United States, the economic activity of individual people and businesses primarily determines our economic health and growth. We make our own decisions about how to save and spend most of our income. We can accept employment as we choose, become **entrepreneurs** and build businesses of our own, and seek education and training to whatever level best serves our goals. These freedoms are based on **laissez-faire capitalism**, the ideas of 18th-century economist Adam Smith, who believed that if individuals are free to act in their own best interests economically, the sum total of their actions will be in the best interests of the society as a whole.

Throughout the history of the United States, **free enterprise** and **competition** have played important roles in the development of our economy. Businesses have incentives to grow larger—either by expanding their **capacity** or by integrating a broader set of functions into their **operations**—in order to make more **profit**. However, businesses are expected to compete with each other on the merits of their products and operations. Businesses are not allowed to form **monopolies**—single companies that control whole industries—and they also are not allowed to form **oligopolies**—tight-knit groups of companies that control whole industries.

Because the U.S. economy is not under government control, no one can predict or control exactly how the economy will behave. Our economy tends to move through a **business cycle** with identifiable phases, but the length and strength of a cycle and its phases vary greatly. The first phase of a cycle is the growth phase, in which businesses invest and expand optimistically. At some point, growth is slowed or stopped by one or more factors—limited resources, limited production capacity, tight employment, or market **saturation**—and the economy enters a slowdown phase. As businesses lay off workers, stop investing their capital, and cut back production, the economy enters a **recession** or **depression** phase. Unemployment rises, consumer spending slows down, and businesses act very conservatively, holding down wages and prices, avoiding risks, and managing cash flow tightly. Eventually, the economy moves into a recovery phase, perhaps initiated by a government action. Recovery may be slow or uneven across economic sectors, but eventually the economy moves into a new growth phase. **Inflation**, in which the combined price of goods and services grows faster than the purchasing power of the currency, is only partly related to these business cycle phases.

Banking and investment services, like most U.S. industries, are conducted on principles of free enterprise. A major role of **banks** and **savings and loan associations** is to create pools of savings in order to make money available as credit to businesses and consumers. **Stock exchanges** have a similar purpose; they allow investors to purchase shares of stock, which represent part ownership of a business. Both saving and investing make funds available for businesses to use to grow. When people invest in stock, they take risks because the value of the stock depends on the success of the business. However, the potential **return** is generally much higher than the **interest rate** on a savings account.

PRACTICE 2

Questions 1 through 4 are based on the information on page 76.

1. Why are monopolies not permitted in the United States?

   A. Monopolies are too efficient.
   B. Monopolies are part of laissez-faire capitalism.
   C. Monopolies result from free enterprise.
   D. Monopolies shut out competition.

2. According to the passage, Select... is one characteristic of a recession.

   - increased job growth
   - large investments of capital
   - increased consumer spending
   - rising unemployment

3. Private ownership of property (land or buildings) is a key characteristic of the free enterprise system. Owning property gives people a strong incentive to take care of it and use it productively.

   What is the basis for this incentive?

   A. Property owners have a stake in the future value of the property.
   B. Property owners work harder than tenants do.
   C. Property owners are given tax incentives by the federal government.
   D. Property owners must pay real estate taxes to local government.

4. Which of the following investments carries the most risk?

   A. opening a savings account at a local bank
   B. buying a certificate of deposit at a savings and loan institution
   C. buying stock in a new company, such as an Internet startup
   D. buying stock in an established company, such as Microsoft

Question 5 refers to the following paragraph and graph.

At different times during the business cycle, the gross domestic product—the total value of goods and services produced in a year—rises and falls.

The Business Cycle

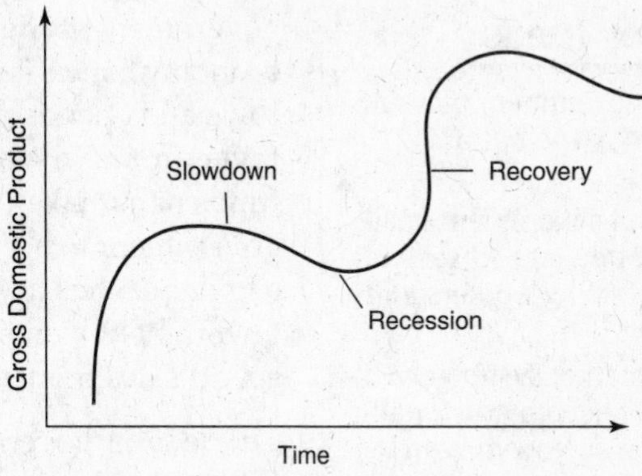

5. Which of the following conclusions is supported by the paragraph and the graph?

   A. High points in the business cycle are generally followed by recoveries.
   B. Low points in the business cycle are generally followed by slowdowns.
   C. During recessions, the rate of unemployment drops.
   D. Despite ups and downs, the gross domestic product generally increases over time.

6. Based on the passage on page 76, what do saving and investing in stocks have in common?

   A. They provide capital for businesses to grow.
   B. They provide a sure rate of return.
   C. They pay a fixed rate of interest.
   D. They are without risk.

Answers and explanations start on page 110.

LESSON

3

ECONOMICS

The Economy and the U.S. Government

Key Ideas

- The U.S. government plays a major part in the nation's economy.
- The federal government facilitates the free market system while protecting workers and consumers.
- The free market system cannot effectively provide for all our needs, so government fills some gaps.

ON THE GED® TEST

Charts, such as the one on page 79, are used to summarize information. You may be asked to find specific information from the chart or to apply information from the chart to a specific situation.

Although the United States has primarily a free market economy, the U.S. government does have important economic functions. Both the executive and the legislative branches of government are involved in setting the U.S. government **budget**. The government has considerable impact on our economy, since it determines our taxes, employs many people, and borrows and spends much money. The federal budget may have a **surplus** of **revenue**, in which case elected leaders may either spend the additional funds or cut taxes; or the budget may have a revenue **deficit**, requiring the government to borrow money to cover its expenses. Government spending sometimes has a very direct impact on the economy. For example, if the government wants to boost the national economy out of a recession, it may spend extra money on projects that create new jobs.

The federal government is also responsible for maintaining good conditions for our free market system. The government must have laws and courts in place to maintain property rights. It must enforce fair legal standards for operating a business. The federal government provides a stable **currency** and operates the U.S. Mint, which makes coins and prints paper money. Our central banking system, the **Federal Reserve System**, manages the total amount of money available for lending and borrowing in the private banking system and partially controls interest rates. The **Federal Deposit Insurance Corporation** (FDIC) insures the money in individual bank accounts in case of bank fraud or failure.

One of the fundamental purposes of the federal government is to promote the general welfare of the nation. Therefore, the government takes over many functions that the free market system does not provide. For example, the free market does not distribute wealth according to what people need to live on, so the government collects taxes to redistribute some money to people who don't earn enough. The government also provides **infrastructure**, such as interstate highways, that indirectly supports economic activity.

Another role for government in the economy is protecting workers from health dangers and exploitation. The **Occupational Safety and Health Administration** (OSHA) is a special federal agency charged to protect workers on the job, particularly in hazardous industries. Many federal and state laws also protect the interests of workers. For example, all states regulate the hours and types of work that children may perform. A number of agencies are involved in enforcing safe and fair working conditions; they visit businesses, investigate reports of problems, identify violations, and initiate prosecution in some cases.

Another group of agencies protects consumers from fraudulent business practices and unsafe products. The **Food and Drug Administration** (FDA) is responsible for making sure that food products are safe, drugs are effective, and cosmetics and drugs are labeled properly. The **Federal Trade Commission** (FTC) ensures that product claims in advertising and on package labels are true and complete.

PRACTICE 3

<u>Questions 1 through 3</u> are based on the passage on page 78.

1. When the U.S. government [Select...], it is an indication that the government has a budget surplus.

- issues bonds through the U.S. Treasury
- attempts to boost the economy by cutting the discount rate
- registers expenditures that exceed its revenues
- registers revenues that exceed its expenditures

2. Which of the following legislative actions would lead to a direct increase in consumer spending?

A. raising Social Security contributions
B. decreasing spending on federal work projects
C. cutting the federal income tax
D. ratifying an international trade agreement

3. Which of the following is an example of infrastructure that supports economic activity?

A. consumer demand
B. the annual federal budget
C. local sales taxes
D. the air traffic control system

4. The federal government has two main ways to manipulate the economy. The first is fiscal policy, in which the government increases or decreases taxes and spending to influence the economy. The second is monetary policy, in which the government increases or decreases the supply of money in order to stimulate or slow the economy.

What is the main similarity between fiscal and monetary policy?

A. Both involve raising taxes.
B. Both involve lowering taxes.
C. Both are budgetary tools of state governments.
D. Both affect the amount of money circulating in the economy.

<u>Questions 5 and 6</u> refer to the following paragraph and chart.

Monetary policy affects the amount of money in circulation. When there is rapid economic growth and a risk of inflation, the Federal Reserve System (the "Fed") slows it down by tightening the money supply. This makes it more difficult for people and businesses to borrow and spend money. When the economy is sluggish, the Fed increases the money supply to stimulate borrowing and spending.

The Fed's Monetary Policy Options

To Take Money out of Circulation	To Put Money into Circulation
Sell government securities (bonds and Treasury bills) to investors ○	Buy back government securities from bond holders ○
Raise the discount rate member banks are charged to borrow from the Fed ○	Lower the discount rate member banks are charged to borrow from the Fed ○
Raise the reserve requirement, the amount banks must keep on hand to cover deposits ○	Lower the reserve requirement ○

5. Place a dot in the circle in each box that indicates a step the government might take in order to stimulate the economy.

6. Since the Fed's monetary policy options have such specific effects, why does the Fed sometimes fail to head off recession or stimulate recovery?

A. The Fed's board meets only four times a year.
B. The people on the Fed's board lack experience.
C. Our complex economy takes time to respond.
D. Our economy can be controlled only by international economic forces.

Answers and explanations start on page 110.

LESSON

4

ECONOMICS

Labor and Consumer Issues

Key Ideas

- Workers earn wages and some benefits and protections in exchange for their labor.
- The U.S. economy is now in a time of rapid change, and workers must prepare themselves to adapt.
- Consumers must protect themselves by being aware of risks and by spending their money wisely.

ON THE GED® TEST

Some of the economics questions on the test will be based on everyday topics faced by workers and consumers.

As workers, we earn **wages** and other **benefits** in exchange for our labor. People who are paid hourly wages are paid only for the number of hours they work. Their earnings may fluctuate depending on how much their labor is needed. People who earn salaries typically receive the same constant pay all the time, although the hours they work may fluctuate. Some people are paid for "piecework"—that is, for each piece of work they complete. Many workers receive benefits in addition to their wages, such as health insurance, vacation pay, and special savings plans. A worker's total **compensation** for a job is the combined value of wages and benefits.

Workers and their employers must pay taxes and buy insurance to cover work-related problems, including injury, disability, and **unemployment**. Workers who lose their jobs because they are fired or laid off usually can receive unemployment benefits for a time or until they find new jobs. Sometimes workers lose their jobs because of major economic changes. For example, rapid changes in the steel industry drove out much of the steel manufacturing in the United States. Plants closed, and workers who thought they would spend their lives making good wages in steel mills suddenly found their skills worthless. In most cases, these workers had to learn new skills. This kind of rapid change is common in our modern times. Because so many markets are international, and because transportation, communication, and shipping are possible even over very long distances, businesses can change strategies very quickly and change their workforce as a result. Workers need to anticipate changes in their industries and continually seek new training in order to be prepared for change.

Most workers have direct individual agreements with their employers. However, **labor unions** are common in certain industries and professions. Through **collective bargaining**, unions negotiate contracts for wages and working conditions on behalf of all union members. If these negotiations fail, the union can call a **strike**, in which workers refuse to work. When labor-management negotiations break down, federal **mediators** may be asked to intervene. The National Labor Relations Board helps companies and unions resolve disputes.

We all participate in the U.S. economy as **consumers**. The free market system offers U.S. consumers an amazing array of choices for the goods and services we want. As retailers and marketers woo our business relentlessly, we should all remember the maxim, "Let the buyer beware." Although government agencies must protect consumers, consumers must also protect themselves. For example, federal laws require that potentially hazardous products have special labeling and instructions. But these will not protect us as consumers unless we read them. Parents are required by law to strap their small children into automobile safety seats. But if the seats are incorrectly installed, the children are still at risk. Retailers who offer credit payment plans are required to disclose the interest rate, payment amount, and number of payments, but it's up to consumers to work out the total expense and compare the total with the purchase price of the item.

PRACTICE 4

Questions 1 through 4 are based on the information on page 80.

1. What is a worker's total compensation?

A. wages only
B. benefits only
C. wages and benefits
D. the amount received in unemployment benefits

2. Reread the second paragraph on page 80. Which of the following statements is a conclusion rather than a supporting detail related to the paragraph?

A. Workers must learn skills throughout their lives to be prepared for changes in their industries.
B. Most steel manufacturing moved out of the United States.
C. Many steelworkers had to retrain themselves and learn new skills.
D. Workers sometimes lose their jobs because of major economic restructuring.

3. A Select... is acting as a consumer.

- person working in a shopping mall
- professor teaching economics at a community college
- woman buying a computer
- teen starting a babysitting cooperative

4. Which of the following proverbs or slogans expresses the principle that underlies labor unions?

A. All for one and one for all.
B. Strike while the iron is hot.
C. Work expands to fill the time available.
D. Many hands make light work.

Questions 5 and 6 refer to the following graph.

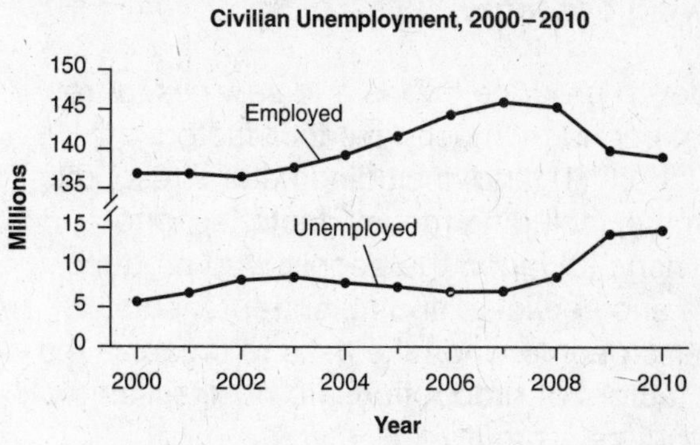

5. When was civilian unemployment at its lowest during the decade shown on the graph?

A. in 2000
B. in 2002
C. in 2006
D. in 2008

6. Which of the following statements is supported by the data in the graph?

A. People who have stopped looking for work are not counted among the unemployed.
B. As the number of employed civilians rose steadily from 2003 to 2006, the number of unemployed slowly declined.
C. The rate of civilian unemployment during the 2000s exceeded the rate of civilian employment.
D. Unemployed civilians made up about 25 percent of the total civilian workforce from 2000 to 2010.

Answers and explanations start on page 110.

ECONOMICS PRACTICE QUESTIONS

Questions 1 through 3 refer to the following passage.

In order to produce goods and services, a free market economy must have four factors of production: (1) land, including natural resources; (2) capital, including money, factories, and machinery; (3) labor, the people who produce goods and services; and (4) entrepreneurs, business people who take risks to organize the other factors of production into businesses that will produce a profit.

1. Which of the following best defines the factors of production?

   A. the political organizations that support an economy
   B. the various types of resources needed for an economy to produce goods and services
   C. the way in which the work flow is organized in a factory or office
   D. all the transactions involved in producing goods and services

2. In a communist economy, a central government makes all of the economic decisions.

   Which factor of production is not part of a communist economy?

   A. land
   B. natural resources
   C. labor
   D. entrepreneurs

3. Which of the following is an example of capital?

   A. an office building
   B. a deposit of iron ore
   C. a skilled engineer
   D. the founder of a publishing business

4. Many fiscal conservatives believe that the U.S. budget should be balanced, with spending equal to income. They think it is wrong for the government to influence the economy by manipulating taxes or by borrowing. Instead, they feel that a balanced budget reassures business leaders that the economy is solid.

   Which of the following statements is a fact?

   A. In a balanced budget, revenues equal expenditures.
   B. The government should not use the budget to tinker with the economy.
   C. The government should not borrow money to balance the budget.
   D. A balanced government budget is the best indicator that the economy is healthy.

Question 5 refers to the following graph.

U.S. Personal Income Sources, February 2013 (Billions of Dollars)

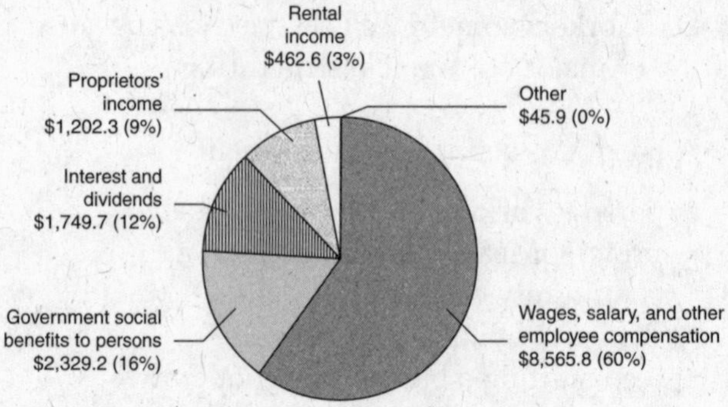

5. Which of the following statements is supported by the data on the graph?

   A. More than half of all personal income was earned through work in February 2013.
   B. Government social benefits accounted for more than one-quarter of personal income in February 2013.
   C. Interest and dividends accounted for one-third of personal income in February 2013.
   D. Per capita income was roughly $8,565 in February 2013.

Questions 6 and 7 refer to the following cartoon.

Reprinted with permission of the *Green Bay Press-Gazette,* Green Bay, Wisconsin.

6. Who does the man in the plaid shorts represent?

   A. a retiree
   B. an American taxpayer
   C. a corporate executive
   D. an investor

7. Why is the man in the plaid shorts calm about his ride on the roller coaster?

   A. He enjoys riding on roller coasters.
   B. He has made money buying bonds.
   C. He is accustomed to stock market ups and downs.
   D. All of his retirement savings are in stocks.

8. Employers withhold, or take out, federal income tax from their employees' paychecks. However, some people need to make estimated tax payments. According to the Internal Revenue Service, "Estimated tax is the method used to pay tax on income that is not subject to withholding (for example, earnings from self-employment, interest, dividends, rents, alimony, etc."

   A [Select...] is most likely to need to make estimated tax payments.

   - factory worker
   - student working part-time at the university
   - person who runs a home day-care center
   - gas station attendant

9. In a free market economy, people make their own decisions about working, buying goods and property, and starting businesses. Which of the following is most likely to be highly valued in nations with free market economies?

   A. cooperation
   B. individualism
   C. job security
   D. economic equality

Questions 10 and 11 refer to the following graph.

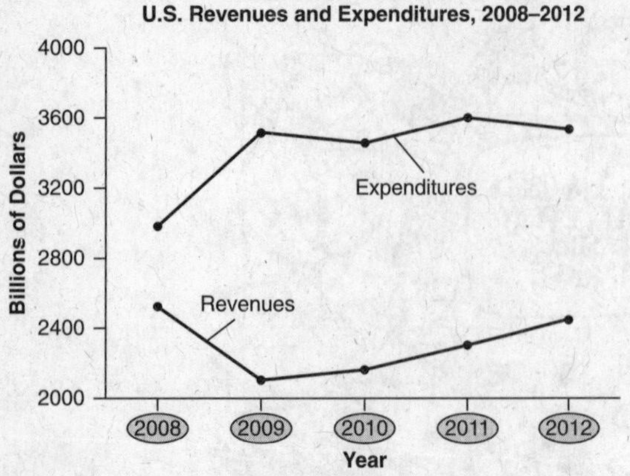

10. At the bottom of the chart, select the year between 2008 and 2012 in which the United States ran its largest budget deficit.

11. If a family wanted to make a graph of its economic situation similar to this graph of U.S. revenues and expenditures, what set of documents for the years 2008 to 2012 would be most useful?

    A. records showing all family members' sources of income
    B. income tax returns and expense records
    C. credit card bills and rent or mortgage statements
    D. records showing the value of the family's possessions

12. The Interstate Highway System, begun in 1956, consists of more than 45,000 miles of four- to eight-lane highways connecting most large U.S. cities. The federal government pays for almost 90 percent of the building and maintenance of interstate highways out of receipts from excise taxes on gasoline, tires, truck parts, and other related products.

    Which of the following best summarizes this information?

    A. In 1956, the federal government established the Interstate Highway System.
    B. The Interstate Highway System consists of thousands of miles of large highways.
    C. The federal government collects excise taxes on transportation-related items.
    D. The national network of interstate highways is paid for mostly by federal excise taxes.

13. In recent years, the United States has lowered protective tariffs (charges on goods imported from other countries), arguing that lower tariffs encourage free trade and benefit consumers by decreasing the cost of imported goods.

    From the perspective of a U.S. factory worker, what is the flaw in this argument?

    A. When cheaper imported goods force out U.S.-made goods, U.S. factory workers often lose their jobs.
    B. Free trade leads to cheaper imported goods because the cost of labor is less in many other nations.
    C. Factory workers cannot afford to buy imported consumer goods even if they are cheaper than U.S.-made goods.
    D. Lower protective tariffs actually raise the prices of all goods whether they are made in the United States or in foreign countries.

Question 14 refers to the following chart.

U.S. Consumer Protection

Agency	Function
Food and Drug Administration	Protects public from poorly processed and improperly labeled foods and drugs
Federal Trade Commission	Protects consumers from misleading and/or fraudulent advertising
Consumer Product Safety Commission	Protects consumers from risk of injury or death from hazardous products
Securities and Exchange Commission	Protects investors from being misled about stocks and bonds
National Highway Traffic Safety Administration	Protects consumers by testing vehicle safety and monitoringn ationwide speed limits

14. In the table above, place a dot or dots in the circle(s) next to the agency or agencies that could be involved in a dispute over a commercial that implied something about a product that was not true.

15. Equilibrium occurs when the supply of a product or service equals the demand for it. A product tends to be priced at the equilibrium point. When the price is greater than the equilibrium point, demand decreases and there is an oversupply of the product on the market.

Select... is the result of the price falling below the equilibrium point.

- A shortage of the product
- A surplus of the product
- The equilibrium point decreasing
- The equilibrium point increasing

16. One approach to the study of economics is called macroeconomics. Macroeconomics deals with economies as a whole. For instance, a macroeconomist might study the causes of inflation or the factors that determine why some national economies grow quickly and others do not.

Which of the following is most likely to be studied by a macroeconomist?

A. how a firm prices its products or services
B. what causes high rates of unemployment
C. what determines consumer demand for a product
D. how a factory makes production decisions

Question 17 refers to the following graph.

Supply Graph

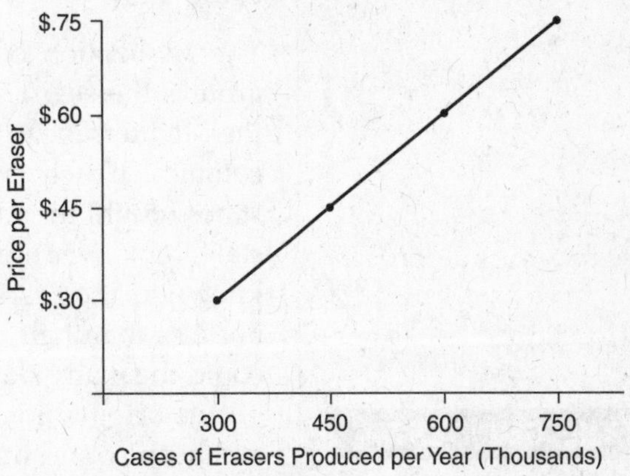

17. Which of the following conclusions is supported by the data on the graph?

A. As the price per eraser decreases, manufacturers supply more erasers.
B. As the price per eraser increases, manufacturers supply fewer erasers.
C. As the price per eraser increases, manufacturers supply more erasers.
D. As the supply of erasers increases, the demand for erasers decreases.

Answers and explanations start on page 111.

LESSON

1

GEOGRAPHY AND THE WORLD

Early Civilizations

Key Ideas

- Ancient civilizations developed where people could settle in one place with a secure food supply.
- The ancient republics of Greece and Rome were incubators for important ideas in modern government.
- Ancient civilizations also left legacies in art, architecture, science, and astronomy.

ON THE GED® TEST

The world history questions require that you have familiarity with major topics in world history. You do not need to memorize names or dates.

One of the earliest known **civilizations** is ancient Egypt. By 5000 B.C.E., people who lived along the **Nile River** had begun to take advantage of the fertile soil left behind by floods. The river and irrigation systems allowed the Egyptians to grow enough food to support a large population. Around 3000 B.C.E., Egyptian civilization grew under the rule of Egypt's kings, or **pharaohs**. Believing their pharaohs to be part god, Egyptians built the famous **pyramids** to house these rulers in their next lives. Many who built the pyramids and did the hard work to build this civilization were slaves.

Around the same time, in the **Fertile Crescent**—an area northeast of Egypt—**Sumerian** city-states were also developing irrigation and flood control methods. They also created a system of writing. In about 1800 B.C.E., the Sumerians were conquered by the Babylonians. One of the Babylonian kings, Hammurabi, is remembered for codifying laws. The **Code of Hammurabi** was written on a huge stone in a public place so all Babylonians could know and follow the law.

The civilization of **ancient Greece** did not develop around a river, but around the sea. The Greeks built an **empire**: they established colonies on the Mediterranean Sea and the Black Sea; then they imported food from the colonies. However, Greece itself was not politically unified. As its city-states fought for control of each other's land, Sparta, a particularly warlike state, took over a number of other city-states. Athens, another city-state, is known as the first political **democracy**. All Athenian citizens could vote—but less than half of Athenians were citizens. Women could not vote, nor could the many slaves. The Greek Empire lasted only a few hundred years, but its original ideas, such as democracy, and its stunning arts, including architecture and literature, remain influential even now.

Eventually, the Greek Empire fell to **Roman** conquerors. Rome began as a city on the Italian Peninsula, governed by its wealthy citizens through an elected Senate. Roman citizens were governed by a system of laws that is still influential in the United States. For example, the Romans believed that a person accused of a crime was innocent until proven guilty. The power of Rome grew, and the Romans took over many lands surrounding the Mediterranean Sea, pushing north as far as England and east into Asia by about 100 C.E. Roman leaders built systems and infrastructure to make their empire strong: schools, roads and bridges, hospitals, a tax system, and an army. The ancient Roman Empire lasted until 476 C.E.

Ancient Egypt, Greece, and Rome were only a few of the early civilizations in which people made important scientific discoveries and developed enduring ideas. In Central America, the **Maya**, whose culture was strongest from 300 to 900 C.E., invented a pictographic writing system in which they recorded remarkable discoveries in mathematics and astronomy. The **Inca Empire** in South America had a sophisticated system of government. The Incas built amazing roads and bridges in their rugged mountain lands. In Mexico, the **Aztecs** invented a written language and a calendar system and expanded their farmlands by dredging mud from lakes.

PRACTICE 1

Questions 1 through 4 are based on the information on page 86.

1. Which of the following Central American civilizations is particularly noted for achievements in both mathematics and astronomy?

   A. the Sumerians
   B. the Maya
   C. the Aztecs
   D. the Incas

2. According to the information on page 86, two ancient civilizations were particularly influential on the form of government adopted by the United States of America. Select the two civilizations that had the greatest impact on America's systems of law and government and write them into the blanks below.

Sumer

Ancient Egypt

Ancient Greece

Incas

Ancient Rome

3. What did the ancient civilizations of Egypt and the Fertile Crescent have in common?

   A. Both developed flood control and irrigation technologies to boost food production.
   B. Both had a public code of law engraved on a huge stone.
   C. Both were centered on the shores of the Mediterranean Sea.
   D. Both developed systems of political democracy in which citizens could vote.

4. Once a society developed agriculture and domesticated animals, food surpluses and rising populations made possible which of the following developments?

   A. a nomadic lifestyle
   B. towns
   C. stone tools
   D. stone carvings

Questions 5 and 6 refer to the following map.

Ancient China

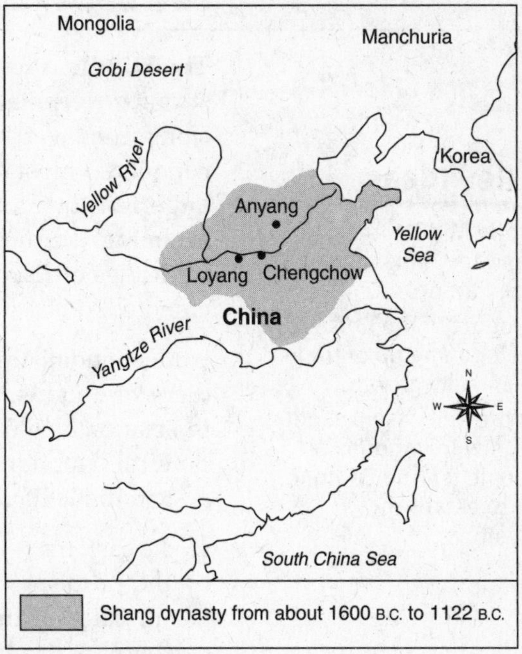

5. In the Yellow River valley, floods deposit a fertile yellow soil called loess that is easily worked by farmers.

   Which of the following civilizations arose under geographic conditions similar to those in ancient China?

   A. the Aztecs
   B. ancient Greece
   C. ancient Rome
   D. ancient Egypt

6. Which of the following statements is supported by the information in the map?

   A. The Yellow River is the only major river in China.
   B. The Shang dynasty, or ruling family, controlled China for almost a thousand years.
   C. The Yellow River was probably the main trade route between Loyang and Chengchow.
   D. The Shang civilization traded more with Korea than with Manchuria.

Answers and explanations start on page 112.

LESSON

2

GEOGRAPHY AND THE WORLD

Feudalism to Nation States

Key Ideas

- During the Middle Ages, the feudal system helped to stabilize Europe.
- A by-product of the Crusades was the opening up of trade routes and city growth.
- During the Renaissance, education grew in importance, and people left the Catholic Church to establish Protestantism.

GED® TEST TIP

To summarize a graph such as the one on page 89, ask yourself: What is the topic of the graph? What is the main point of the data? How could I say this in a sentence or two?

The **Middle Ages** in Europe lasted from about A.D. 500 to 1500. As the once strong government of Rome weakened, Europe became vulnerable to invasions from warring groups or tribes. A tribal ruler named **Charlemagne** conquered most of Europe by 800. Charlemagne was able to stabilize this large territory for a time. He established laws, spread Christianity, and encouraged education and commerce. When Charlemagne died in 814, the territories of Europe became unstable again, and the system of **feudalism** emerged.

Under feudalism, kings granted control of land to nobles. A noble's soldiers, or knights, protected the noble's estate, or manor. **Peasants** farmed at the manor. Nobles paid taxes to kings; peasants paid taxes to nobles. As the political boundaries among the kings' lands became established, the feudal system made life in Europe more peaceful over several hundred years.

To the east, the religion of **Islam** was founded during the early Middle Ages by the prophet Muhammad, who was born in A.D. 570. The followers of Islam, called **Muslims**, conquered large territories in the Middle East, northern Africa, Spain, Persia, and India. They established a series of empires. Many people in these conquered lands converted to Islam while contributing their own knowledge and arts to the Muslim culture. Although the Islamic Empire itself did not last, Islam and its culture have remained strong.

During the late Middle Ages, Christians and Muslim Turks fought over the holy city of Jerusalem in a series of wars called the **Crusades**. Christians gained control of Jerusalem from the Turks, but they ruled the city for less than 90 years. A more lasting effect of the Crusades was to open up trade between Europe and the Middle East and even China. As trade, money, and merchants grew in importance in Europe, feudalism declined. People left the manors and went to live and work in cities, where opportunities were greater. Cities gained political, economic, and cultural importance.

During the Middle Ages, European nations began to form as **monarchs** combined territories of small rulers and took advantage of the wealth of cities. England's monarchy was established by 1100. France won the Hundred Years' War against England and emerged as a strong nation under its monarch. Spain united through the marriage of two rulers, Ferdinand and Isabella, who had each controlled smaller states.

The **Renaissance**, which spread from Italy across Europe between 1300 and 1600, brought growth in education, science, and the arts. The Renaissance also led to changes in the Catholic Church. During the **Reformation** in the 1500s, reformers criticized the church for abusing its power. Those who believed that people should read the Bible themselves rather than follow the pope split from the Catholic Church and formed the **Protestant** religion. King Henry VIII of England broke from the Catholic Church and formed the Church of England so he would not have to obey the pope.

PRACTICE 2

1. According to the passage on page 88, what was the role of the knights in feudal Europe?
   - A. to collect taxes for the king
   - B. to take care of livestock
   - C. to protect their noble's land from attack
   - D. to administer justice

<u>Question 2</u> is based on the text on page 88 and the following map.

2. Given the information on page 88, select the modern European nation in which you are most likely to find evidence of Muslim arts and culture.

---

3. During the late Middle Ages, the growth of trade spurred a migration of peasants from the manors to the towns. To which of the following events is this most similar?
   - A. the migration of Puritans to the New World to escape religious persecution in the 1600s
   - B. the migration of people from farms to industrial cities in the 1800s
   - C. the migration of political refugees to the United States in the 1900s
   - D. the migration of individuals with health problems from cold, damp regions to warm, dry regions

4. At the time of the Reformation, which of the following was one of the main differences between Roman Catholics and Protestants?
   - A. Roman Catholics accepted the authority of the pope and Protestants did not.
   - B. Roman Catholics lived on the manors and Protestants lived in the towns.
   - C. Roman Catholics supported the monarchies in their nations and Protestants did not.
   - D. Roman Catholics led the Church of England under Henry VIII and Protestants did not.

5. In England in the 1100s, any free man could bring a case before a royal court headed by a circuit judge, who formed juries of local people. The decisions of these courts were recorded and formed the basis for common law, which was applied to everyone in the kingdom. In contrast, justice in the manor courts, which were run by the nobles, could be fickle. There were few written laws, and the verdicts could be overturned by the lord.

   People usually preferred to be tried in royal courts rather than manor courts because the royal courts valued which of the following?
   - A. accepted legal principles
   - B. harsh punishment
   - C. power for the local lord
   - D. fines rather than imprisonment

<u>Question 6</u> refers to the following graph.

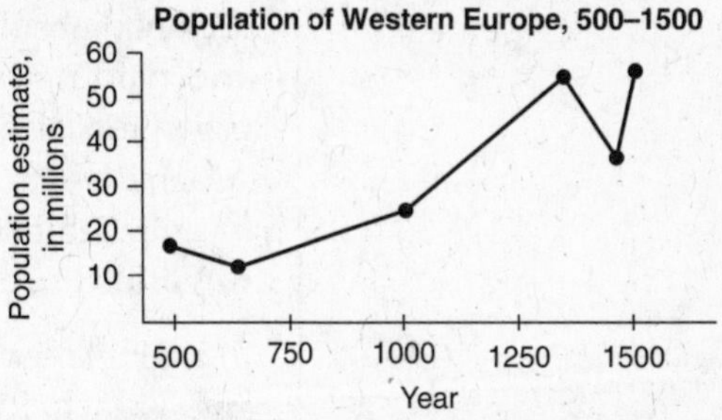

Source: Carlo M. Cippola, ed. *The Fontana Economic History of Europe: The Middle Ages* and Carlo M. Cippola *Before the Industrial Revolution: European Society and Economy, 1000–1700.*

6. Which of the following best summarizes the information shown on the graph?
   - A. The population of Western Europe showed the most growth between the years 750 and 1000.
   - B. There were fewer than 50 million people living in Western Europe at any given time.
   - C. The population of Western Europe showed almost constant growth with only brief periods of decline.
   - D. The population of Western Europe fell to its lowest around the year 1450.

Answers and explanations begin on page 112.

LESSON

3

GEOGRAPHY AND THE WORLD

The Age of Revolutions

Key Ideas

- In the American and French Revolutions, people fought against unjust governments.
- Revolution spread to Latin America, ending many colonial governments there.
- The Industrial Revolution caused sweeping changes in work, living conditions, and social mobility.

ON THE GED® TEST

As part of the GED® Social Studies Test, *you may be provided with basic historic information and asked to make comparisons—such as the similarities and differences between two revolutions.*

Political revolutions often happen when people are unhappy about the conditions resulting from their system of government. Political revolutions may also be fueled by new ideas about who is best suited to govern. In the Age of Revolutions, many people wanted more political power.

One important cause of the **American Revolution** was British taxation. Although British citizens in England were represented in government through **Parliament**, the American colonists did not have representatives in that body. The colonists believed that they should not have to pay the special taxes levied on them, since they had had no voice in determining the tax laws. Although the colonists began by arguing for representation in the British government, by 1776 they had declared themselves a sovereign nation, the United States of America.

Revolutionaries in France were inspired by democratic ideas expressed in the American colonies' **Declaration of Independence** and the **U.S. Constitution**. Unlike England, France had no Parliament; the French monarch had absolute power. The nobility and the Church had many privileges and paid no taxes, while ordinary citizens paid heavy taxes and had few rights or freedoms. In 1789, the French people organized a National Assembly—a law-making body to represent them. When King Louis XVI fought against the establishment of the National Assembly, the **French Revolution** began. Its turmoil lasted for ten years.

In Latin America, many colonized people, inspired in part by the American and French Revolutions, began to shake off European rule. In Haiti, an island in the Caribbean Sea, slaves led by Toussaint L'Ouverture overturned French rule and established an independent nation in 1804. Mexican revolutionaries finally won their independence from Spain in 1821. In South America, revolutions rocked the continent until 1824, by which time most countries had gained their independence.

Important revolutions are not always political. The **Industrial Revolution** started in the late 1700s in the textile industry, when new equipment was invented for spinning thread and weaving cloth. Instead of workers using their own tools at home, factories could house many workers using machines to produce much greater quantities. This factory model for large-scale production spread along with **steam engines** and electricity. Workers moved into factory towns and cities to work for wages. The Industrial Revolution brought a mixture of benefits and problems—useful inventions, increasing wealth, and new **social mobility** were offset by dangerous factory jobs, **child labor**, crowded cities, and **pollution**.

The Industrial Revolution also brought sweeping social changes. The economic mainstay of the European **aristocracy** had been farmland. After the Industrial Revolution, manufacturing and trade became more important economically than agriculture. Thus, the merchant classes became more powerful. New ideas about political equality affected how people thought about social equality as well.

PRACTICE 3

1. According to the passage on page 90, which of the following had a great influence on the French Revolution?

   A. the Industrial Revolution
   B. the Mexican Revolution
   C. the U.S. Declaration of Independence
   D. the British monarchy

Question 2 refers to the following paragraph and graph.

Before the French Revolution, the French were divided into three groups by law, each with different privileges. In the First Estate were the higher clergy, who were nobles, and the parish priests, who were commoners. The Second Estate consisted of nobles who were not members of the clergy. The Third Estate was made up of commoners, including the middle class and peasants.

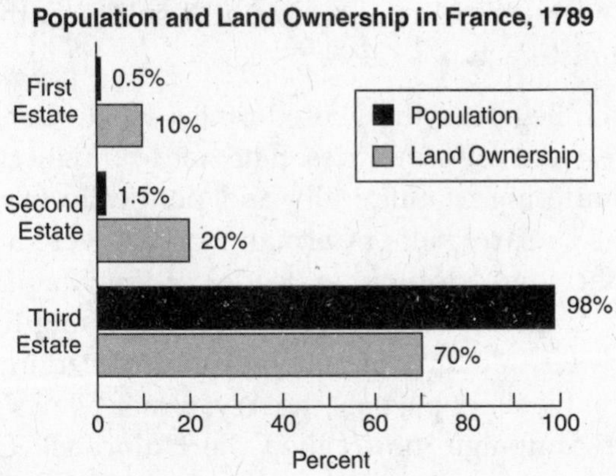

2. Which of the following statements is supported by the paragraph and the graph?

   A. All members of the nobility belonged to the First Estate.
   B. The members of the First Estate owned more property than members of the Second Estate.
   C. The distribution of wealth in prerevolutionary France favored the Third Estate.
   D. Members of the Third Estate owned the least amount of land per person.

3. According to the information on page 90, the main difference between the English and French governments before 1789 is that England (1) Select... , while France (2) Select... .

Select (1)	Select (2)
was a monarchy	was not a direct democracy
had a parliament	did not have a parliament
was a democratic republic	was not a monarchy

4. On what was the economic power of the aristocracy based in 18th-century Europe?

   A. moral superiority
   B. attaining a high level of education
   C. possessing large landholdings
   D. belonging to the Church bureaucracy

5. Which of the following does the writer of the text on page 90 take for granted that you know, but does not state outright?

   A. The American colonists demanded representation in the British government before they declared independence.
   B. A sovereign nation is independent, having the power to govern itself.
   C. Many colonies were influenced by the American and French revolutions to seek independence.
   D. As manufacturing and trade became more important, the merchant classes gained power.

6. The Information Revolution of the late 20th century, spurred by the availability of personal computers and the Internet, is most similar to which of the following revolutions?

   A. the American Revolution
   B. the French Revolution
   C. the Mexican Revolution
   D. the Industrial Revolution

Answers and explanations start on page 112.

LESSON

4

GEOGRAPHY AND THE WORLD

Exploration, Colonialism, and Wars

Key Ideas

- Two devastating world wars occurred during the first half of the 20th century.
- The United States and Soviet Union emerged as superpowers after World War II.
- The superpowers faced off during the Cold War, which ended with the breakup of the Soviet Union in 1991.

GED® TEST TIP

You may be familiar with some of the world events covered on the GED® Test. However, answer questions based on the information provided on the test, even if it differs from what you remember.

World War I resulted from **nationalism** and **imperialism**—the desire of nations to extend their empires. This desire for expansion led to military buildup. When war broke out in 1914 between Serbia and Austria-Hungary over the assassination of an Austrian leader visiting Serbia, a chain reaction started as other countries also declared war. Germany and Austria-Hungary were the mainstays of the **Central Powers**, who fought against the **Allies**—England, France, Russia, Serbia, and eventually the United States. When the Central Powers finally lost the war, millions of people had been killed. The war had devastated Europe, leaving many people jobless and homeless. In the 1918 **Treaty of Versailles**, Germany was blamed for the war and forced to pay **reparations** to the Allies.

Revolution in Russia began during World War I. The Russian **Czar** refused to pull out of the war, even though most Russians did not support involvement. In 1917, the Czar and his family were assassinated, and the **Russian Revolution** ended with Bolshevik leader Vladimir Lenin in power. The Bolsheviks founded the Soviet Union as a **communist** nation with one political party—the Communist Party.

The Great Depression, which began in the United States when the stock market crashed in 1929, affected many countries. One hard-hit nation was Germany, which was still suffering economically and politically from its defeat in World War I. By 1933, nearly half of German workers were unemployed, and people were starving. Adolf Hitler, leader of the Nazi Party, rose to power by appealing to German nationalism and promising to put people back to work. Hitler's terrible form of nationalism involved imprisoning and killing people who were not part of "the Aryan race." Jews were the main targets of Hitler's campaign, now called the **Holocaust**. Hitler wanted to take over all Europe, and because other powerful nations wanted to avoid war, they let him annex Austria, then Czechoslovakia. But when Hitler invaded Poland in 1939, England and France declared war on Germany, and **World War II** began. Many nations went to war, including the United States. Once again, Germany and the other **Axis Powers** (including Italy and Japan) were defeated by the Allies. The United States dropped the first **atomic bomb** on Hiroshima to end the war.

After World War II, the United States and the Soviet Union emerged as **superpowers**. Former allies, they each led opposing groups of countries, one group democratic, the other group communist. The two groups of nations so distrusted each other that the period following World War II was called the **Cold War**—a war fought through political and diplomatic contests instead of battles. To catch up with the United States, the Soviet Union started to build its own nuclear weapons, and the **arms race** began, soon followed by the "space race."

However, by 1990 the Soviet bloc was falling apart. The Soviet Union itself split into 15 countries in 1991. People who had lived under repressive governments for many years struggled to establish democracy—not only in the former Soviet bloc, but also in Africa, Latin America, and Asia.

PRACTICE 4

Questions 1 through 4 are based on the information on page 92.

1. As a result of the 1918 Treaty of Versailles, what did Germany have to do?

   A. pay the Allies money to repair war damages
   B. develop its military forces to protect Europe
   C. adopt a communist government
   D. promote nationalism among its people

2. What event was the immediate cause of England and France declaring war on Germany at the beginning of World War II?

   A. the annexation of Austria
   B. the annexation of Czechoslovakia
   C. the invasion of Poland
   D. the invasion of France

3. Before the atomic bomb was dropped on Hiroshima, the Allies warned Japan they would suffer "complete and utter destruction" unless they surrendered. Despite the fact that 80,000 people were killed and 40,000 wounded by the bombing of Hiroshima, Japan still refused to surrender. The United States then dropped a second atomic bomb on the city of Nagasaki, killing 40,000 more people. After the second bombing, the Japanese surrendered.

   Japan's refusal to surrender after the bombing of Hiroshima suggests that the Japanese placed a high value on which of the following?

   A. negotiation
   B. national pride
   C. the lives of military personnel
   D. a lasting peace

4. Which of the following is a similarity between World War I and World War II?

   A. Both were confined to Europe.
   B. Both occurred after the Russian Revolution.
   C. Both involved the use of atomic weapons.
   D. Both were won by the Allies.

Questions 5 and 6 refer to the following chart.

Casualties in World War II

Nation	Military Dead	Military Wounded	Civilian Dead
Great Britain	398,000	475,000	65,000
Soviet Union	7,500,000	14,102,000	15,000,000
United States	292,000	671,000	very few
Germany	2,850,000	7,250,000	5,000,000
Japan	1,576,000	500,000	300,000

Source: *The Second World War* by Henri Michel.

5. What was the main difference between the casualties sustained by the United States and those sustained by other nations in World War II?

   A. The United States had more military dead than wounded.
   B. The United States sustained only a few civilian casualties.
   C. The United States had the fewest wounded.
   D. The United States had more civilian than military casualties.

6. The main reason that the Soviet Union had so many casualties is that it was invaded by the German army, which got as far as the outskirts of Moscow and Leningrad. There the Germans halted in 1941. Severe winters, long supply lines back to Germany, and stiff resistance from the Soviets ultimately defeated the Germans.

   Which of the following events is most similar to the German invasion of the Soviet Union?

   A. the 1812 French invasion of Russia, which failed due to harsh weather and lack of supplies
   B. the occupation of Singapore by Japan in World War II, which gave Japan control of Malaya
   C. the 1941 Japanese attack on Pearl Harbor, which drew the United States into World War II
   D. the 1945 Allied invasion of Europe, which liberated Europe from German control

Answers and explanations start on page 113.

LESSON

5

GEOGRAPHY AND THE WORLD

Humans and the Environment

Key Ideas

- When populations grow, decline, or shift, changes in geographic regions occur.
- Populations change as a result of many different political and economic factors.
- Population growth and urbanization have a negative impact on the environment.

GED® TEST TIP

Some questions give a definition and ask you to apply it. To answer an application question such as number 2 on page 95, check each of the answer options against the given definition.

Populations—particularly the movement and growth of population groups—play a major role in defining and altering geographic regions. A population may be **native** to a geographic area, as the Taino, for example, were native to the Caribbean when Columbus arrived there. Sometimes population groups **migrate** over long distances, as did many Irish people who came to the United States during the Potato Famine in the mid-1800s. However, when people feel strong ties to a place, they may stay there even when conditions are unfavorable; they may even develop new economic and cultural strategies that strengthen their population. The **distribution** of population within a region depends on many factors, not all of which humans can control. People tend to move where there are resources, jobs, and other favorable conditions. But these conditions are ever changing, depending on politics, climate, economic development, and so on.

Urban and **rural** development have a strong impact on the distribution of a population. Industrialized regions generally see their populations shift away from rural areas into cities and towns. **Suburban** development very often follows urban growth. As cities become crowded, the urban population spreads into the countryside, often taking up agricultural lands for housing and commercial development. Agriculture also changes in most industrialized regions. Farming is done on a larger scale by fewer people using more mechanized tools. Industrialized regions usually can support a larger population at a higher standard of living than nonindustrialized regions. However, these regions also may lose some of their distinctive traditional cultures, arts, farming methods, and so on.

When political boundaries are in dispute, or ethnic groups declare war on each other, local population shifts may dramatically change the character of a region. For example, during World War II, Hitler depopulated Europe of millions of Jews through deportation and death camps. After World War II, the state of Israel was established in the Middle East, drawing many Jews to the region. Continuing conflicts within the Middle East have led to further population shifts of different Arab and Jewish groups there.

When human populations grow, they significantly affect the natural environment. **Manufacturing** and **urbanization** cause air and water **pollution**. Commercial agriculture tends to degrade both soil and water. Eventually food and water supplies become endangered. For example, these problems, along with a loss of farmland to urbanization, are very prominent in China today, where the government has been trying since the 1970s to reduce population growth.

Overall, government policies and international agreements have not been strong enough nor widely enforced when it comes to reducing the destructive impact of growing populations, large cities, and damaging agricultural methods in many parts of the world.

PRACTICE 5

Questions 1 through 4 are based on the information on page 94.

1. What is migration?

   A. a form of society in which people move on after they consume an area's resources
   B. temporary travel to another geographic region to scout for resources
   C. the move of an individual or population from one geographic area to settle in another
   D. the relative distribution of populations in urban and rural areas

2. Migration within a country's borders is called internal migration. Which of the following is an example of internal migration?

   A. the movement of the Irish to the United States during the Potato Famine in the 1800s
   B. the westward movement of the American population from the 1700s to the present
   C. the movement of Mexican workers into the southwest United States during the 1900s
   D. the movement of people from former British colonies to Great Britain

3. Urban areas [Select...] suburban areas.

   - are more densely populated than
   - have been more recently settled than
   - contain more remnants of farms than
   - have more agricultural workers than

4. Which of the following technologies was the most likely contributor to the rapid growth of suburbs in the United States?

   A. the telephone
   B. the telegraph
   C. the airplane
   D. the automobile

Questions 5 and 6 refer to the following graph.

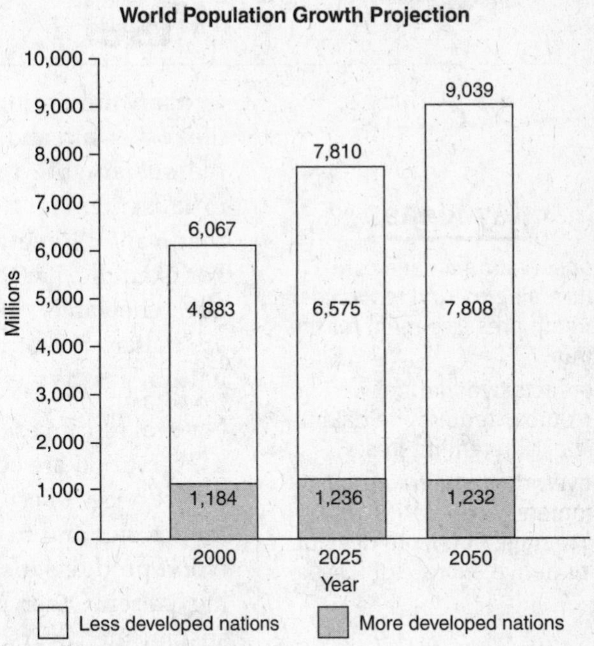

Source: Population Reference Bureau

5. What does the figure 9,039,000,000 represent?

   A. the projected population of less developed nations in 2025
   B. the projected population of less developed nations in 2050
   C. the projected population of more developed nations in 2050
   D. the projected total world population in 2050

6. Which of the following conclusions is supported by the data on the graph?

   A. The total world population will double in the 50 years from 2000 to 2050.
   B. About half the world's population lives in the more developed nations.
   C. Most of the population growth in the 50 years from 2000 to 2050 will occur in the less developed nations.
   D. Most of the population growth in the 50 years from 2000 to 2050 will occur in the more developed nations.

Answers and explanations start on page 113.

LESSON

6

GEOGRAPHY AND THE WORLD

Using Resources Wisely

Key Ideas

- Conservation means carefully using natural resources to help preserve them for the future.
- Conflicts over natural resources require the balancing of different interests.
- Government programs can promote conservation and encourage people to develop alternative energy sources.

ON THE GED® TEST

Some questions are based on important current topics such as the development and conservation of resources. Reading the newspaper will help you become familiar with many of these issues.

Conservation means using natural resources—such as soil, plant and animal life, water, air, and mineral reserves—carefully. Conservationists encourage the **sustainable use** of resources—using resources in ways that do not exhaust them for the future. Natural resources are either **renewable** or **nonrenewable.** Renewable resources can be sustained through replacement. For example, harvested plants can be replanted. Solar and wind energy are also renewable, since their supply never runs out. Nonrenewable resources are materials that humans use but cannot replace—such as petroleum and natural gas, as well as minerals such as coal, copper, and iron.

Natural resources need to be protected for many reasons. Some reasons for conservation are economic: natural resources are needed to produce goods and services of economic value. Petroleum provides fuel to run equipment in factories and to transport materials and goods. We also need wood and wood products for building structures, making furniture, and manufacturing paper. Other reasons for conserving resources relate to our need to sustain the diverse **ecosystems** of Earth to help keep the planet healthy. These diverse ecosystems help maintain the following resources: water; air; and plant, animal, and human life. Finally, natural resources inspire our sense of beauty and wonder; natural areas and materials play important roles in people's cultural and spiritual traditions.

When natural resources are **scarce** or become threatened, different people's interests can come into conflict. For example, water resources in a region might not be adequate to provide clean drinking water, irrigate local farms, sustain wildlife, and supply water for industrial development. If these interests are not balanced, some people will lose what they need. These problems become even more difficult when political boundaries are involved. Perhaps one nation's water supply comes from a river that flows through another nation; if the second nation builds a dam on the river, it could cut back the flow of water to the first nation. Such conflicts can be very difficult to negotiate. Industry, agriculture, natural ecosystems, clean air and water, and historical and cultural preservation—all these factors influence how people decide to allocate natural resources.

Many countries have laws that protect **endangered species** of plants and animals. Industrial and agricultural interests have to be balanced against **biodiversity**—the maintenance of many different species of organisms. New international agreements attempt to protect the **ozone layer** in the atmosphere, which is critical to maintaining Earth's climate patterns. In some nations—although not in the United States—high taxes on gasoline pay for clean air programs and encourage people to reduce their use of cars. **Fossil fuels** are relatively inexpensive and available, so industrialized regions are highly dependent on them. But they are nonrenewable and cause a great deal of pollution. Globally, we will have to develop more sustainable sources of energy on a large scale—such as **solar** and **wind energy**—to keep our planet healthy in the long run.

PRACTICE 6

Questions 1 through 5 are based on the information on page 96.

1. What are renewable resources?

   A. materials that will never run out or can be replaced if used
   B. materials that we do not use and so can use at a later date
   C. materials that we use but cannot replace
   D. an incentive to conserve materials

2. Which of the following is an example of the sustainable use of a resource?

   A. burning fossil fuels
   B. strip mining
   C. overgrazing livestock
   D. rotating crops

3. Since conflicts over scarce or polluted resources sometimes cross national boundaries, which of the following methods would be most likely to solve problems related to these resources?

   A. negotiating in an international forum
   B. taking unilateral action
   C. importing resources
   D. selling resources

4. In the United States, there is disagreement about how to reduce dependence on foreign oil. Some favor exploiting domestic sources of oil even if that means polluting the environment. Others prefer to concentrate on developing alternative, renewable sources of energy.

   Which of the following best characterizes the underlying difference in points of view between the pro-oil and pro-alternative energy factions?

   A. self-sufficiency versus interdependence
   B. competition versus cooperation
   C. short-term benefit versus long-term benefit
   D. patriotism versus internationalism

5. Which of the following actions could a family take to conserve nonrenewable resources?

   A. incinerate the trash
   B. carpool to work and school
   C. plant trees in the yard
   D. burn more firewood

Questions 6 and 7 refer to the following chart.

Current Natural Gas Resources and Reserves (in trillion cubic feet)

Region	Current Production	Proved Reserves	Reserves to Production Ratio
N. America	25.5	312.7	12/1
S. America	2.1	189.1	90/1
Europe	9.2	216.3	24/1
Former U.S.S.R.	25.7	2,057.5	80/1
Africa	2.6	341.6	131/1
Middle East	3.9	1,594.3	409/1
Asia/Oceania	6.5	350.6	54/1

Source: Congressional Research Service.

6. Select the world region that currently produces the most natural gas.

7. Natural gas is a nonrenewable resource. As gas is produced for consumption, reserves are depleted. Assume that each of the regions listed above continues to produce natural gas at its current rate and does not discover any additional reserves. Rank the regions below in the order in which they will run out of natural gas, with (1) meaning the region will run out of natural gas first and (4) meaning the region will run out of natural gas last.

(1)	
(2)	
(3)	
(4)	

North America	Europe
Former U.S.S.R.	Africa

Answers and explanations start on page 113.

Geography and the World Practice Questions

1. The Germanic tribes that invaded the Roman Empire had relatively simple governments. There were few government officials and taxes. Rulers depended on the loyalty of their warriors rather than on a government bureaucracy. Germanic laws were based on custom and designed to prevent warfare between families.

   Which of the following is the best title for this passage?

   A. How Germanic Tribes Governed
   B. Germanic Tribes and the Roman Empire
   C. The Invasion of the Roman Empire
   D. Loyalty Among the Germanic Tribes

2. The mechanization of the textile industry, the invention of the steam engine, and the development of the coal and iron industries contributed to Great Britain's lead in the Industrial Revolution. However, after 1850, other nations began to challenge Great Britain's lead. Belgium, France, and Germany all industrialized quickly. By 1900, natural resources and railroad building helped make the United States the leading industrial nation.

   Which of the following is the best summary of this passage?

   A. The development of natural resources made Great Britain the leader in the Industrial Revolution.
   B. The Industrial Revolution started in Great Britain and spread throughout the world.
   C. The Industrial Revolution started in Great Britain and spread to Europe, but by 1900 the United States was the leading industrialized nation.
   D. Plentiful natural resources and a vast railroad system were the underpinnings of the Industrial Revolution in the United States.

Questions 3 and 4 refer to the following map.

Early Civilizations in Africa

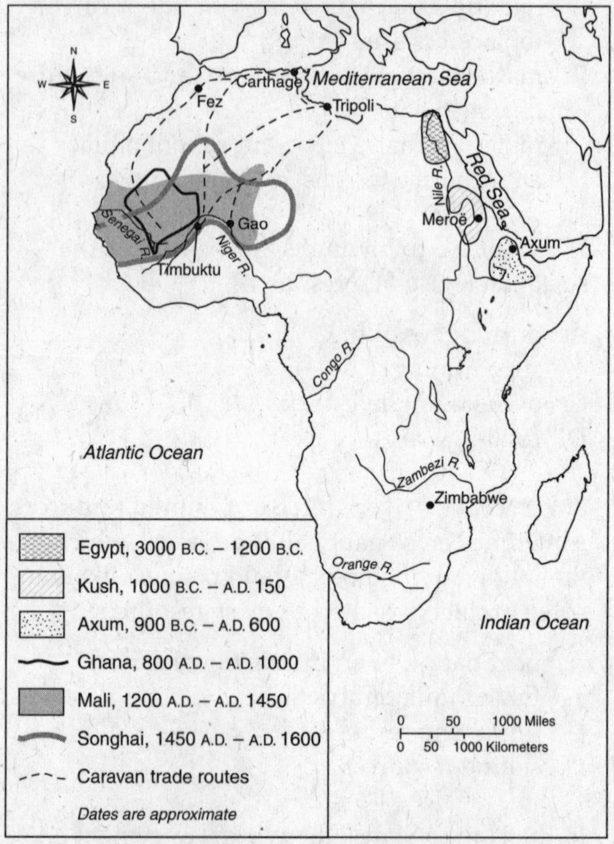

3. Select the area on the map where the earliest civilizations in Africa developed.

4. Which of the following statements is supported by information on the map?

   A. Over 800 years, several civilizations succeeded one another in western Africa.
   B. The Kingdom of Mali dominated western Africa for more than 500 years.
   C. Timbuktu was an important center of learning in Songhai.
   D. Gold and salt were transported along caravan trade routes in western Africa.

Questions 5 through 8 refer to the following timeline.

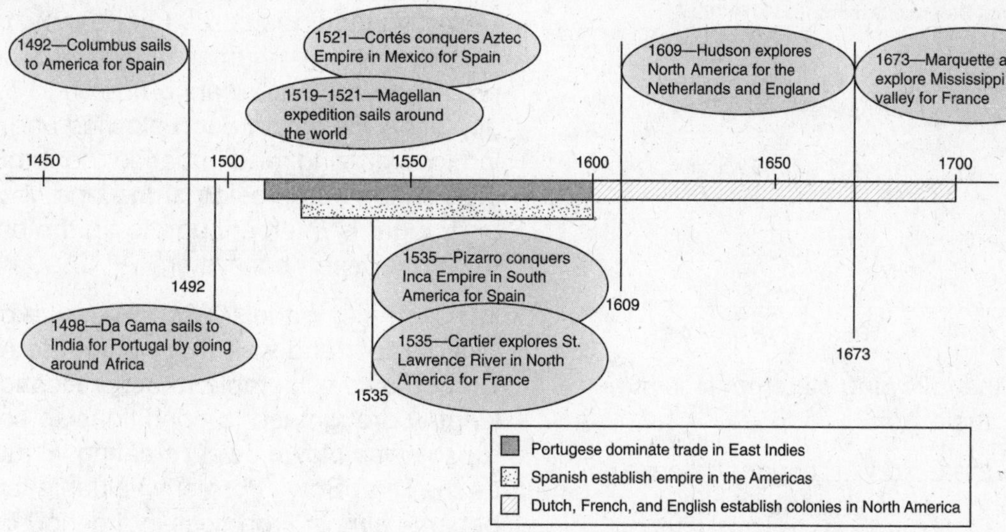

5. Portugal dominated trade in the East Indies for most of the 1500s. Select the event on the timeline that most likely first triggered Portugal's superiority in the region.

6. Which of the following statements is supported by information on the timeline?

   A. Spanish and Portuguese domination of exploration gave way to that of the Dutch, French, and English.
   B. Henry Hudson discovered more places in North America than did Marquette and Joliet and Cartier.
   C. Both Cartier and Da Gama explored North America on behalf of France.
   D. French explorers cooperated with American Indians in establishing trade.

7. Instead of financing expeditions themselves, the rulers of Spain allowed conquistadors to establish outposts in the Americas. The conquistador financed his own expedition, but if he succeeded, he was allowed to keep four-fifths of any treasure he found. Cortés was a conquistador who became rich by conquering the Aztecs in Mexico.

   Select... was also a conquistador.

   - Da Gama
   - Pizarro
   - Cartier

8. Which of the following is the best title for this timeline?

   A. The Spanish Explorers and Empire
   B. The Age of Exploration
   C. History of the 16th and 17th centuries
   D. European Colonies in the Americas

Question 9 refers to the following graph.

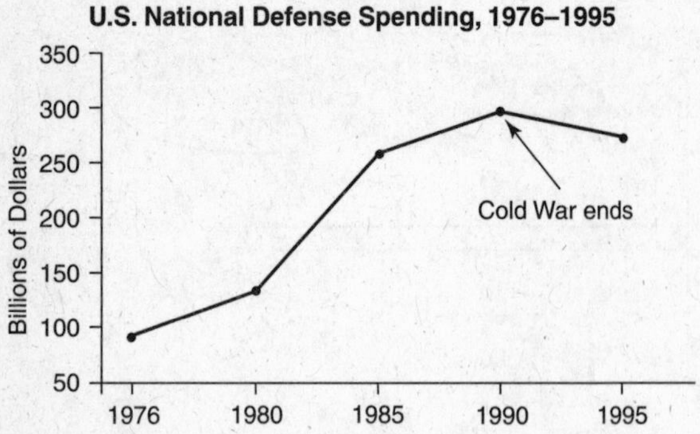

9. Which of the following statements is supported by the graph?

   A. Before the Cold War began, defense spending was at an all-time high.
   B. Defense spending remained steady throughout the Cold War.
   C. Defense spending declined steadily during the period 1976 to 1990.
   D. After the Cold War ended, defense spending began to fall.

10. When establishing colonies, European nations wanted their colonies to be economically self-sufficient. That meant that each colony paid for its government salaries and the cost of building and maintaining roads, railroads, and government buildings. To do this, European colonists or the colonial governments exported natural resources like gold or copper or grew cash crops like sugar or rubber.

    Which of the following statements is an opinion rather than a fact?

    A. European countries had similar goals in establishing their colonies.
    B. Colonies should be economically independent.
    C. European nations built railroads, roads, and government buildings in their colonies.
    D. Colonies provided natural resources that colonists could export.

Questions 11 and 12 refer to the following passage.

Desertification, the spread of deserts, is usually caused in part by human activity. Agricultural practices, such as clearing trees and brush, depleting the soil through plowing and planting, overgrazing, and irrigation, contribute to the sterilization and erosion of the land. A period of drought is often enough to tip the balance toward a desert ecosystem.

For example, in the 1930s, excessive plowing, overgrazing, and well-digging left the American Great Plains vulnerable to desertification. A lengthy drought led to conditions so severe the topsoil was blown away, creating what is known as the Dust Bowl. Formerly valuable farmland became almost worthless in a period of years. The area was spared permanent desertification only because normal rainfall eventually resumed.

11. Which of the following was the most likely result of the Dust Bowl?

    A. the Great Depression of the 1930s, an economic downturn
    B. the migration of thousands of farm families to other regions
    C. the permanent cessation of agriculture in the Great Plains
    D. restoration of the Great Plains ecosystem as it was before agriculture

12. Which of the following is an example of desertification?

    A. the shrinking of the Greenland ice sheet
    B. the shifting sandbars along the coast of Lake Michigan
    C. the extension of grazing onto land that is part of the National Forest system
    D. the spread of the Sahara into the grazing land on its southern border

13. According to experts in world agriculture, the poor nutrition and starvation of millions of people stems not from a global scarcity of resources, but from the uneven distribution of resources among nations. Experts claim the world has the resources to feed its population if the political will of the richer nations were brought to bear on this problem.

    Which of the following is an opinion rather than a fact?

    A. Millions of people worldwide are undernourished.
    B. The world has abundant natural resources.
    C. Natural resources are distributed unevenly among nations.
    D. The problem of feeding the world's population is a matter of political will rather than one of resources.

14. The 2000 Census showed that the United States has 281,421,906 people, an increase of 13.2 percent over the 1990 Census. Population growth and immigration accounted for this increase. The state population counts showed the largest relative gains in the South and West, with Nevada's population increase the highest at 66.3 percent. Because state population figures are used to allocate seats in the House of Representatives, every ten years a shift in political power occurs. In 2000, states in the Northeast and Midwest lost seats, and states in the West and South picked up seats.

    Which of the following is implied by the paragraph?

    A. Nevada had a 66.3 percent population increase.
    B. Nevada gained seats in the House.
    C. People moved away from the Northeast and Midwest.
    D. The U.S. population in 2000 was about 281 million people.

Questions 15 and 16 refer to the following map.

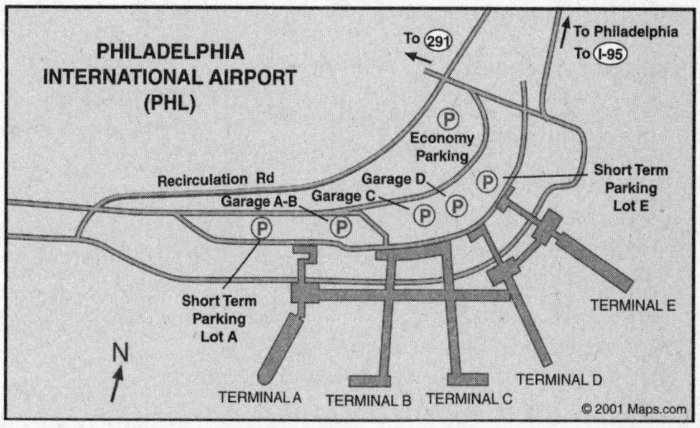

15. Which of the following people is most likely to use the map above?

    A. a geologist surveying land features in the Philadelphia area
    B. a visitor to Philadelphia
    C. an employee of the Federal Aviation Administration
    D. a commercial airline pilot

16. Which of the following statements is supported by the data on the map?

    A. More than 20 airlines have landing rights at Philadelphia International Airport.
    B. Route 95 borders the south side of Philadelphia International Airport.
    C. It is possible to get to Philadelphia International Airport by plane, car, or rail.
    D. Labels for terminals and parking areas are coordinated to provide convenient parking.

Answers and explanations start on page 114.

PRACTICE QUESTIONS ANSWERS AND EXPLANATIONS

Social Studies Practices

Lesson 1: Determine Central Idea and Draw Conclusions

Practice 1, page 27

1. **C. the characteristics of Greek tragedy** The passage describes tragedy as "central to Greek culture" and supports this point with details about the plots, staging, characters, and themes of Greek tragedy.
2. **D. The main character in Greek drama has a tragic flaw that causes his downfall.** Choice (D) cites one of the details the author uses to try to establish the central role of tragedy in Greek culture. The other choices are all too broad (choice (A)) or misrepresent what the passage actually said (choices (B) and (C)).
3. **A. Ancient Greeks did not expect to see an original story each time they attended the theater.** Choice (A) is the only answer choice supported by information in the passage. The writer tells you that tragedies "told stories familiar from myths and epics," so it must have been the case that theatergoers knew the general story that would be acted out.
4. **D. Where do the incomes of senior citizens come from?** Choice (D) is correct because the graph tells you the sources of income for American senior citizens. The graph doesn't give any actual dollar amounts, nor does it state how many senior citizens there are in the United States You would need those numbers to answer the questions in choices (A), (B), and (C).
5. **B. Social Security benefits are the most widespread means of support for most senior citizens.** Each bar in the graph represents the percentage of all seniors who receive some of their income from that source. Since the Social Security bar is the tallest (representing more than 86% of all seniors), choice (B) must be true based on the graph.

Lesson 2: Interpret Words and Ideas

Practice 2, page 29

1. **C. political and social instability in some Northern European countries** In the first paragraph of the passage, the author mentions "riots, civil unrest, and open rebellion" as some of the factors that pushed German citizens to migrate. Those events are examples of "political and social instability," so choice (C) is correct.
2. **D. a painting of pioneers settling and farming productive prairie land** In the passage, the author discusses "abundance" in the second paragraph, giving examples of the kinds of optimistic messages that attracted people to the United States. The image of pioneers opening up productive farmland is symbolic of the economic opportunity promised to 19th century immigrants to the United States, so choice (D) is correct.
3. **C. a growth in the population of the United States** In the first paragraph, the author tells you that the number of immigrants arriving in the United States. between 1820 and 1870 was greater than the entire U.S. population just 10 years before that time period. You can conclude from the passage that the U.S. population grew.
4. **B. Internal migration led to overgrazing.** According to the timeline, aggressive agriculture occurred prior to 1930 and the "black blizzards," caused in part by overgrazing, began in 1931. Internal migration did not begin until around 1933. Inferring that internal migration (which began later) caused overgrazing (which had already occurred) would be illogical, so choice (B) is correct.
5. **C. depleted topsoil** The "aggressive, mechanized farming techniques" that depleted the topsoil in the American Midwest and Southern plains occurred prior to and contributed to the dust storms and "black blizzards" that characterize the Great Dust Bowl. Internal migration (choice (B)) and failed farms (choice (C)) were results, not causes, of the Dust Bowl.

Lesson 3: Analyze Author's Purpose and Point of View

Practice 3, page 31

1. **C. propagandistic** Page 30 explains that propaganda uses emotional language to influence readers' behavior. Here, asking the readers to "have a part in Victory" is just such language.
2. **C. Citizens who plant war gardens help supply the war effort with essential resources.** As the passage explains, war gardens were encouraged so that, with citizens supplying more of their own food, the government could use its limited resources to feed and equip soldiers, sailors, and airmen. Choice (C) paraphrases this nicely.
3. **A. describe war gardens and explain their popularity in the United States** The author's tone is neutral and explanatory; she simply wants to explain what war gardens were and why they were popular during the two world wars. The author is not advocating a point of view (choice (B)), trying to compare or contrast the United States with any other country (choice (C)), or arguing against anyone else's position (choice (D)).
4. **C. a cancer** By using a frightening and often fatal disease such as "cancer" to describe the impact of the proposed regulations, the citizen is making an emotional comparison. The analogy is especially aggressive given that the issue addresses health and safety.

Lesson 4: Evaluate Author's Reasoning and Evidence

Practice 4, page 33

1. **A. Damming the Mekong could solve Cambodia's energy problems.** The author argues for cooperation among Cambodia and its neighboring

countries, all of which share the Mekong river. The reason this is important, the author asserts, is because hydroelectric power from the Mekong would help solve Cambodia's energy problems. Nowhere in the argument, however, does the author support this contention.

2. **B. Strikes have a detrimental impact on workers.** The cartoon shows a laborer using a strike as a means of "cutting off" production, depicted as a tree branch. The joke is that the worker sits on the wrong side of the branch he's cutting. Once the worker is successful in cutting off production, the cartoonist implies, he will fall to the ground along with production. Choice (B) neatly sums up the cartoonist's point.
3. **D. Ancient Greece pioneered democracy.** The one reason the author gives for believing that Ancient Greece was the greatest of the early civilization is that it was the birthplace of democracy. Thus, choice (D) is correct. Choice (A) is the author's opinion, not a fact supporting that opinion. Choices (B) and (C) are both reasons that ancient Babylon and Egypt (and not the author's favorite, Greece) might be considered great.
4. **B. The Constitution grants more power to the federal government than did the Articles of Confederation.** In each category compared in the chart, the federal government has more power under the Constitution than it had under the Articles of Confederation, so choice (B) is a valid inference, though it is not explicitly stated anywhere on the chart. All three wrong answers cite specific facts stated in the chart.

Lesson 5: Analyze Relationships Between Materials

Practice 5.1, page 35

1. **A. housing and food** Study the circle graph (pie chart) to see that the two largest portions are labeled with white (33%) and vertical lines (20%). Checking the legend to the right shows that these "slices" correspond to housing and food, respectively.
2. **D. Brazil has a higher divorce rate than Mexico.** This bar chart directly supports choice (D): Brazil's divorce rate is 0.6 per thousand, while Mexico's is 0.4 per thousand. Choice (B) is incorrect because this chart shows five countries in the Western Hemisphere, not all of them. One of the countries not shown on the chart may have a divorce rate even lower than Mexico's. Choice (C) is incorrect because this chart conveys nothing about how divorce rates have changed over time.
3. **fluctuated** As you read the line graph left to right, showing the change over time, you see that percentage of votes for third-party presidential candidates went up and down multiple times, so "fluctuated" is accurate.
4. **C. Third party candidates have never captured more than 10 percent of the popular vote in any presidential election.** The statement in choice (C) is disproved by 1968 (14 percent) and 1992 (more than 19 percent).
5. **C. how agriculture spread in the Americas** The map shows two places at which agriculture originated independently (indicated by black stars) and where agriculture spread out from those two points (indicated by the white arrows). The map shows no political boundaries (choice (A)) or physical features (choice (B)) of the Americas, nor does it claim to name all of the ancient civilizations on the two continents (choice (D)).
6. **B. Both the Andes civilization and Mesoamerica domesticated beans.** Check right below the names of the two civilizations named on the map and you'll find the crops they learned to grow. "Beans" is the only crop listed for both the Andes and Mesoamerican groups.

Practice 5.2, page 37

1. **D. Sea otters have been able to live in habitats from which they were once eliminated.** Choice (D) is directly supported by the third paragraph of the passage, which refers to successful "programs to reintroduce the sea otter into previously populated areas." Choice (C) is incorrect because, although the passage says that the sea otters in California have regained about two-thirds of their former habitat range, it does not indicate that they have reached two-thirds of their former population numbers. Choices (A) and (B) are not mentioned at all in the passage.
2. **D. The current range of the sea otter in California is larger than what it was in 1911.** According to the passage, the sea otter's range in 1911 "was limited . . . to a small area around Monterrey Bay." The map makes it clear that the sea otter's range now extends significantly to both the north and south of Monterrey Bay. Putting the information from the passage together with that from the map shows that choice (D) must be true.
3. **C. Without conservation efforts and reintroduction programs, the range of sea otters in California would be smaller than what is shown on the map.** In the third paragraph of the passage, the author states that conservation and reintroduction programs "have contributed to" the expansion of the sea otter's habitat range in California. This directly supports the statement in choice (C).

Lesson 6: Interpret Data and Statistics

Practice 6, page 39

1. **D. 36** Median refers to the middle term in a set of numbers arranged from smallest to largest. Since more than half of New Mexico's 2010 population was age 35 or older, the median age could have been 36. For that same reason, ages 30 (choice (A)), 32 (choice (B)), and 34 (choice (C)) are all too small to represent the state's median age in 2010.

2. **B. the average margin of victory was higher in years when a Democrat won than in years when a Republican won** In both years in which a Republican won the presidential election (2000 and 2004) the final electoral vote count was very close. In each of the four years in which a Democrat won (1992, 1996, 2008, and 2012) the Democratic candidate captured a much larger portion of the electoral vote. Thus, choice (B) is supported by the graph.
3. **C. 1920** Of the years shown on the graph, 1920 is the point when the rural and urban populations are closest in number. Prior to 1920, the rural population was much larger than the urban population. After 1920, the urban population begins to be much larger than the rural population.
4. **C. 34 million** To determine the correct answer to this question, you need to subtract the range of the rural population from the range of the urban population. The rural population was around 54 million in 1930, up from approximately 25 million in 1860. That's a range of approximately 29 million. The urban population was around 68 million in 1930, up from just 5 million in 1860. That gives a range of approximately 63 million. Subtracting 29 million from 63 million produces a difference of 34 million, choice (C).

Lesson 7: Write an Extended Response

Practice 7, page 41

Refer to the *Social Studies Extended Response Evaluation Guide* on page 135 to evaluate your response.

Social Studies Practices Practice Questions, pages 42–45

1. **B. The unemployment rate declined consistently until shortly before the war's end.** Checking the timeline, you can see that World War II began in 1939 and ended in 1945. Unemployment went down every year between 1939 and 1944, and rose just slightly in 1945. Thus, choice (B)'s description of the war's impact on unemployment is correct.
2. **A. the stock market crash** Immediately after the stock market crash in 1929, unemployment increases dramatically and directly until 1933. That makes choice (A) correct. After 1933, unemployment declines gradually until the end of the war, and the decline is interrupted by a small increase during 1937–1938.
3. **D. The Seneca Falls Convention was a shocking event that undermined the nature of women.** There is no objective way to prove that something is "shocking and unnatural." Those words reveal that the statement in choice (D) was the opinion of one newspaper's editors.
4. **D. The Seneca Falls Convention was important in the fight for women's rights.** The passage's primary purpose is to explain how the women's movement "gained strength" at the Seneca Falls Convention.
5. **A. More than half of the reported cases of human plague in the United States between 1970 and 2010 were reported in four states.** Even if you don't recognize the four states in question as Arizona, California, Colorado, and New Mexico, the map clearly shows the overwhelming concentration of reported plague cases as occurring there. Choice (A) is justified by the information in the map.
6. **C. Several cases of plague were reported on the East Coast of the United States between 1970 and 2010.** The statement in choice (C) is clearly false given the information in the map. No cases of plague were recorded east of Illinois during the time period depicted by the map.
7. **D. The effects of the cotton gin on the cotton industry actually led to an increased demand for slaves in the South.** The fact stated in choice (D) is directly supported by the end of the passage where the writer explains the effects of the cotton gin: "with the boom in the cotton industry, more slaves were used to pick cotton at a faster rate."
8. **C. 2,000,000** The increase in the number of cotton bales produced between 1840 and 1860 was approximately 3,500,000. The increase in the number of slaves living in the United States during the same twenty year period was approximately 1,500,000. The difference between the two figures is 2,000,000.
9. **C. In most years, the percent population increase in South Dakota was greater than that in North Dakota.** Choice (C) is correct. In seven of the eleven years shown (every year from 01–02 to 07–08) South Dakota's annual population increase was greater than that of North Dakota. The increases were approximately equal in 08–09, and North Dakota's increase was greater in the remaining three years. Choice (B) makes a statement about the populations of these states, but the graph only contains information about *percent increase*, or proportional increase, of the population.
10. **less than** Though North Dakota had far greater growth than South Dakota toward the end of the period, North Dakota averaged an increase of approximately 0.77 percent per year over the 11 years, while South Dakota averaged approximately 0.93 percent per year.
11. **70 percent** The mean voter turnout for the years shown is 39.67 percent in midterm elections, and 55.98 percent in presidential elections. 36.67 percent divided by 55.98 percent equals 70.9 percent.
12. **C. 13.8 percent** "Median" refers to the middle term in a set of numbers arranged from smallest to largest.
Arrange the terms from the chart in order: 11.1 percent, 11.6 percent, 13.8 percent, 13.9 percent, 14.0 percent. The middle term is 13.8 percent, corresponding with the correct answer, choice (C).
13. Refer to the *Social Studies Extended Response Evaluation Guide* on page 135 to evaluate your response.

U.S. History

Lesson 1: Exploration, Colonialism, and the American Revolution

Practice 1, page 47

1. **the Spanish** According to the map and the key, Spain had the southernmost colony along the east coast of what would eventually become the United States.
2. **B. The English established several colonies in the New World.** The map shows several English colonies along the New England coast and in what is now Virginia and Maryland.
3. **D. Haitian refugees who fled to the United States to escape a dictatorship** Like the early colonists, the Haitian refugees of the mid- and late 1900s came to the United States seeking freedom from political persecution.
4. **B. increased British taxes and restrictions on the colonies** The fourth and fifth sentences of paragraph 4 link increased taxes and restrictions to the outbreak of the American Revolution.
5. **B. They were concerned about the government becoming tyrannical.** The first amendment guarantees citizens' rights to pressure their government. The passage explains that the framers of the U.S. Constitution did not want the government to become overly powerful. While choices (A) and (C) were both rights listed amongst the guarantees of the First Amendment, they do not explain *why* the Framers listed them. Choice (B) discusses their motivations and is correct.

Lesson 2: Westward Expansion, the Civil War, and Reconstruction

Practice 2, page 49

1. **D. whether slavery should be permitted in territories in the West** This is implied in the third and fourth paragraphs of the passage. Choice (B) is incorrect because the fourth paragraph says that Abraham Lincoln promised to halt the spread of slavery, not to end it where it already existed.
2. **C. To balance the admission of Missouri, they agreed to a compromise in which Maine was admitted as a free state.** The third paragraph of the passage describes how the U.S. government tried to maintain a balance of power between the North and the South by adding states in pairs: one slave state and one free state. Since Missouri was a slave state, the most likely response of Northerners would be to propose the addition of a free state. (Indeed, Maine and Missouri were the 23rd and 24th states to join the United States.)
3. **concluded with the reunification of the nation** The information in the question indicates that North and South Vietnam were reunited under the Communists at the end of the Vietnam War. The passage implies that at the end of the U.S. Civil War, the North and the South again were united under the United States federal government.
4. **C. In 1868, many African Americans served in the government of South Carolina.** There are more than 20 African Americans included in this composite photograph of the South Carolina legislature. The other choices are opinions that cannot be confirmed by the photograph.
5. **A. Over the course of Reconstruction, African Americans in the South gained and then lost political power.** The number of African Americans in the composite photograph of the South Carolina state legislature of 1868 indicates that near the beginning of the Reconstruction period, African Americans had considerable political power. The last paragraph of the passage on page 48 states that by the 1870s, whites were preventing African Americans from exercising their newly won right to vote. This indicates that African Americans were losing political power as Reconstruction ended.

Lesson 3: Industrialization, Immigration, and the Progressive Era

Practice 3, page 51

1. **B. an increase in manufacturing** By definition, industrialization is related to increased manufacturing. This meaning is implied in the passage in paragraphs one and two.
2. **C. the development of the Bessemer process, which made it easier to produce steel** The first paragraph of the passage relates rapid industrialization to the invention of new industrial processes. The Bessemer process was one such process. It made steel more readily available for tools, railroads, construction, and other uses.
3. **C. cooperation with others to improve worker safety** The fourth paragraph indicates that union workers pledged to work together (cooperate) for better working conditions. The passage states that better working conditions include improved worker safety.
4. **D. fairness** The fifth paragraph discusses the Progressive Era. The fact that reformers were working to improve conditions for poor people and to give people a greater voice in government indicates that fairness was a strong ideal for them.
5. **Asia and the Americas** The second circle graph indicates that, in the years 2000–2009, 77 percent of persons obtaining legal resident status came from Asia and the Americas.
6. **C. In the 1890s, that number was roughly three times what it was in the period of 2000–2009.** The question asks you to compare the number of persons from Europe in the first circle graph to the number of persons from Europe in the second circle graph. Keep in mind that the total numbers represented by the two graphs are different. Calculate that number for the period 1889–1890: 97 percent of 3,689,609 is about 3,578,920. (You could use your calculator or estimate to find an approximate number.) Then calculate that number for the

period 2000–2009: 13 percent of 10,299,430 is about 1,338,925. (Use your calculator or estimate.) Now, compare those two numbers: 3,578,920 is a little less than three times 1,338,925.

Lesson 4: The United States as an Emerging World Power

Practice 4, page 53

1. **Military** The building of a naval base indicates that the correct category is "military."
2. **B. In World War II, the Allies included England, France, and Russia.** The author assumes that you realize that the Allies of World War II included the same major powers as the Allies in World War I. If you do not recognize this unstated assumption, you will not understand who fought whom in World War II.
3. **C. Unemployment fell after the start of the New Deal and continued to fall as the United States entered World War II.** The graph shows a decline in the unemployment rate after the New Deal went into effect in 1934. It shows that unemployment went up in 1938 but then dropped after that and dropped considerably after the United States' entry into World War II in 1941.
4. **D. America took a strong leadership role during and after World War II.** The paragraph focuses on the role the United States played during and after World War II. The other choices are details from the paragraph or they bring up information not included in the paragraph.

Lesson 5: The Cold War and the Civil Rights Era

Practice 5, page 55

1. **Blank (1) no direct combat; Blank (2) dissolution of the Soviet Union** The first paragraph of the passage implies that the name "Cold War" was used because there was no direct fighting. The first sentence of paragraph two explains that the Cold War ended when the Soviet Union broke up.
2. **C. The buildup of nuclear arms increases fear and instability, not peace.** The statement about peace and stability made by the man on the right in the bottom frame of the cartoon is supposed to be ironic. The cartoonist's reference to the man's trembling arms suggests that the situation is not stable, and that perhaps we should be afraid.
3. **C. Americans were in complete agreement about pulling out of Vietnam.** Paragraph one states that even when defeat for South Vietnam seemed fairly certain, a few Americans still wanted to continue contributing to the fighting. Therefore, it is an overstatement to say that Americans were in complete agreement that pulling out of Vietnam was the right thing to do.
4. **B. petitioning for a city ordinance requiring those selling real estate to select a buyer without regard to race** Paragraph three states that the aim of the civil rights movement was to end segregation and discrimination in the United States. Preventing the selective selling of real estate was one important way civil rights activists worked to end discrimination, making decreased segregation possible.
5. **A. Reliance on technology has increased pollution.** This is a conclusion—a general statement about a topic. The other choices are details—facts or examples—that support this conclusion.

U.S. History Practice Questions, pages 56–59

1. **B. Although the Cherokee adopted many aspects of white culture, they were driven off their ancestral lands.** This statement is the only one with a large enough scope to be considered a conclusion. The other choices are details that are either included in, related to, or not based on the time line.
2. **A. If the government can't protect us from white settlers here, now, how could it protect us from whites moving west in the future?** This question shows the lack of logic in the government's claim that location was what made it difficult to protect Cherokee rights. Location had nothing to do with the government's lack of protection of Cherokee land in the South. The government did not have the political will to enforce laws protecting the Cherokee.
3. **D. equal rights and opportunities for women** Adams's statements that women are not inferior and her invention of the term *Lordess* both indicate that she advocated equality for women.
4. **Select any four of: Maryland, Delaware, West Virginia, Kentucky, and Missouri** The map shows that these were all slave states loyal to the Union.
5. **A. The nation's capital was located nearby.** If the nation's capital, located adjacent to the state of Maryland, had been surrounded by Confederate states, it would have been extremely difficult for the U.S. army to defend it. This would have given a great edge to the Confederacy during the Civil War. The other choices are untrue, irrelevant, or not verifiable by the map.
6. **D. to weaken the South by enlisting former slaves in the Union army** This was implied by the text of the Proclamation that is quoted. None of the other choices are supported by the text.
7. **the Voting Rights Act of 1965** The chart explains that this act prohibited literacy (reading) tests for voting.
8. **C. African Americans were granted the vote soon after the Civil War, but laws enforcing these rights had to be passed a century later.** This is implied by the passage of the 15th Amendment in 1870 and by the passage of the Voting Rights Act of 1965. Congress would not have passed the later law if the 15th Amendment were being upheld and enforced. Choice (A) is true, based on the chart, but is not a summary of the information in the chart.

9. **B. They both prohibited the legal separation of people by race in public places.** The chart shows that both the 1875 and the 1964 Civil Rights Acts banned racial segregation in public places.
10. **D. The telephone was the greatest electrical invention ever.** This statement is said to have been made by leading scientists of the time; this is not in the author's voice. It is the only opinion. Choices (A), (B), and (C) are all facts stated in the passage.
11. **B. the framers of the U.S. Constitution** The clothes of the men in the picture indicate that this cartoon is set in the late 1700s. Impeachment is discussed in the caption. Impeachment was a provision that the framers of the Constitution included in order to prevent the kind of abuse of presidential power carried out by Nixon. Impeachment of elected officials was not discussed in the Declaration of Independence, which laid out the reasons for the United States' independence from Great Britain, so choice (A) is incorrect.
12. **A. the pursuit of justice** By investigating the circumstances of Watergate, Congress was trying to make sure that the nation's laws were carried out.
13. **C. the escalation and failure of the Vietnam War** Of the choices listed, only choice (C) describes an event just prior to the Watergate scandal. The bloodshed and failure of the Vietnam War caused many people to question authority, including the government, and to question decisions made by the government.
14. **C. 1,000,000** The scale on the vertical axis of the bar graph shows that population is measured in millions. The bar for Cuba stands one unit high. This means that about 1,000,000 people of Cuban descent lived in the United States in 1990.
15. **B. Mexico** The bar graph shows that most people in the United States who are Hispanic originally came from Mexico. Therefore, Mexico is the most likely nation of origin of the unknown family.

Civics and Government

Lesson 1: Historic Basis for U.S. System

Practice 1, page 61

1.

Direct democracy	In Country D, laws are made by the vote of all citizens.
Monarchy	In Country B, laws are made by a sovereign king and are subject to no review.
Representative democracy	In Country C, laws are made by Congress, an elected group of representatives.
Aristocracy	In Country A, laws are made and administered by lords who inherit their land and titles.

2. **B. They were concerned about protecting the rights of individuals.** According to the passage on page 60, the Founding Fathers were influenced by the Enlightenment philosophers, who did place importance on the rights of the individual.
3. **C. Parliament of England** Similar to the United States Congress, the parliamentary system in England allows for citizens to elect representatives to a lawmaking body.
4. **D. England during the Age of Enlightenment** According to the passage on page 60, England adopted a bill of rights for the individual during the Enlightenment. This action limited the monarchy's power over the individual.
5. **D. The president would be appointed by the majority party in parliament.** In most parliamentary democracies, the majority party in the Parliament appoints the president. Nothing in the text indicates whether this would make the office of the president more or less powerful than it currently is, so choices (A) and (B) are unsupported.

Lesson 2: Constitutional Government

Practice 2, page 63

1. **B. elected representatives exercising government power on behalf of citizens** According to the first paragraph of the passage, the key characteristic of a republic is elected officials governing for the voters.
2. **C. The details of government would be worked out in the future, as the need arose, within the framework of the Constitution.** The leaders who drafted the Constitution were wise enough to realize that they could not anticipate every eventuality, so instead of trying to cover everything in the Constitution, they made it a general framework within which specific future decisions and laws could be made.
3. **C. the power of an office, not an individual** Roosevelt's long tenure worried many people as they saw his power growing with time. They pursued term limits to prevent any individual from amassing too much power as president.
4. **The U.S. Supreme Court declaring an Illinois state law unconstitutional** The supremacy clause asserts the supremacy of federal law when it conflicts with state law. Therefore, the declaration that a state law is unconstitutional is an exercise of the supremacy clause.
5. **A. State governments do not usually act together.** The third and fourth methods of passing a constitutional amendment both require concerted action by state governments. Therefore, choice (A) would explain why those methods have never been used. Choices (B) and (D) are contradicted by information in the chart. Choice (C) repeats information in the chart, but does not provide a useful explanation.

Lesson 3: Levels and Branches of Government

Practice 3, page 65

1. **A. division of power between national and state governments**

According to the second paragraph of the passage on page 64, a federalist form of government divides power between the national and state levels of government.

2. **D. the State Department** The State Department is part of the executive branch; its head is a member of the president's cabinet. The Democratic National Committee, choice (A), is not part of the government at all. Choice (B) is part of Congress, and therefore part of the legislative branch. Courts, choice (C), are in the judicial branch.
3. **A. Federal judges need not worry about pleasing their constituents in order to be reelected.** Because they do not need to please any constituents in order to be reelected, federal judges can preside without worrying about making unpopular decisions. This leaves them freer to be impartial judges of the law.
4.

Checks and balances	Limits that one branch of government can place on the other branches
Veto	The president's power to strike down a law
Senators	Legislators who serve six-year terms
Constituents	The people whom political leaders represent
Representatives	Legislators who serve two-year terms

5. **B. a member of Congress** Although this person subscribes to the idea that the government is divided into three branches, he can only think of one of them—the one to which he belongs. Since he is probably in the legislative branch, he is likely to be a member of Congress. The way the desks are arranged and the way the man is standing to make his point are visual cues that the setting of the cartoon is Congress.
6. **A. mutual respect and convenience** Although in theory each state could insist on its own laws being followed even by residents of other states, in practice that would be too cumbersome. So on many matters, such as driver's licenses, states respect one another's laws because it is convenient to do so.

Lesson 4: The Electoral System

Practice 4, page 67

1. **C. receiving a majority in the Electoral College** According to the second paragraph of the passage on page 66 a president must have a majority in the Electoral College to be elected.
2. **A. Exit polls may be inaccurate if the people polled are not representative of the political unit as a whole or if the election is very close.** It is more likely that a poll will be wrong if an unrepresentative sample is used or if the election is very close. Under those circumstances it is hazardous to call an election based on exit poll results, as was shown in the 2000 presidential election, in which the media gave Florida's vote first to Gore, then to Bush, and only hours later declared the state too close to call.
3. **D. Two city council members are on a ballot to determine which one will run for mayor as a Democrat.** A primary is an election to choose among candidates of the same party. The winner of the primary then faces an opponent of another political party in the general election.
4. **B. In total, individuals contributed a greater dollar amount to House candidates than they did to Senate candidates.** Although Senatorial candidates received a higher percentage (greater by 4 percent) of their contributions from individual donors, the total dollar amount received by the House candidates was much higher (greater by approximately $350,000,000). Therefore, the total dollar amount of individual contributions received by the House candidates was ultimately greater than that received by the Senate candidates.
5. **A. In 2010, self-funding was a larger source of funds for Senate candidates than it was for House candidates.** The Senate candidates' own contributions accounted for 13 percent of the total Senate Candidates' Funds while the House Candidates' own contributions accounted for only 6 percent of the total House Candidates' Fund. In addition, calculations based on the total amount of funds reveal that Senate candidates spent more total dollars on self-funding than did House candidates.

Lesson 5: The Role of the Citizen

Practice 5, page 69

1. **The U.S. Constitution** According to the third paragraph of the passage, the Constitution sets forth the rights of citizens.
2. **A. resident alien** Because she moved here permanently as the wife of an American citizen, Louvina is a resident alien and will remain so until she qualifies for citizenship through naturalization.
3. **C. They would become enemy aliens.** If the country of aliens residing in the United States declares war on the United States, that nation becomes an enemy state, and the aliens become enemy aliens.
4. **B. privacy** The protection against unreasonable search and seizure is essentially a protection of citizens' privacy rights. The government must demonstrate a good reason before it is allowed to search or seize property.
5. **C. If the 2012 presidential election is representative of elections generally in the United States, voter turnout increases with age.** This is the only statement general enough to be a conclusion. All the other options are details from the graph that support this conclusion.

Civics and Government Practice Questions, pages 70–73

1. **B. In 2013, a different major party controlled the House than controlled the Senate.** According to the numbers of the 113th Congress, the Republicans had majority control in the House and the Democrats had majority control in the Senate. Choice (A) is too broad to be a summary of this chart which focuses on political divisions. The conclusions in choices (C) and (D) require more information than the chart provides.
2. **Bill of Rights of the U.S. Constitution, which guarantees citizens certain rights** Like the Magna Carta, the Bill of Rights of the U.S. Constitution accords citizens certain rights and protections. Note that the scope of the Bill of Rights is broader in that it protects the rights of all citizens, not just a special group, as the Magna Carta did.
3. **C. a $3,000 contribution to a party fund for TV ads on political issues** Of all the choices, this is the only donation that is going to a political party fund rather than to a specific candidate, so it is a "soft money" contribution.
4. **A. People were less aware of soft money because disclosure was not required.** During the 1980s, political parties did not have to reveal the amount and sources of their soft money contributions, so the extent of this type of campaign financing was not generally known. Only when a law was passed requiring disclosure did people become aware of the scale of soft money donations and so began to raise their concerns about the issue.
5. **C. Jill Stein won a greater percentage of the popular vote than of the electoral vote in 2012.** Jill Stein won 0.36% of the popular vote, but she did not win any electoral votes in the 2012 election.
6. **D. 2012 Presidential Election: Popular and Electoral Votes** This is the only option that covers the topic of the paragraph as well as that of the graphs.
7. **A. The board of election is the county, city, or town office responsible for local voting.** Nowhere in this excerpt from the voter's guide is the board of election defined or explained; the writer assumes that the reader knows what it is.
8.

The Democratic Party, which nominates candidates and tries to win elections	
The National Association of Manufacturers, which lobbies for businesses	★
The Federal Communications Commission, which regulates broadcasters	
The Cabinet, an advisory body for the president	
Public Citizen, a nonprofit consumer rights advocacy group	★

Of all the choices, these two are the only groups that consist of people with common interests and goals—in this case, manufacturers and consumers—working by lobbying to influence government policies. The other choices are either political parties or part of the executive branch.

9. **B. Most registered voters don't vote.** Despite the fact that voting is one of the obligations of citizens, in most elections, less than half of the nation's registered voters actually vote.
10. **C. civic duty** The cartoonist is appealing to voters to take their civic duty to vote more seriously.
11. **A. China, where the top leaders of the Communist party control the government** Of the national governments described, only China is an oligarchy, a government with rule by a small group of people. The other options are not oligarchies; they are either democracies or autocracies.
12. **A. retribution** These laws all embody the urge to take revenge on wrongdoers, or to exact retribution. The other principles underlie the modern criminal justice system and other modern legal systems.
13. **C. 32** Look for the map key to determine the symbol for death penalty states. According to the map, 18 states do not have the death penalty, so 32 out of 50 states have the death penalty.
14. **D. Two of the five states with the lowest per capita homicide rates have abolished the death penalty.** If that argument were correct, then the states with the lowest homicide rates should all be death penalty states, but that is not the case. Two states—Vermont and Hawaii—that have homicide rates among the lowest in the nation do not have the death penalty.
15. **C. The 1978 Panama treaties sold out U.S. interests to Panama.** Choice (C) states an opinion about the Panama treaties, not a fact that can be tested or proved. The word in the passage that signals an opinion is "believed."
16. **D. The mayor has ceremonial duties.** In both the mayor-council and the council-manager forms of city government, at least part of the time, the mayor plays a ceremonial role.

Economics

Lesson 1: Basic Economics Concepts

Practice 1, page 75

1. **B. to convert capital and raw materials into products and services** According to the first paragraph of the passage, labor transforms capital and raw materials into goods and services that may be sold.
2. **D. a plastic material** A producer good is something used in the production of a finished good. Of all the choices, only plastic is a producer good. The remaining choices are consumer goods, in other words, finished products.
3. **A. When the supply of houses is low, demand is high and sellers can raise their prices.** Because of the law of supply and demand, when the supply of houses is lower than the demand, sellers have more

control over the terms of sale. In that situation, they can raise the asking price. Because there are many potential buyers, chances are high that a seller will get a good price.

4. **B. Toys are not critical to a nation's economic and political well-being.** The U.S. government prefers the free-market system and generally provides price supports only for industries that are extremely important to the nation's welfare, such as agriculture and transportation.
5. **D. 16** On the vertical axis, locate $.30, and then see where a horizontal line drawn through $.30 would meet the sloping demand line. The answer is 16 apples.
6. **C. As the price of apples rises, Keisha buys fewer apples.** The demand line on the graph shows that Keisha's apple purchases are related to the price of apples. As the price rises, her demand for apples falls, and she buys fewer apples. None of the other choices is supported by the data on the graph.
7.

a tool manufacturer	a bicycle repair shop ★
a paper mill	a microchip factory
a car wash ★	a beauty salon ★

According to the passage, a service business does not produce or sell tangible goods but instead offers services. Of all the choices, a car wash, a repair shop, and a beauty salon all sell services; the remaining choices are businesses that produce goods for sale.

Lesson 2: The U.S. Economic System

Practice 2, page 77

1. **D. Monopolies shut out competition.** When a company has a monopoly on a market, it has great power to squelch competing firms that try to enter the market. This is implied in the last two sentences of the second paragraph of the passage.
2. **rising unemployment** Of all the economic factors listed, only high unemployment is associated with recessions, according to the third paragraph of the passage.
3. **A. Property owners have a stake in the future value of the property.** Since property can increase or decrease in value, its owner is motivated to do things that will maintain or increase its value.
4. **C. buying stock in a new company, such as an Internet startup** In general, investing in stocks is riskier than choice (A), saving money in a bank, or choice (B) buying a certificate of deposit (or CD, as they're commonly called). Choice (C), investing in a startup that has no track record of turning a profit, is also riskier than choice (D), investing in a big, well-established company like Microsoft.
5. **D. Despite ups and downs, the gross domestic product generally increases over time.** Even though the gross domestic product rises and falls with business cycles, the general trend shown by the graph is for the gross domestic product to rise over the long term.
6. **A. They provide capital for businesses to grow.** One of the similarities between saving and investing in stocks is the ultimate use of the money. In both cases, the money allows businesses to start or expand operations as banks loan money they hold in savings accounts and the purchase of stock directly funds the company issuing the stock.

Lesson 3: The Economy and the U.S. Government

Practice 3, page 79

1. **registers revenues that exceed its expenditures** As implied in the first paragraph of the passage on page 78, a budget surplus occurs when the government takes in more tax and other revenue than it spends.
2. **C. cutting the federal income tax** If Congress cut the federal income tax, consumers would have more money to spend. This strategy has been used to stimulate the economy. The other choices would decrease consumer spending or have no direct effect on consumer spending.
3. **D. the air traffic control system** Like the federal highway system, the air traffic control system facilitates transportation, which is critical for economic activity.
4. **D. Both affect the amount of money circulating in the economy.** Fiscal and monetary policies are two tools the government uses to control the money supply. Increasing the money supply by lowering taxes or lowering interest rates stimulates the economy, and decreasing the money supply slows the economy.
5.

Money out of Circulation	**Money into Circulation**
Sell government securities (bonds and Treasury bills) to investors	Buy back government securities
Raise the discount rate member banks are charged to borrow from the Fed	Lower the discount rate member banks are charged to borrow from the Fed
Raise the reserve requirement, the amount banks must keep on hand to cover deposits	Lower the reserve requirement

According to the passage, policies that increase the amount of money in circulation are used to stimulate the economy. Therefore, all three of the choices listed on the chart under *Money into Circulation* could be used by the government to stimulate the economy.

6. **C. Our complex economy takes time to respond.** Since the economy is made up of the actions of millions of people, any Fed action takes time to have an overall effect that is measurable.

Lesson 4: Labor and Consumer Issues

Practice 4, page 81

1. **C. wages and benefits** According to the first paragraph

of the passage on page 80, the money a worker earns plus the value of his or her benefits equals total compensation.

2. **A. Workers must learn skills throughout their lives to be prepared for changes in their industries.** This is the conclusion that the writer comes to after describing the steelworkers who lost their jobs and had to retrain when much of their industry moved overseas.
3. **woman buying a computer** Of all the choices, this is the only one in which a person is buying a product, so that person is a consumer.
4. **A. All for one and one for all.** When workers unite in labor unions, all of them together have the power to benefit each of the individual members. Similarly, each member supports the goals of the union as a whole.
5. **A. in 2000** The lower line on the graph shows the number of unemployed civilians. That line is at its lowest point at the year 2000.
6. **B. As the number of employed civilians rose steadily from 2003 to 2006, the number of unemployed slowly declined.** The graph shows that the number of employed civilians rose from about 137 million to about 144 million from 2003 to 2006. At the same time, the number of unemployed civilians dropped slightly—by about 2 million.

Economics Practice Questions, pages 82–85

1. **B. the various types of resources needed for an economy to produce goods and services** According to the passage, the factors of production include all the resources—natural, human, and man-made—needed to produce products and services.
2. **D. entrepreneurs** In a communist nation with centralized economic decision making, there is no place for individual entrepreneurs. The government decides what will be produced and how it will be produced.
3. **A. an office building** An office building is a capital resource. Choice (B) is a natural resource, choice (C) is labor, and choice (D) is an entrepreneur.
4. **A. In a balanced budget, revenues equal expenditures.** This explanation of a balanced budget is a fact. The remaining choices express opinions held by many fiscal conservatives.
5. **A. More than half of all personal income was earned through work in February 2013.** According to the chart, the primary source of personal income in 2013 (approximately 60 percent) was from wages, salary, and other forms of employee compensation.
6. **D. an investor** The man in the plaid shorts represents an investor who buys and sells stock on the stock market.
7. **C. He is accustomed to stock market ups and downs.** Like the roller coaster in the background, stocks gain and lose value, often precipitously. The investor is calm because he has experienced the ups and downs of the stock market, so a roller coaster ride feels familiar to him.
8. **person who runs a home daycare center** This is a person who is running a business out of his home and so is self-employed. Therefore, no federal income tax is withheld from her earnings, and he must pay estimated tax.
9. **B. individualism** Individualism is one of the core values of a society with a free enterprise economic system, because each person is free to make his or her own economic decisions.
10. **2009.** A budget deficit occurs when the government is spending more money than it is collecting in revenue. The larger the gap between the revenues and the expenditures, the larger the country's deficit. In the five-year span depicted on the chart, the largest gap between the revenues and expenditures exists in the year 2009.
11. **B. income tax returns and expense records** The federal budget is similar to a family budget; it differs primarily in scale. For a family, income tax returns provide documentation of revenues (income), and expense records such as grocery receipts and credit card bills provide a record of expenditures. None of the other choices includes records of both income and expenditures.
12. **D. The national network of interstate highways is paid for mostly by federal excise taxes.** Of all the choices, (D) contains the main details of the paragraph. Choices (A), (B), and (C) each focus on only one supporting detail.
13. **A. When cheaper imported goods force out U.S.-made goods, U.S. factory workers often lose their jobs.** Free trade may benefit the economy as a whole in the long term, but as the economy adapts, some individuals (in this case, factory workers) lose in the short term.
14.

Agency	Function
Food and Drug Administration	Protects public from poorly processed and improperly labeled foods and drugs
Federal Trade Commission	Protects consumers from misleading and/or fraudulent advertising
Consumer Product Safety Commission	Protects consumers from risk of injury or death from hazardous products
Security and Exchange Commission	Protects investors from being misled about stocks and bonds
National Highway Traffic Safety Administration	Protects consumers by testing vehicle safely and monitoring nationwide speed limits

According to the chart, the Federal Trade Commission exists to protect consumers from misleading and/or fraudulent advertising.

15. **A shortage of the product** When a product's price falls below the equilibrium point, demand for

the product increases, and thus the supply decreases, causing a shortage of the product.

16. **B. what causes high rates of unemployment** The unemployment rate is a factor in the economy as a whole, so it is a subject of study to a macroeconomist. All of the other choices relate to the economic actions of individuals or companies, which are not the main interest of a macroeconomist.
17. **C. As the price per eraser increases, manufacturers supply more erasers.** According to the graph, as prices rise, manufacturers are willing to supply more erasers as they see an opportunity for more profit.

Geography and the World

Lesson 1: Early Civilizations

Practice 1, page 87

1. **B. the Maya** According to the passage, the Maya recorded their discoveries about mathematics and astronomy in a pictographic writing system.
2. **Ancient Greece; Ancient Rome** As stated in the passage, the Greek idea of democracy, in which citizens voted, and the representative government and laws of ancient Rome were great influences on the founders of the United States.
3. **A. Both developed flood control and irrigation technologies to boost food production.** Both ancient Egypt and the civilizations of the Fertile Crescent grew up along rivers. The passage points out that in both areas, people learned to control floods and irrigate fields in order to improve food production.
4. **B. towns** The food surpluses that result from agriculture mean that not everyone must grow or gather her own food. Therefore, some people are free to live in towns where they can pursue a craft or business in exchange for food from farmers. The other options occur without the gathering together of people in settlements.
5. **D. ancient Egypt** Ancient China developed along a great river, the Yellow River. Of the civilizations listed, only ancient Egypt also grew up along a river, the Nile. In both ancient China and ancient Egypt, the river kept the soil rich and damp.
6. **C. The Yellow River was probably the main trade route between Loyang and Chengchow.** Not only were rivers the source of water for irrigation, they were major thoroughfares for the transport of goods. Since both cities are on the Yellow River, trade between them most likely took place by river at that time.

Lesson 2: Feudalism to Nation States

Practice 2, page 89

1. **C. to protect their noble's land from attack** According to the passage, the role of the knights in feudal society was to protect their noble's estate, or land.
2. **Spain** Of the lands mentioned in the passage that were conquered by the Muslims, only Spain is in Europe. Thus, of the European nations marked for selection in the map, Spain is the one in which you would most expect to find evidence of Muslim culture.
3. **B. the migration of people from farms to industrial cities in the 1800s** Like the migration to the cities in the 1800s, the migration from manors to towns in the late Middle Ages resulted from economic causes. In both migrations, people were seeking better economic opportunities than farming offered.
4. **A. Roman Catholics accepted the authority of the pope and Protestants did not.** According to the passage, this was one of the main differences between the two branches of Christianity.
5. **A. accepted legal principles** Since the manor court did not rely on a written body of legal rulings, its actions were unpredictable. Most people felt they would get a fairer ruling in the royal courts, which were bound by written common law that applied to everyone in the kingdom.
6. **C. The population of Western Europe showed almost constant growth with only brief periods of decline.** This is the best summary because it contains the main idea (Europe's population rose from 500 to 1500) and important details (two brief periods of decline).

Lesson 3: The Age of Revolutions

Practice 3, page 91

1. **C. the U.S. Declaration of Independence** According to the passage, the American Revolution and its goals of democracy (as expressed in the Declaration of Independence and the Constitution) were big influences on the French.
2. **D. Members of the Third Estate owned the least amount of land per person.** With 98 percent of the population but only 70 percent of the land, the Third Estate owned the least land in proportion to its numbers. Members of the First and Second Estates owned more land in proportion to their percentage of the population.
3. **had a Parliament; did not have a parliament** This contrast is stated in the third paragraph of the passage. It is one of the reasons French citizens were dissatisfied with their lack of representation in the monarchy of Louis XVI.
4. **C. possessing large landholdings** The last paragraph of the passage on page 90 states that farmland had been the economic mainstay of the aristocracy up until the time of the Industrial Revolution, which began late in the eighteenth century.
5. **B. A sovereign nation is independent, having the power to govern itself.** In the passage, the word *sovereign* is used but not explained; the author takes for granted you know what it means. The remaining options are all stated in the passage.
6. **D. the Industrial Revolution** Like the Industrial Revolution, the Information Revolution is an economic revolution that has brought about social change. The other revolutions are all political in nature.

Lesson 4: Exploration, Colonialism, and Wars

Practice 4, page 93

1. **A. pay the Allies money to repair war damages** According to the passage, paying reparations was one of the provisions of the Treaty of Versailles.
2. **C. the invasion of Poland** The third paragraph of the passage indicates that to avoid going to war, the Allies permitted Germany to take over, or annex, Austria and Czechoslovakia. However, Germany's invasion of Poland spurred England and France to declare war.
3. **B. national pride** The Japanese had a great deal of national pride, which they found difficult to put aside. Thus it took the destruction of two cities and thousands of deaths to overcome their reluctance to surrender.
4. **D. Both were won by the Allies.** Of the options listed, the fact that the Allies won both wars is the only similarity. Choices (B) and (C) are true only of World War II, and choice A is not true: both wars involved other parts of the world.
5. **B. The United States sustained only a few civilian casualties.** The chart indicates "very few" civilian dead in the United States; every other cell in the chart has a number in the thousands or millions.
6. **A. the 1812 French invasion of Russia, which failed due to harsh weather and lack of supplies** Both the French and German invasions failed due to weather and lack of supplies, making them similar. The campaigns and actions mentioned in the other answer choices failed for different or unspecified reasons.

Lesson 5: Humans and the Environment

Practice 5, page 95

1. **C. the move of an individual or population from one geographic area to settle in another** The first paragraph of the passage on page 94 implies that the key characteristics of migration are the movement of people and their settling in a new place.
2. **B. the westward movement of the American population from the 1700s to the present** Because this migration took place within the U.S. borders, it is an internal migration. The other choices all involve people moving from one country to another.
3. **are more densely populated than** The passage describes suburban areas appearing as a consequence of urban areas becoming too crowded. Thus, the text implies that urban areas (cities) are more densely populated than suburbs (neighboring towns).
4. **D. the automobile** Automobiles make it possible for many people to live in the suburbs, where the distances between a home and retail stores and workplaces can be considerable and public transportation may be lacking.
5. **D. the projected total world population in 2050** To answer this question, first locate 9,039,000,000 on the graph. (Note that the figures are given in millions, so the number to locate is written as 9,039.) It represents a total world population figure. Then look at the bottom axis to see what year that bar represents.
6. **C. Most of the population growth in the 50 years from 2000 to 2050 will occur in the less developed nations.** The bar graph shows that the proportion of the world population living in the more developed nations (shown in gray) is relatively small, and shows that it is predicted to remain relatively small over the next 50 years. In contrast, the graph predicts that the population in the less developed nations (shown in white) will grow much more. The remaining choices are not supported by the data on the graph.

Lesson 6: Using Resources Wisely

Practice 6, page 97

1. **A. materials that will never run out or can be replaced if used** According to the first paragraph of the passage on page 96, a renewable resource can be replaced (for example, replanting a field that's been harvested) or is in endless supply (for example, wind and solar power).
2. **D. rotating crops** In crop rotation, a farmer plants different crops in succeeding growing seasons in order to conserve nutrients in the soil. The other choices are all examples of a nonsustainable use of a resource; eventually, each will cause the resource to be used up.
3. **A. negotiating in an international forum** An international forum provides a framework for nations to work to resolve conflicts over resource use before the problems escalate.
4. **C. short-term benefit versus long-term benefit** Finding and using new oil deposits is a short-term solution to U.S. energy problems because it doesn't solve the underlying problem in the long run. Developing alternative sources of energy requires more investment of time and capital with an uncertain outcome, but it has the potential to help meet long-term U.S. energy needs.
5. **B. carpool to work and school** Carpooling saves gas, a nonrenewable resource.
6. **former U.S.S.R.** The second column lists current production figures; the highest figure in the column is 25.7, that of the former U.S.S.R.
7.

(1)	North America
(2)	Europe
(3)	former U.S.S.R.
(4)	Africa

To answer this question, look at the column labeled "Reserves to Production Ratio." This column indicates the relationship between the amount produced annually and the total amount the region has. Regions with lower ratios will run out of gas before regions with higher ratios.

Geography and the World Practice Questions, pages 98–101

1. **A. How Germanic Tribes Governed** The focus of the passage is the minimal governmental structure of the Germanic tribes.
2. **C. The Industrial Revolution started in Great Britain and spread to Europe, but by 1900 the United States was the leading industrialized nation.** This summary statement has all the major details from the paragraph—the start of the Industrial Revolution in Great Britain, its spread to Europe, and the lead taken by the United States. The other choices either focus too narrowly on a couple of details or are too broad to be an effective summary.
3. **Egypt (along the Nile River)** The map key gives the dates of each civilization shown on the map. Egypt, Kush, and Axum were the earliest civilizations. They are all located along the Nile River in the northeast part of Africa.
4. **A. Over 800 years, several civilizations succeeded one another in western Africa.** The civilizations of Ghana, Mali, and Songhai developed one after the other in the same region of Africa. None of the other choices is supported by information on the map.
5. **1498: Da Gama sails to India for Portugal by sailing around Africa.** Da Gama's voyage opened up new trading opportunities for the Portuguese. Note from the time line that the Portuguese dominated trade in the East Indies from about 1510 to 1600.
6. **A. Spanish and Portuguese domination of exploration gave way to that of the Dutch, French, and English.** According to the time line, most Spanish and Portuguese exploration and conquest took place during the 1500s. From the 1600s on, other nations such as England, France, and the Netherlands increased their activity considerably. The other choices are incorrect or cannot be determined from the information in the time line.
7. **Pizarro** Like Cortés, Pizarro explored on behalf of the Spanish rulers. He conquered the Inca Empire in South America.
8. **B. The Age of Exploration** This title describes the era and events shown. The other choices are too narrow, too broad, or simply incorrect.
9. **D. After the Cold War ended, defense spending began to fall.** The graph shows defense spending decreasing in the period 1990–1995, after the Cold War ended in 1990. None of the other choices is supported by data on the graph.
10. **B. Colonies should be economically independent.** Of all the choices, only this one is an opinion. The other choices are facts that are stated in the paragraph.
11. **B. the migration of thousands of farm families to other regions** The Dust Bowl temporarily disrupted farming in the Great Plains, forcing farmers to migrate to find work. While the Dust Bowl contributed to the Great Depression, (choice (A)), it was not the Great Depression's only or primary cause.
12. **D. the spread of the Sahara into the grazing land on its southern border** The Sahara, the desert that covers much of northern Africa, has been spreading steadily southward into the Sahel, a dry grasslands region that has been overused as grazing land.
13. **D. The problem of feeding the world's population is a matter of political will rather than one of resources.** This is an opinion attributed to agriculture experts in the passage. The remaining choices are all facts stated in the passage.
14. **B. Nevada gained seats in the House.** The passage tells you that the population shifts were large enough that seats in the House were reallocated. Since Nevada had a large population gain, it is likely that it also gained seats in the House. Choices (A) and (D) are stated outright rather than implied by the passage. Choice (C) does not have to be true based on the information in the passage. Because immigration also played a role in population changes, it does not have to be the case that people moved away from the Northeast and Midwest.
15. **B. a visitor to Philadelphia** This is a special-purpose map designed to help visitors find their way around the airport and locate transportation routes to and from the airport.
16. **D. Labels for terminals and parking areas are coordinated to provide convenient parking.** The map shows Terminal E by Lot E, Terminal D by Garage D, and so on.

Practice Test

1. To practice for the actual GED® Social Studies Test, you can take the following practice test. When you do, follow the same time limits you will face on the actual test:

   - **Social Studies, 34 Questions and one Extended Response, 1½ Hours**

Just as on the actual tests, you will work with a variety of formats:

- For the **multiple-choice questions**, you may fill in the circles next to the correct answers in this book, or you can write your answers on a separate piece of paper.
- For **other formats**, directions will indicate where you can write in boxes, on lines, or place a dot on a specific place on a graphic.
- You can write the **extended response** on a computer, or, if one is not available, on a sheet of paper.

NOTE: Writing your responses on a computer is preferable because you will be composing your responses on a computer when you take the GED® test. However, if you do not have a computer available when you take these tests, write your responses on paper so that you can evaluate your writing samples.

2. **You may use your calculator** as needed during the Social Studies Test.
3. **Check** your answers using the ***Practice Test Answers and Explanations*** that begin on page 131, and fill in the ***Practice Test Evaluation Charts*** on page 133. These charts will allow you to see which study areas may still need work.
4. **Confirm** your readiness to take the actual GED® Social Studies Test.

Directions: Use 65 minutes to answer the following 34 questions. You may fill in the circles next to the correct answers or write your answers in boxes or on lines as indicated.

Question 1 is based on the following paragraph and graph.

When the value of exported goods – those sold abroad—is greater than the value of imported goods—those bought from foreign nations—there is a favorable balance of trade. On the other hand, when imports are greater than exports, there is an unfavorable balance of trade.

Source: *Statistical Abstract of the United States*

1. Which of the following statements is supported by the paragraph and the graph?
   - A. Exports equaled imports at the start of the 2000s.
   - B. Exports exceeded imports throughout the 2000s.
   - C. The United States had a favorable balance of trade in merchandise during the 2000s.
   - D. The United States had an unfavorable balance of trade in merchandise during the 2000s.

Question 2 is based on the following table.
You MAY use your calculator.

2. In an opinion poll, people were asked, "In politics, as of today, do you consider yourself a Republican, a Democrat, or an independent?" The chart below represents the results, by month, for the first six months of 2013.

	Republicans %	Independents %	Democrats %
Jan 2013	27	38	33
Feb 2013	28	38	32
Mar 2013	27	36	35
Apr 2013	26	40	33
May 2013	28	39	32
Jun 2013	26	41	31

Source: Gallup

During the first six months of 2013, what percent of the people surveyed, on average, considered themselves independents? (Assume that the same number of people were surveyed each month.) Round your answer to the nearest percentage and write your answer in the box below.

Questions 3 and 4 are based on the following information and graph.

What standard of living do people in other countries enjoy? There are different ways to answer that question. Many economists hold that one good way is to calculate *gross domestic product* (GDP) *per capita*. GDP per capita is found by adding up the value of all the goods produced and services performed in a given country in a year and then dividing that total (the GDP) by the number of people living in that country.

The map below shows GDP per capita for each country in the world in 2008. Some, but not all, of the countries are labeled with the name of the country.

Map of GDP Per Capita by Country

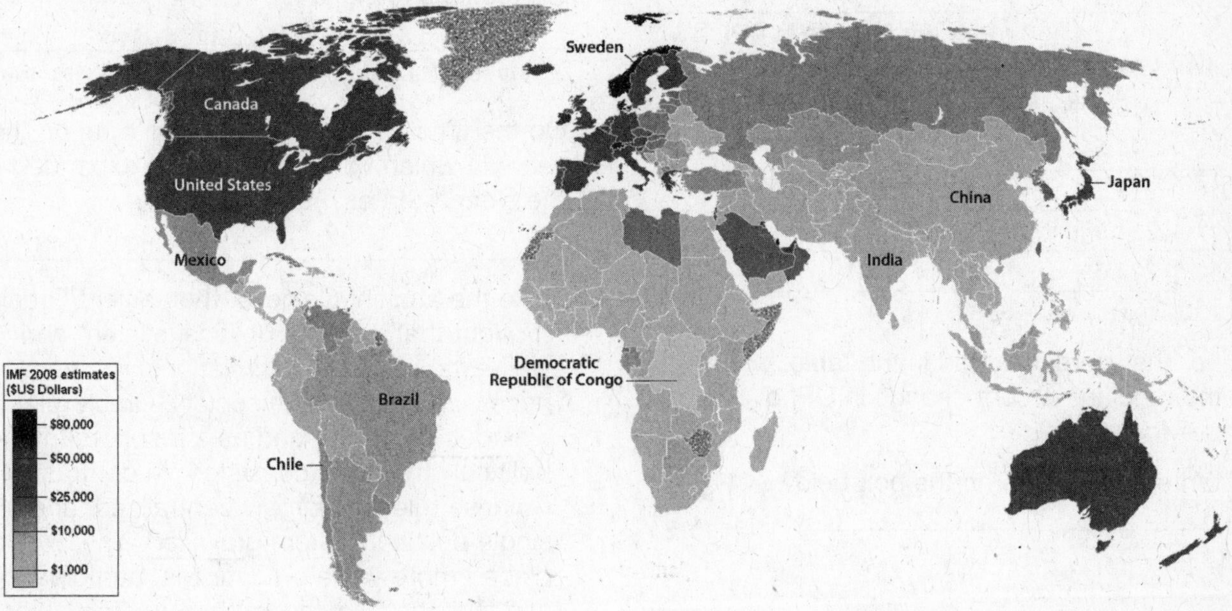

3. In the map above, place a dot on the continent that, in 2008, had the highest percentage of countries with a GDP per capita of less than $10,000 per year.

4. Place the countries below in order from highest GDP per capita to lowest GDP per capita.

Highest	
Second highest	
Third highest	
Lowest	

Democratic Republic of Congo
United States
Mexico
India

Question 5 refers to the following information and chart.

The Consumer Price Index (CPI) is a measure of the average prices paid by consumers for a typical assortment of goods and services, including housing, food, clothing, transportation, recreation, and medical care. A higher CPI indicates that prices have risen. The table below shows the CPI for several years, as well as the percent change in CPI over the previous year.

Year	CPI	Percent change in CPI over previous year
2008	215.3	3.8
2009	214.5	−0.4
2010	218.1	1.6
2011	224.9	3.2
2012	229.6	2.1

Source: Bureau of Labor Statistics

5. For the years included in the table, what was the median percent change in CPI over the previous year?

   Write your answer in the box below.

6. The 15th Amendment to the Constitution, ratified in 1870, declared that U.S. citizens' right to vote "shall not be denied ... on account of race." However, some states found ways to continue to restrict voting rights for almost a century. For example, Mississippi's 1890 constitution restricted African Americans' voting rights by imposing a poll tax and a literacy test. In the Voting Rights Act of 1965, Congress outlawed such restrictions and put protections in place for minority voters.

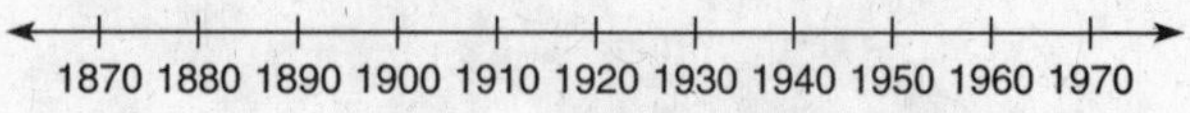

   On the timeline above, place two dots on the years in which voting rights were expanded in the United States.

7. Like the ancient Chinese, the ancient Greeks thought that a sound political system and well-established social relationships were necessary for a stable society. Greek rule was decentralized, and as a result, many political structures coexisted. In contrast, Chinese rule was largely centralized, and a single political system prevailed. The Greeks placed more value on councils, participation, and law; the Chinese, on bureaucracy, hierarchy, and rules.

   Based on the paragraph, what did the ancient Greeks and the ancient Chinese have in common in regard to politics and government?

   - A. Both governed through a hierarchical bureaucracy.
   - B. Both valued a stable political framework for society.
   - C. Both had centralized councils.
   - D. Both had decentralized political systems.

Question 8 refers to the following chart.

The Effect of World War II on Industry

Measure	1939	1940	1941
Index of manufacturing output (1939 = 100)	100	116	154
Corporate profits before taxes	$6.4 billion	$9.3 billion	$17 billion
Corporate profits after taxes	$5 billion	$6.5 billion	$9.4 billion

Source: Fute, Gilbert C., and Reese, Jim E. *An Economic History of the United States*

8. Which of the following best explains why the war had the effect on industry indicated by the chart?

A. Even before the United States entered the war, corporate profits had increased sharply.
B. Manufacturing output increased by over 50 percent in two years.
C. The war created a huge demand for military equipment and supplies.
D. With men gone to serve as soldiers, more women were employed in factories.

---

9. The U.S. president has a great deal of influence over foreign policy. In part, this is because international relations often require quick and decisive action, which is best undertaken by an individual. In times of foreign crisis, the public usually rallies to the support of the president, at least at first.

Which of the following values probably underlies Americans' initial approval of a president's emergency foreign policy actions?

A. patriotism
B. imperialism
C. self-expression
D. self-sacrifice

10. To combat the anticompetitive nature of monopolies or "trusts" such as US Steel, Standard Oil, and the American Tobacco Company, the US Congress passed the Sherman Antitrust Act in 1890. That act made it illegal for an individual to monopolize or conspire to monopolize an industry or to act with others to restrain trade or commerce among the States or abroad. While the Sherman Antitrust Act was, and remains, very influential, it was not sufficient to solve all of the problems raised by monopolies. Because of its broad language and its focus on the intent to create monopolies, courts interpreted the Sherman Antitrust Act differently and inconsistently in the many cases to which it was applied. As a result, Congress passed the Clayton Antitrust Act in 1914, which targeted specific actions—such as favorable price discrimination and exclusive dealings contracts—that were used to create monopolies.

In the passage above, the writer's main point is that

A. courts struck down the Sherman Antitrust Act because its broad language made it unconstitutional
B. problems with consistently enforcing the Sherman Antitrust Act led to further legislation to prevent monopolies
C. monopolies like US Steel, Standard Oil, and the American Tobacco Company successfully avoided prosecution under the Sherman Antitrust Act
D. the Sherman Antitrust Act ended monopolies like US Steel, Standard Oil, and the American Tobacco Company, but did not prevent new monopolies from arising

11. Since the mid-twentieth century, environmental scientists have been warning the United States about the impact of unchecked carbon emissions into the atmosphere, a threat that many researchers conclude has already led to climate change. Of the many long-term dangers of climate change, which refers to the trend toward greater global temperature extremes, some of the most destructive involve lengthy droughts, diminishing fresh water supplies, and decreased world food production. Although some point to the potential benefits of the temperature changes in particular hemispheres, benefits such as longer growing seasons and more temperate climates for certain populations, the hazards far outweigh any potential advantages. Since the United States has the second highest rate of carbon emissions per person, it must lead the way by dramatically cutting industrial emissions and finding alternate sources of fuel that do not release carbon dioxide as a byproduct. Positive efforts are underway, particularly through the Environmental Protection Agency, which has fostered several international partnerships to limit the production of carbon dioxide, among other greenhouse gases.

Place the letter of each statement within the correct column. You may or may not fill up each column.

The author would agree with this statement:	The author would disagree with this statement:	The author does not address this information:

a. The United States has failed to take any action against carbon emissions.
b. The dangers of climate change are more significant than the possible benefits.
c. Wind energy is preferable to solar energy.
d. Climate change will not impact the world food supply.

Questions 12 through 13 refer to the following map.

Forced Resettlement of American Indians, 1830s

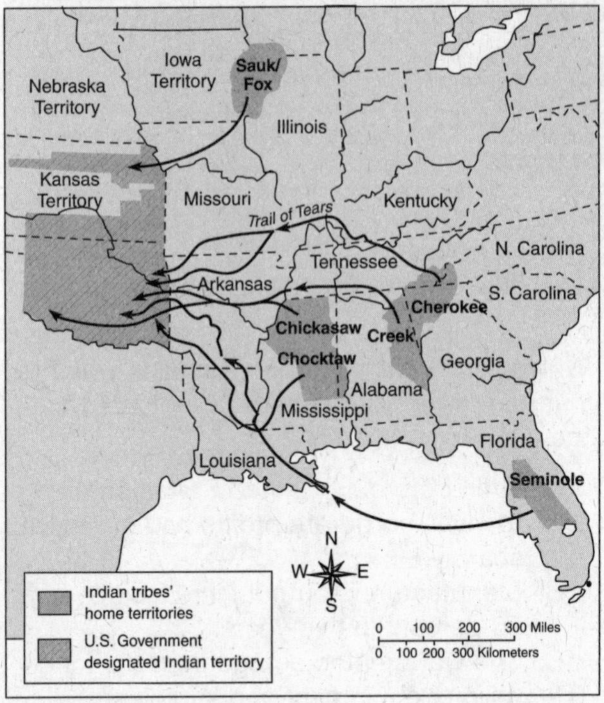

12. Which of the following is the most likely reason that American Indians were forcibly relocated in the 1830s?
   - A. Whites wanted lands in the Kansas and Nebraska territory for settlement.
   - B. Whites wanted to take over Indian lands in the eastern states.
   - C. Indians of different tribes wanted to settle in a single Indian territory.
   - D. Indians in the eastern states wanted to look for gold in the West.

13. Which American Indian tribe was moved the farthest from its tribal lands?
   - A. the Sauk/Fox
   - B. the Cherokee
   - C. the Chocktaw
   - D. the Seminole

Question 14 refers to the following cartoon.

14. With which of the following opinions would the cartoonist be most likely to agree?
  - A. People shouldn't have to stand around waiting to see their elected representatives.
  - B. Senators should pay attention to special interest groups as well as to voters.
  - C. Special interest groups are treated better than voters by members of Congress.
  - D. Senators are nicer to their constituents than are members of the House.

15. In the late 1800s, industrialization caused a large-scale migration from rural to urban areas in the United States. Parents who moved to cities with their children left behind the social support of their extended families. In addition, city families found that children, who were an asset on the farm because they could work at an early age, were more of an economic drawback in the city. As a consequence, the birthrate dropped during this period and average family size shrank.

Which of the following is the best summary of this passage?
  - A. Industrialization led to increased urbanization in the late 1800s.
  - B. City families lost the social support of their extended families back on the farm.
  - C. Industrialization and urbanization caused many changes in family life in the late 1800s.
  - D. In the late 1800s, average family size shrank due to the fall in the birthrate.

Questions 16 and 17 refer to the following chart.

Acts of Parliament Directed at the American Colonies

Act	Description
Revenue Act of 1764 (Sugar Act)	Imposed duties (tariffs) on foreign sugar and luxuries to raise money for Great Britain
Quartering Act of 1765	Required colonists to provide food and shelter for British soldiers
Stamp Act of 1765	Required colonists to purchase revenue stamps for all important documents, including legal documents, newspapers, and ads
Declaratory Act of 1766	Asserted the right of Parliament to make laws for the colonies
Townshend Acts of 1767	Imposed new duties on the import of tea, glass, and paper

16. How did the Declaratory Act differ from all the other acts of Parliament shown in the chart?
  - A. It did not involve the quartering of British soldiers.
  - B. It related only to the import of luxury goods.
  - C. It did not impose direct economic costs on the colonists.
  - D. It was enacted long after the other acts of Parliament.

17. The information in this chart would have been most useful for the writing of which of the following documents?
  - A. The Declaration of Independence, which explained why the colonies broke away from Great Britain
  - B. The Articles of Confederation, which established a central government consisting of a congress
  - C. The U.S. Constitution, which established the structure of government for the newly independent nation
  - D. Washington's Farewell Address, in which he warned the new nation of policies and practices he thought unwise

Questions 18 and 19 are based on the following map.

Percentage of Undernourished People Worldwide

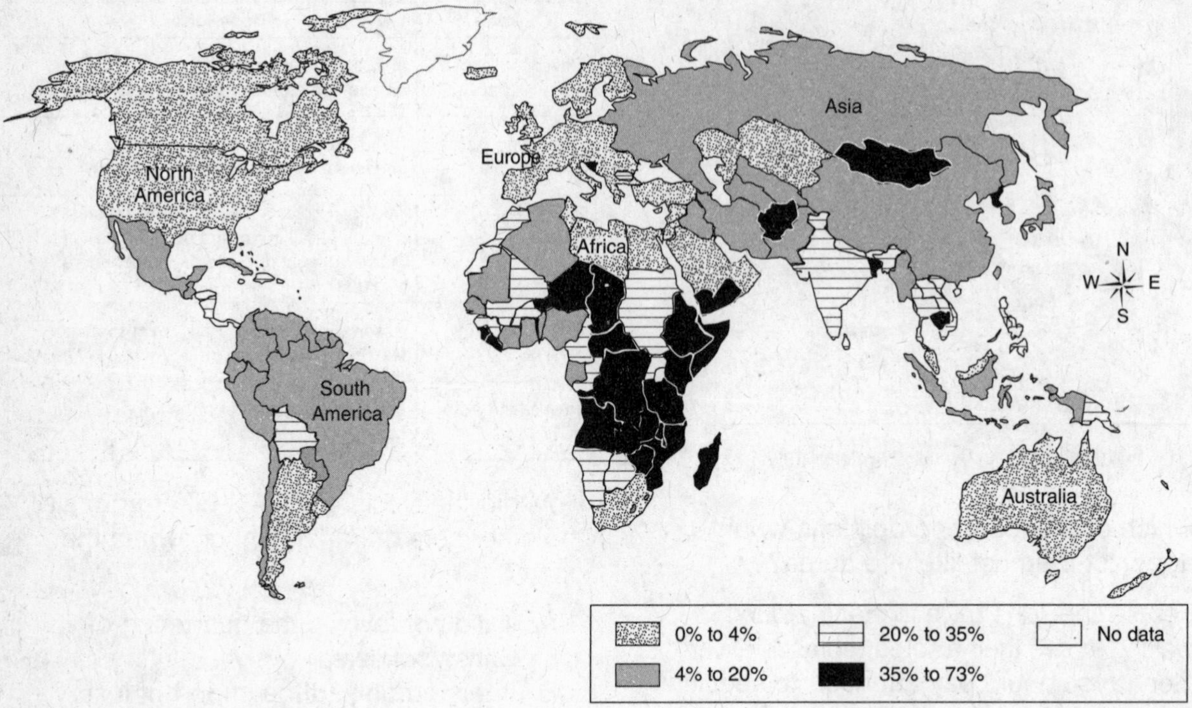

Source: The United Nations, World Food Program.

18. According to the map, what is the percentage range of people in the United States who do not get enough food and nutrients?
   - A. 0% to 4%
   - B. 4% to 20%
   - C. 20% to 35%
   - D. 35% to 73%

19. Which of the following statements is supported by the information on the map?
   - A. All areas with more than 35% of the population undernourished are inland nations.
   - B. World hunger would disappear if food were distributed more fairly.
   - C. There are no areas of hunger in Europe or Australia.
   - D. Hunger is a major problem in many countries in Africa.

Questions 20 through 22 refer to the following chart.

Important Political Documents Preceding the Declaration of Independence and the U.S. Constitution

Year	Document	Description
1215	Magna Carta	Limited the power of the English king and granted rights to the nobles
1620	Mayflower Compact	Set rules by which the Pilgrims would govern themselves in Plymouth colony
1628	Petition of Right	Limited the English king's powers further
1636	Great Fundamentals	Established the first basic system of laws in the English colonies, in Massachusetts Bay Colony
1688	English Bill of Rights	Declared that the king rules with the consent of the people's representatives in Parliament; granted ordinary people certain rights

20. What do the Mayflower Compact and the Great Fundamentals have in common?

- A. Both limited the power of the king.
- B. Both granted rights to the nobles.
- C. Both established methods of self-government in English colonies.
- D. Both applied to the government in England.

21. One of the major grievances the American colonists had against the British was that the British taxed the colonists without granting them representation in the British Parliament. Part of the Declaration of Independence is a list of political and economic rights that American colonists complained that the British king had deprived them of.

By which of the following documents were the writers of the Declaration probably most influenced as they drafted their list?

- A. the Mayflower Compact
- B. the Petition of Right
- C. the Great Fundamentals
- D. the English Bill of Rights

22. Which document first set limits on the British monarch's powers?

- A. the Magna Carta
- B. the Mayflower Compact
- C. the Petition of Right
- D. the English Bill of Rights

23. The civil rights movement of the 1950s and 1960s inspired historians to reinterpret slavery's impact on U.S. society in general and on African Americans in particular. One interpretation that emerged was that slaves and owners were always in conflict and that slavery was destructive. The extent of slavery's destructiveness was debated. Some historians argued that slavery destroyed the culture and self-respect of the slaves and their descendants. Others thought that slaves overcame hardship by developing a unique African American culture that included, among many different things, strong religious and musical traditions.

Based on the paragraph, which of the following statements is an opinion rather than a fact?

- A. The civil rights movement took place during the middle of the twentieth century.
- B. The civil rights movement caused historians to take another look at slavery.
- C. Historians debated slavery's negative effects on slaves and their descendants.
- D. Slavery destroyed the culture of the slaves, diminishing their self-respect.

Questions 24 and 25 refer to the following paragraph and graph.

The market price of a product tends to change in a way that brings supply and demand into balance, a condition called equilibrium. This is illustrated in the graph below, which shows supply and demand for apples.

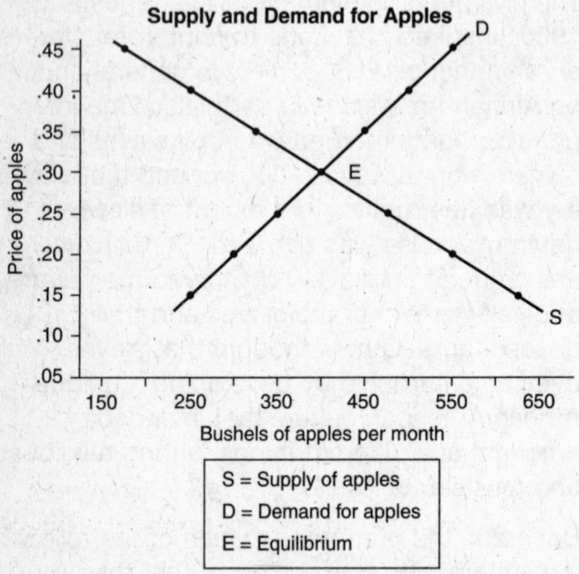

24. According to this graph, what is the market price of apples—also known as the price at equilibrium?

- A. 45 cents
- B. 30 cents
- C. 20 cents
- D. 15 cents

25. Which of the following would result if part of the apple crop were destroyed but demand remained the same?

- A. Supply would increase.
- B. The market price would remain the same.
- C. The market price would go down.
- D. The market price would go up.

Question 26 refers to the following paragraph and map.

The Battle of Fort Sumter was the first battle of the American Civil War. South Carolina had seceded from the Union and insisted that Union troops in South Carolina leave. A small band of Union soldiers was finally forced to evacuate Fort Sumter, on the South Carolina coast. After that, President Lincoln called for 75,000 volunteers to help put down the rebellion in the south. Following his call, four additional states seceded from the Union and joined the Confederacy. The progress of secession is shown here.

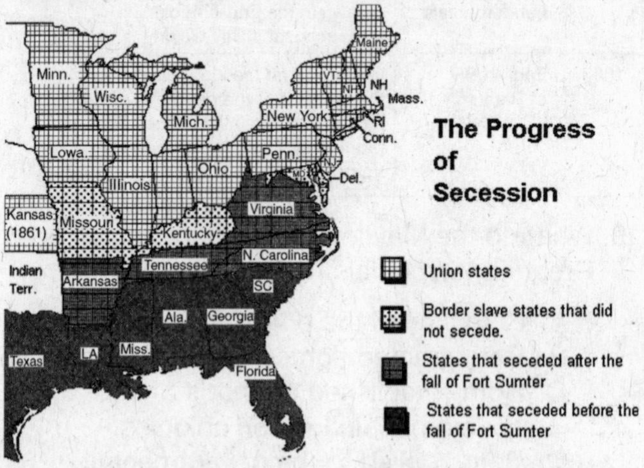

Reprinted from "The South Secedes," U.S. History Online Textbook, ushistory.org.

26. Match each of the following states to the appropriate column(s) in the table. A state may be matched to both columns, or to none at all. You may or may not fill up each column.

Belonged to the Confederacy before the battle of Fort Sumter	Belonged to the Confederacy after the battle of Fort Sumter

Iowa

North Carolina

Delaware

Alabama

Questions 27 through 29 refer to the following paragraph and diagram.

Most cases that arise under federal law are tried in the federal court system. The federal court system has several levels of courts and several routes by which cases may be appealed to a higher court.

Routing Cases Through the Federal Court System

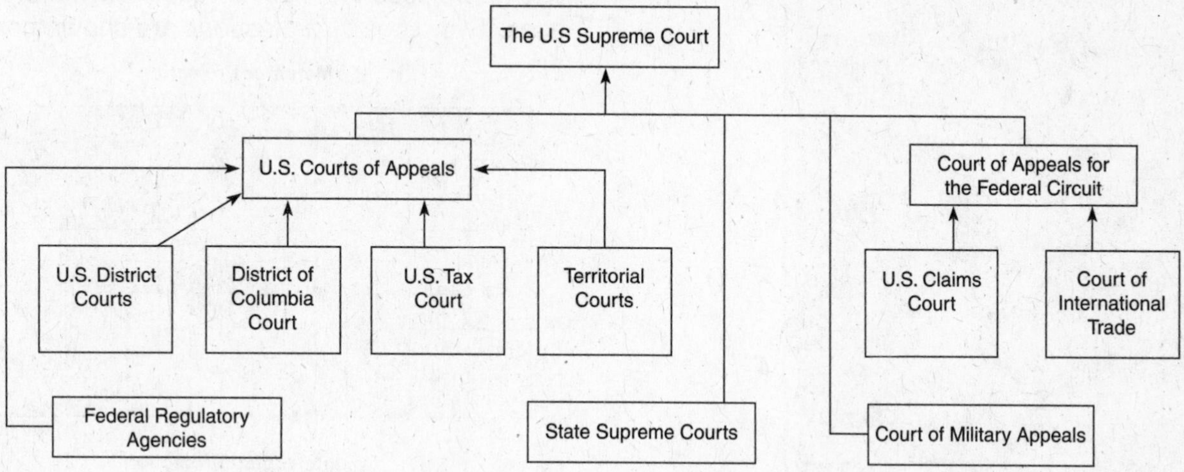

27. A U.S. import-export firm files a lawsuit against a foreign trading company. In which court is the suit most likely to be filed?
    - A. the United States Claims Court
    - B. the United States Court of Appeals
    - C. the Court of International Trade
    - D. the United States Tax Court

28. The U.S. Constitution established only the Supreme Court, but it gave Congress the power to create inferior (lower) federal courts.

    Which of the following is the most likely reason that Congress established other federal courts?
    - A. The justices of the U.S. Supreme Court were not well versed enough in the law to handle all federal cases.
    - B. The volume and variety of federal cases were too great for a single court to handle.
    - C. A system of inferior federal courts gave the United States prestige in the eyes of the rest of the world.
    - D. The Supreme Court's power to interpret the Constitution was established in *Marbury v. Madison.*

29. If cases are not resolved in any of the lower federal courts, to which court may they eventually, finally be appealed?
    - A. the Supreme Court of the United States
    - B. the United States Courts of Appeals
    - C. the Court of Appeals for the Federal Circuit
    - D. the Court of Military Appeals

Question 30 refers to the following poster.

The poster below was published during World War I.

Source: Library of Congress. Poster by James Montgomery Flagg

30. Which of the following opinions is the artist attempting to propagate?

- A. Americans are not yet part of civilization.
- B. The war effort needs the help of everyone, including men, women and children.
- C. Every man, woman and child should rest in preparation for the war effort.
- D. Americans are part of a lazy civilization.

Questions 31 and 32 refer to the following paragraph and maps.

Mapmakers have devised many solutions to the problem of projecting the curved surface of Earth onto a flat piece of paper. However, all map projections involve some distortion, and each type of projection has advantages and disadvantages. Two types of projections are shown here.

Mercator Projection

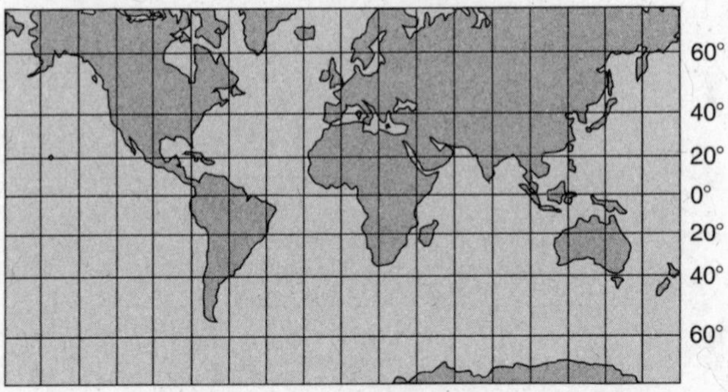

Interrupted Projection

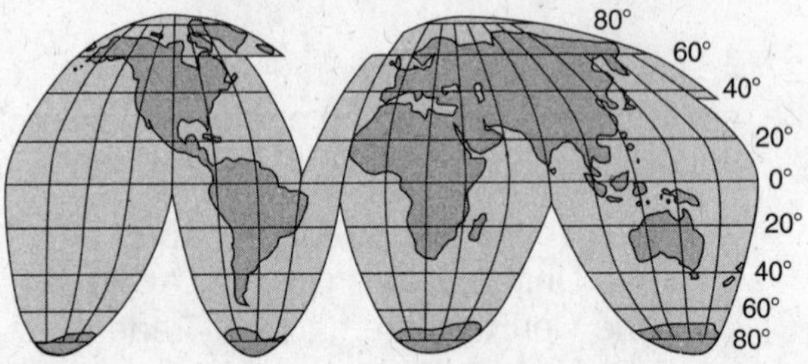

31. Approximately where is there the least distortion on these projections?

- A. at 60° north and south latitude
- B. at 40° north and south latitude
- C. at 20° north and south latitude
- D. at 0° latitude

32. A sailor who wanted to plan an around-the-world sailing trip decided to use the interrupted projection. What was wrong with his decision?

- A. The interrupted projection distorts distances across the continents at midlatitudes.
- B. The interrupted projection distorts distances across the oceans.
- C. The interrupted projection distorts the shapes of mid-latitude land masses.
- D. The interrupted projection shows only a few of the world's oceans.

Question 33 refers to the following paragraph and map.

After the Roman Empire had reached its greatest extent in the 2nd century C.E. emperors consolidated its borders in various ways: where the frontiers were over land, they were seen as vulnerable, and so the emperors often built heavy fortifications, such as forts or walls to defend the borders; where there was a natural barrier like a river or a desert, light fortifications, such as watchtowers, were viewed as adequate; and where there were major barriers, such as the ocean, the emperors concluded that no defense was needed.

Northwestern Frontiers of the Roman Empire, 2nd Century C.E.

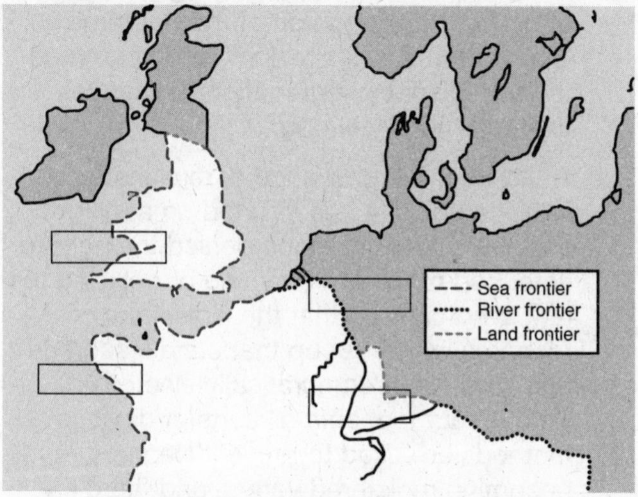

33. Based on the information in the paragraph above, match the appropriate degree of fortification to each part of the frontier on the map. You may use some labels twice.

Heavy

Light

None

34. Constitutional guarantees of fairness and equality under the law, our basic civil liberties, are called due process of law. The Fifth and Fourteenth Amendments state that government shall not deprive anyone of "life, liberty, or property, without due process of law." The Fifth Amendment protects people from actions of the federal government. The Fourteenth protects people specifically from actions of governments of the individual states.

What is a main difference between the Fifth and Fourteenth Amendments?

- A. The Fifth Amendment applies to adults, and the Fourteenth Amendment, to children.
- B. The Fifth Amendment applies to due process, and the Fourteenth Amendment, to freedom of speech.
- C. The Fifth Amendment applies to the federal government, and the Fourteenth Amendment, to state governments.
- D. The Fifth Amendment applies to life, and the Fourteenth Amendment, to liberty.

Directions: Based on both articles, write a response to the prompt on page 129. This task may take up to 25 minutes to complete.

Passage A

In 1963, a group of civil rights activists began a campaign of sit-ins and other demonstrations in the highly segregated city of Birmingham, Alabama. As part of that campaign, the group broke laws forbidding demonstrations and requiring racial segregation. Dr. Martin Luther King, Jr., one of the leaders of the Birmingham Campaign, was arrested and wrote a famous letter from his jail cell. The passage below is excerpted from that letter.

Excerpted from "Letter from a Birmingham Jail"

You may well ask: "Why direct action? Why sit-ins, marches and so forth? Isn't negotiation a better path?" You are quite right in calling for negotiation. Indeed, this is the very purpose of direct action. . . . I have earnestly opposed violent tension, but there is a type of constructive, nonviolent tension which is necessary for growth. . . .

. . . Perhaps it is easy for those who have never felt the stinging darts of segregation to say, "Wait." But when you have seen vicious mobs lynch your mothers and fathers at will and drown your sisters and brothers at whim; when you have seen hate-filled policemen curse, kick and even kill your black brothers and sisters; when you see the vast majority of your twenty million Negro brothers smothering in an airtight cage of poverty in the midst of an affluent society; . . . I hope, sirs, you can understand our legitimate and unavoidable impatience.

You express a great deal of anxiety over our willingness to break laws. This is certainly a legitimate concern. Since we so diligently urge people to obey the Supreme Court's decision of 1954 outlawing segregation in the public schools, at first glance it may seem rather paradoxical for us consciously to break laws. One may well ask: "How can you advocate breaking some laws and obeying others?" The answer lies in the fact that there are two types of laws: just and unjust. . . . One has not only a legal but a moral responsibility to obey just laws. Conversely, one has a moral responsibility to disobey unjust laws. I would agree with St. Augustine that "an unjust law is no law at all."

Now, what is the difference between the two? How does one determine whether a law is just or unjust? A just law is a man-made code that squares with the moral law or the law of God. An unjust law is a code that is out of harmony with the moral law. . . . Thus it is that I can urge men to obey the 1954 decision of the Supreme Court, for it is morally right; and I can urge them to disobey segregation ordinances, for they are morally wrong.

. . . Let me give another explanation. A law is unjust if it is inflicted on a minority that, as a result of being denied the right to vote, had no part in enacting or devising the law. Who can say that the legislature of Alabama which set up that state's segregation laws was democratically elected? Throughout Alabama all sorts of devious methods are used to prevent Negroes from becoming registered voters, and there are some counties in which, even though Negroes constitute a majority of the population, not a single Negro is registered. Can any law enacted under such circumstances be considered democratically structured?

—Martin Luther King, Jr., "Letter from a Birmingham Jail"

Passage B

In 1872, Susan B. Anthony broke the law by voting in a federal election. At that time, women were not permitted by law to vote. She was arrested, convicted, and ordered to pay a fine, which she never paid. The passage below is an excerpt from a public speech Anthony gave around the time of her trial.

Excerpted from "Is It a Crime for a Citizen of the United States to Vote?"

I stand before you to-night, [accused of] the alleged crime of having voted at the last Presidential election, without having a lawful right to vote. It shall be my work this evening to prove to you that in thus voting, I not only committed no crime, but, instead, simply exercised my citizen's right, guaranteed to me and all United States citizens by the National Constitution, beyond the power of any State to deny. . . .

[The Declaration of Independence says:] "All men are created equal, and endowed by their Creator with certain unalienable rights. Among these are life, liberty and the pursuit of happiness. That to secure these, governments are instituted among men, deriving their just powers from the consent of the governed."

. . . And here, in this very first paragraph of the declaration, is the assertion of the natural right of all to the ballot; for, how can "the consent of the governed" be given, if the right to vote be denied. . . .

. . . One-half of the people of this nation to-day are utterly powerless to [erase] from the statute books an unjust law, or to write there a new and a just one. The women, dissatisfied as they are with this form of government, that enforces taxation without representation, that compels them to obey laws to which they have never given their consent, that imprisons and hangs them without a trial by a jury of their peers, that robs them, in marriage, of the custody of their own persons, wages and children, are this half of the people left wholly at the mercy of the other half. . . .

[The Fourteenth Amendment to the Constitution says:] "No states shall make or enforce any law which shall abridge the privileges or immunities of citizens; nor shall any state deprive any person of life, liberty or property, without due process of law, nor deny to any person within its jurisdiction the equal protection of the laws."

. . . [W]omen are citizens, and no state has a right to make any new law, or to enforce any old law, that shall abridge their privileges or immunities. Hence, every discrimination against women in the constitutions and laws of the several states, is to-day null and void [that is, invalid], precisely as is every one against negroes.

—Susan B. Anthony, "Is It a Crime for a Citizen of the United States to Vote?"

Write an Extended Response to Both Passages

Both Dr. Martin Luther King, Jr., and Susan B. Anthony were arrested for breaking the law. The passages describe their reactions to being arrested and their attitudes toward the law.

Write an essay in which you compare and contrast King's and Anthony's responses to their arrests. What ideas did they seem to have in common? In what ways did their explanations of their actions differ? Use specific and relevant details from both passages in your essay.

Type your response on a computer, if one is available. If one is not, write your response neatly on paper. This task may require 25 minutes to complete.

Use the *Social Studies Extended Response Evaluation Guide* on page 135 to evaluate your response.

Answers and explanations begin on page 131.

STOP

Congratulations! You have completed the GED® Social Studies Practice Test.

Reminder: your next step is to check your answers with the Practice Test Answers and Explanations and fill in the evaluation charts that follow those explanations.

Pages 115–129

1. **D. The United States had an unfavorable balance of trade in merchandise during the 2000s.** According to the passage, the balance of trade is the difference between exports and imports. When imports are greater than exports, the balance of trade is unfavorable. Since the graph shows that imports consistently exceeded exports during the 2000s, you can conclude that the balance of trade in merchandise was unfavorable during the decade.
2. **39** To calculate the average percent of people surveyed who considered themselves independents, add up the January – June numbers, 38 + 38 + 36 + 40 + 39 + 41 = 232. Divide 232 by the total number of terms, 6, and round to the nearest percentage to get 39 percent.
3. Look for the continent with the highest percentage of countries colored in the lightest gray. Place a dot on **Africa**.
4.

Highest	United States
Second highest	Mexico
Third highest	India
Lowest	Democratic Republic of Congo

5. **2.1** The median is the middle number in a set of numbers. Here, the question asks for the median in the percent change figures, or the third column. Arrange those numbers in order, and 2.1 will be the middle number.
6. **1870, 1965** The 15th Amendment (1870) and the Voting Rights Act of 1965 expanded the right to vote.
7. **B. Both valued a stable political framework for society.** The paragraph indicates that this was one thing the ancient Chinese and the ancient Greeks had in common.
8. **C. The war created a huge demand for military equipment and supplies.** The chart shows that there was a substantial increase in manufacturing output between 1939 (when World War II began in Europe) and 1941. Even though the United States did not enter the war until late 1941, industry had already geared up to sell equipment and supplies to the Allies in Europe. Choices (A) and (B) may be true, but do not explain the war's impact.
9. **A. patriotism** The tendency of the American public to support a president's emergency foreign policy actions is sometimes called the "rally 'round the flag" effect.
10. **B. problems enforcing the Sherman Antitrust Act consistently led to further legislation to prevent monopolies** In the passage, the author explains the intention behind the Sherman Antitrust Act: to make monopolies illegal. He goes on to outline the limitations of the act, arguing that its broad language rendered it insufficient to solve the problems created by monopolies. He concludes the paragraph by telling how Congress responded to the problems in the Sherman Antitrust Act by passing additional laws to control monopolistic practices.
11.

The author would agree with this statement:	**The author would disagree with this statement:**	**The author does not address this information:**
b. The dangers of climate change are more significant than the possible benefits.	a. The United States has failed to take any action against carbon emissions.	c. Wind energy is preferable to solar energy.
	d. Climate change will not impact the world food supply.	

12. **B. Whites wanted to take over Indian lands in the eastern states.** The graphic shows the Indians being moved away from eastern states to Kansas and Oklahoma. The question asks about "forcible" relocation, so the correct answer can't be about what Indians wanted.
13. **D. the Seminole** The Seminole tribe's home territory was in Florida, which was farthest from the new, government-declared Indian Territory in the Midwest.
14. **C. Special interest groups are treated better than voters by members of Congress.** The cartoonist is using irony in the caption to indicate that he thinks members of Congress treat voters badly, but treat people who represent special interest groups well.
15. **C. Industrialization and urbanization caused many changes in family life in the late 1800s.** This covers the main points of the passage, which discusses the impact of industrialization and urbanization on the American family. The other choices are all supporting details.
16. **C. It did not impose direct economic costs on the colonists.** All of the other acts of Parliament shown in the chart cost the colonists money, whether by having to pay import taxes, buy revenue stamps, or use their own resources to shelter British soldiers.
17. **A. The Declaration of Independence, which explained why the colonies broke away from Great Britain** The acts of Parliament listed in the chart were grievances used to justify declaring independence.
18. **A. 0% to 4%** First find the United States on the map and see what shade it is colored. Then consult the map key to see the percentage of undernourished people that shade represents. The map indicates that the percentage range is 0% to 4%.
19. **D. Hunger is a major problem in many countries in Africa.** More than 20 nations in Africa have a very high percentage of undernourished people. The remaining options are not supported by the data on the map.

20. C. Both established methods of self-government in the English colonies. Both documents set forth rules and laws for the self-government of specific English colonies.

21. D. the English Bill of Rights The English Bill of Rights tied the king's right to rule to the consent of the people's representatives, and the colonists' major grievance was taxation without representation. The colonists felt they should be granted the same representation and rights as other British citizens, which were listed in the English Bill of Rights.

22. A. the Magna Carta The Magna Carta, signed in 1215, was the first document to set limits on the British king's powers.

23. D. Slavery destroyed the culture of the slaves, diminishing their self-respect. According to the paragraph, this is an opinion, or belief, held by some historians. The other choices are all facts stated in the paragraph.

24. B. 30 cents According to the passage, market price is reached under equilibrium conditions—when supply equals demand. According to the graph, supply and demand cross each other—and so are equal—at 30 cents.

25. D. The market price would go up. When the supply decreases and demand stays the same, the market price increases. The same number of people want to buy fewer apples, so the people will generally be willing to pay more for the apples.

26.

Belonged to the Confederacy before the battle of Fort Sumter	Belonged to the Confederacy after the battle of Fort Sumter
Alabama	Alabama
	North Carolina

Iowa and Delaware never seceded, so they never belonged to the Confederacy. Alabama seceded before the Battle of Fort Sumter, so it belonged to the Confederacy both before and after the Battle of Fort Sumter. North Carolina also belonged to the Confederacy, but it didn't secede until after the Battle of Fort Sumter.

27. C. the Court of International Trade International trade" is commerce with foreign companies, so the case would most likely be filed in the Court of International Trade.

28. B. The volume and variety of federal cases were too great for a single court to handle. It would be impractical to have just one court handling all cases; the workload would be too great.

29. A. the Supreme Court of the United States According to the passage, cases are appealed to higher level courts; according to the diagram, the Supreme Court is the highest court of appeal.

30. B. The war effort needs the help of everyone, including men, women and children. The focus of the poster is to enlist the help of everyone in the country for the war effort. The sleeping woman represents an American population that needs to take action.

31. D. at 0° latitude On both of these projections the distortions are greatest near the north and south poles. Along the equator (0° latitude), the maps look most alike and most similar to a globe; the distortions increase as you go north or south toward the poles.

32. B. The interrupted projection distorts distances across the oceans. The interrupted projection was a poor choice because ocean areas are cut apart on the map, making it very difficult to measure distances on an around-the-world voyage.

33. The one segment (the bottom right box) of the Roman frontier that the map legend identifies as land frontiers would see "Heavy" fortification, the one river frontier (the top right box) would see "Light" fortification, and the two sea coasts (the two left-hand boxes) would see "None." Rivers served as natural barriers, making fortifications less necessary, and the emperors saw no need to defend ocean frontiers.

34. C. The Fifth Amendment applies to the federal government, and the Fourteenth Amendment, to state governments. According to the passage, this is one of the main differences between the two amendments.

Extended Response Evaluation Guide Use the *Social Studies Extended Response Evaluation Guide* on page 135 to give your response a score between 0 and 6. Enter your score on the *Evaluation Chart* on page 133.

SOCIAL STUDIES PRACTICE TEST EVALUATION CHARTS

Questions 1–34

Circle the numbers of the questions that you got correct and then total them in the last column of each row.

	United States History Pages 46–59	Civics and Government Pages 60–73	Economics Pages 74–85	Geography and the World Pages 86–101	Points
Social Studies Practices					
Determine Central Idea and Draw Conclusions Pages 26–27	10, 15	7, 17	(no questions)	(no questions)	____/4
Interpret Words and Ideas Pages 28–29	12	9, 16, 20, 27	8, 25	33	____/8
Analyze Author's Purpose and Point of View Pages 30–31	11, 30	14	(no questions)	(no questions)	____/3
Evaluate Author's Reasoning and Evidence Pages 32–33	23	21, 28, 34	1	32	____/6
Analyze Relationships Between Materials Pages 34–37	13, 26	6, 22, 29	3, 4, 24	18, 19, 31	____/11
Interpret Data and Statistics Pages 38–39	(no questions)	2	5	(no questions)	____/2
SUBTOTAL	____/8	____/14	____/7	____/5	

Extended Response

Use the evaluation guide on page 135 and assign each trait a value. Add to find the subtotal. On the GED® Test, your Extended Response score subtotal will be doubled. Multiply by 2 as shown in the table below.

Creation of Arguments and Use of Evidence	____/2
Development of Ideas and Organizational Structure	____/2
Clarity and Command of Standard English Conventions	____/2
SUBTOTAL	**____/4. Then multiply your subtotal by 2: ____/8.**

Composite Score

Add both Subtotals to get the total number of points you earned on the *Social Studies Test*.

Questions 1–34	____/34
Extended Response	____/8
TOTAL	____/44

If you do not have time to review the entire *Social Studies* unit, you may want to review the sections that need the most work. You can use your total above (____/44) to figure out your percentage correct for the entire *Social Studies* test. Divide the numerator by the denominator and multiply by 100.

GED® Social Studies Resources

Extended Response Evaluation Guide

You can use this guide to evaluate your own writing. You can also provide the guide to another person whom you ask to read your paper. Read a paper three times—once for each trait. Circle a score for each trait in the chart at the bottom of this page. Add to find your total score and then analyze your results.

Trait 1 – Creation of Arguments and Use of Evidence

Rate the response as 2, 1, or 0 based on these criteria:

2 – makes **logical, explicitly stated claim(s)** based on a close reading of text(s); utilizes **mainly accurate analysis of ideas, events, or figures;** provides **largely accurate and relevant understanding** of **historic context** of sources

1 – makes **one strongly stated claim or an implied claim** which may be unclear or inconsistent; **limited analysis of ideas, events,** or **figures;** provides **limited understanding** of **historic context** of sources

0 – makes **vague, illogical, or no claims,** with **minimal or no analysis of ideas, events, or figures;** makes **little or no analysis** of the **claims;** presents **no understanding of historical context** of source texts

Trait 2 – Development of Ideas and Organizational Structure

Rate the response as 1 or 0 based on these criteria:

1 – demonstrates **logical organization;** uses a **clear progression of ideas** with well-chosen **transitions;** connects **supporting details to the main idea;** utilizes **appropriate style, tone,** and **word choice**

0 – demonstrates **insufficient or illogical development** with **unclear progression of** ideas; contains **few supporting details** and/or **does not connect them to the main idea;** utilizes **incorrect** or **inappropriate style, tone, and word choice**

Trait 3 – Clarity and Command of Standard English Conventions

Rate the response as 1 or 0 based on these criteria:

1 – exhibits **mainly correct and varied sentence structure;** uses **transitional words** to connect ideas; **avoids awkward or overly wordy constructions; competent application of grammar, capitalization, punctuation,** and **spelling -** with some mistakes allowed

0 – exhibits **flawed or highly repetitive sentence structure** may use **overly wordy, awkward, or confusing constructions; lacks transitional words and phrases;** exhibits **frequent errors** of **grammar, capitalization, punctuation,** and **spelling**

Trait	Circle Score
1	0 1 2
2	0 1
3	0 1
Added Total	

Analysis of Score Total

0 to 1	Weak – needs improvement with all three traits
2 to 3	Fair – needs work with some traits
4	Strong – mastery of all three traits

NOTE: This guide is Kaplan's simplified interpretation of the official GED® *Social Studies Extended Response* rubric. It has been developed for ease of use in evaluating extended written responses to one passage or paired passages.

TI-30XS Calculator Reference Sheet

An on-screen calculator reference sheet, similar to what appears on these two pages, will be available to you on Test Day. However, you should understand how to use the calculator before you take the GED® Test.

To perform basic arithmetic, enter numbers and operation symbols using the standard order of operations.

Example: 

−25

To calculate with percentages, enter the number, then 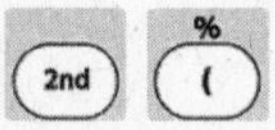

Example: 

224

To perform calculations with scientific notation, use the  key.

Example: 

630000000

To perform calculations with fractions, use the  key. The answer will automatically be formatted in reduced form.

Example: 

$\frac{2}{21}$

To perform calculations with mixed numbers, use 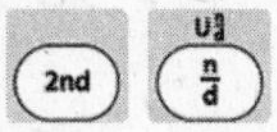

As with fractions, the answer will automatically be formatted in reduced form.

Example: 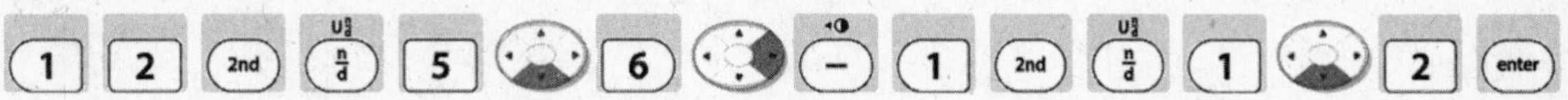

$\frac{34}{3}$

To perform calculations with powers and roots, you will use the following keys:

[x^2] [^] [2nd] [x^2] [2nd] [^]

Example: [1] [.] [2] [x^2] [enter] **1.44**

Example: [7] [^] [4] [enter] **2401**

Example: [2nd] [x^2] [5] [2] [9] [enter] **23**

Example: [3] [2nd] [^] [1] [7] [2] [8] [enter] **12**

The answer toggle key [◂▸] can be used to toggle the display result between fraction and decimal answers, exact square root and decimal, and exact pi and decimal.

Example: [$\frac{n}{d}$] [9] [▾] [1] [0] [enter] [◂▸] **0.9**

Æ Symbol Tool Explanation

Starting in 2014, test-takers will take the GED® Test on the computer. On the computer-based test, some fill-in-the-blank questions require you to insert mathematical symbols.

You can access the "Symbol Selector" by clicking on this icon when it appears on the computer screen:

Choose the symbol you want, and click on Insert at the bottom of the screen. When you are done, close the screen.

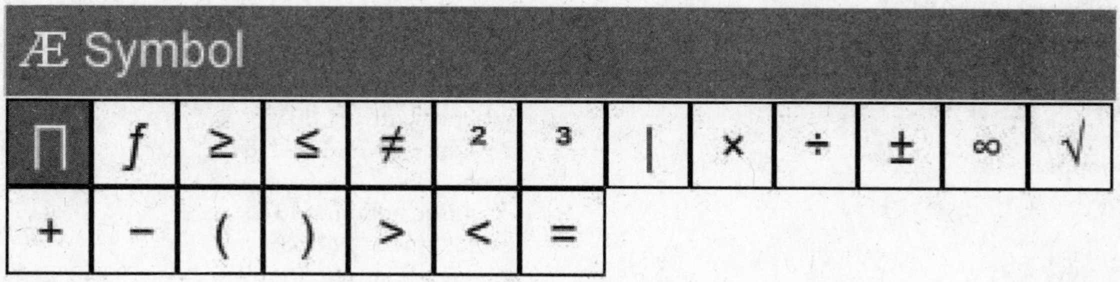

Below are the meanings of the symbols. Learn the meanings before you take the test because only the symbols will be available to you.

Π "pi" symbol π

f "function" symbol

$\geq$ greater than or equal to

$\leq$ less than or equal to

$\neq$ not equal to

^{2} 2 exponent ("squared")

^{3} 3 exponent ("cubed")

| "absolute" value

$\times$ multiplication sign

$\div$ division sign

$\pm$ "positive-or-negative" sign

∞ "infinity" symbol

$\surd$ "square root" symbol

$+$ plus sign or "positive" symbol

$-$ minus sign or "negative" symbol

(open (or left) parenthesis

) close (or right) parenthesis

$>$ "greater than" symbol

$<$ "less than" symbol

$=$ "equals" sign

INDEX

D

E

F

G

T

U

V

W